Playing in the Mind of God

A Guide to the Ultimate Truth-This Book Changes Lives

By

Jeffrey M. Solomon

This book is a work of non-fiction. Names and places have been changed to protect the privacy of all individuals. The events and situations are true.

ISBN: 1-4107-3726-8 (e-book)
ISBN: 1-4107-3727-6 (Paperback)
ISBN: 1-4107-3728-4 (Dust Jacket)

Library of Congress Control Number: 2003092859

This book is printed on acid free paper.

Printed in the United States of America
Bloomington, IN

1stBooks - rev. 08/13/03

There are many people who deserve acknowledgment for this book, not least are those who have challenged me, confronted me and played the role of the "bad person, the tough guy or the gentle persuader" in this lifetime of mine. They are all my teachers. Those who have shared this life with me in the past and those who do so in the present, I acknowledge you and thank you.

Knowing that these people are both my greatest challenge and also my greatest teachers as well as my biggest supporters, I respectfully bow and acknowledge their roles in my growth and understanding of what it means to have a body and to be present on this earth.

The greatest challenge to my mind and to my ego is my teacher Babaji. Babaji who never lets me rest or become complacent. It is Babaji who washes all my illusions, puts me in the spin cycle and hangs me out to dry! Thank you Baba. Bhole Baba Ki Jai! Jai Maha Maya Ki Jai!

To the Divine Mother and the Divine Father, thank you for sharing with me.

To Sri Muniraji, the silent teacher, the King of Silence, for being the role model of how to be in this world but not of it. Thank you for being in my life Guruji.

To Shri Vishnu Dutt Shastriji and his family. Shastriji, thank you for the many hours of bliss in your home in Rajahstan, the lessons in your presence and the many blessings at your feet from one of the greatest souls on earth is beyond my ability to express.

My parents, Daisy and Monty, I thank you for your role as parents and teachers as well as fulfilling our life contract. To my sister Roslyn, may you grow and flower - Rose.

To the many angels who have blessed me, my children Morgan, Micha and Alexander. You have given me the opportunity to be one of your many guides in this lifetime and I am humbled. Thank you for your light and your love. You are loved all-ways.

Leela my chocolate Labrador, if everyone could see the wisdom that comes to you so naturally, how easily we all could manifest our Tummies being tickled!

To Nathaniel who never ceases to amaze me - you are my teacher young man.

To Sharda, who has guided me, challenged my mind endlessly and wrestled with my demons with me and somehow always stayed rooted in Wisdom and Devotion like Saraswati her namesake. Om Namaha Saraswati Ki Jai. How great it is to share this path together as immortal beings.

Thank you for your presence in my life. Thank you for your guidance and your love and devotion.

To Peter - I feel Great! I feel Fine! I feel this way aaall the time!

Om Namaha Shivaya

With love and blessings
Jeffrey Solomon

Book One

Playing In The Mind Of God

Contents

Introduction

We do not inherit the land from our ancestors; we borrow it from our children.
- Native American Proverb

As we stand on the threshold of a new millennium, the human race has the power to destroy itself.

This power is not necessarily through the obvious means, such as nuclear or biological weapons.

The destruction of the biosphere, that is the global environment, which is the air, water, land and the forests, is severe. Our way of thinking, that is how we perceive our role in relation to nature, has not kept up with our technological progress and our ability to alter, pollute and destroy our environment.

We have created drugs that can wipe out disease, and in the process we have created drug resistant species of microorganisms that are more virulent than the original. We have genetically engineered new species without the full knowledge of the consequences and ramifications of these altered life forms. Especially in the field of biological warfare, the germs being produced are super-bugs, so powerful that they could render the world uninhabitable for human life for thousands of years!

A professor at a U.S. university research facility showed me a tank of concentrated HIV (AIDS) virus, the size of an oxygen tank, with enough HIV to wipe out all human life!

I hasten to add that this facility is not even guarded or secure.

So intent is science on the genetic engineering of plants and animals, that many of the hundreds of varieties of corn and potatoes, to name just two of our staple crops, plus hundreds of varieties of fowls, sheep, pigs and cattle are becoming extinct. Yes, rare wild animals are not the only species that are vanishing. Every day we lose domestic species of plants and animals.

Every day the bio diversity of the food chain is diminished in favor of more popular, higher yielding varieties. Without genetic diversity, a plague or plant disease could eliminate an entire species of food crop.

This is not being done for the greater good of mankind. People are still starving. Children are still dying on the streets, even as we throw away enough food in the USA every day to feed the world.

The beneficiaries of this ravaging of our planet are a few hundred huge corporations worldwide, and the even fewer super wealthy families who are the principal beneficiaries of government largesse and political cronyism, which allows the pillaging and pollution to rage unchecked across the globe.

At his stage of human evolution the strongest message mankind must receive is that it is five till midnight on the clock.

The need to become spiritually aware is not so that we get a place in heaven when we die. We need to understand the fundamental nature of what and who we are and how we fit in to the broader picture of life in the universe.

We need to understand spirituality in order to understand ourselves as spiritual beings in a cosmological sense. We need to know with certainty, that the knowledge available to us today on spiritual matters is vast and it is real.

For the most part I exclude organized religion and the teachings in our places of worship. These institutions are a source of divisiveness and egalitarianism in our society. Frequently they are part of the problem and not part of the solution.

Religious organizations have carried out slaughter, discrimination and torture throughout their histories. Almost without exception they claim that they alone represent the Divine presence of God on Earth. They claim that their way alone is the ticket to get to heaven.

And they purport to know Gods will for the world and for you. In short, if you do not follow their theology you are a doomed soul.

This is all wrong. It is religion based on fear, control and exclusion, and it is totally erroneous, as I will discuss later.

One thought that I have on the subject of God is that the concept of God may be limiting to our thought process. Although I have used the word God throughout this book to describe the Universal Energy, most of us have a preconceived idea about the word "God".

Our thoughts are based on our upbringing and religious experience of what God means to us. We may even be hostile to the very concept of God.

I think that it is good to separate the God of your upbringing with the Energy Being that I am dealing with in this book.

In this work you should suspend any thought you may have of the old paradigm of a fatherly being observing our every thought and action and weighing our guilt or innocence against a biblical set of commandments.

I ask you to hold the possibility of an energy force so grand and multi-dimensional in scope and unbounded by time, that the very word "God" can only diminish our understanding.

Yet for the sake of language, I am forced to use the word God as a tool for communication with the reader. At other times I will use terms such as "Universal Energy" to describe this Being and in order to jolt the reader into a more expanded point of reference.

Try to hold this idea in mind as you read this book and do not let old values or conceptions affect how you relate to, or understand this material. I ask that you keep an open mind.

Spirituality is absolutely love based. Spirituality is inclusive of all people, totally forgiving, totally accepting, tolerant of all belief systems, and in line with the Universal Truths of all creation.

It recognizes the grace inherent in every-one of us without judgment or precondition. It strives to help everyone reach their highest state of being and awareness, knowing that even the least among us is also the seed of the greatest in all of us.

Spirituality accepts all souls without preconditions, knowing that within each and every one of you is the majesty of the universe, an unstoppable force waiting release.

There is a Cinderella, a hidden princess, within the rags of poverty and servitude awaiting the noble spark of truth to be free.

This book is dedicated to the hidden potential within us all.

There are spiritual books, tapes and teachers on this planet in abundance today. This is more so now than at any time in history.

This is no coincidence. They are Divinely placed here at this time when we most need them. We MUST learn very quickly and at an accelerated rate, what the true meaning of life is.

We must discover what it truly means to be a conscious being and to love a conscious life in which accept the sole responsibility of our actions.

We need to understand our relationship with God, the universe, and earth and especially with each other. And we need to rededicate our lives anew to a higher and more conscious principle.

We can create a new, caring, loving reality on earth, in direct opposition to that which exists today.

This is the most important thing you can do in your life right now.

Learn, understand and realize how important you really are to the world.

Your life has tremendous meaning for each and every one of us!

You are a flame of the universe, unkindled.

Mankind's very survival depends on you!

Nothing less than this awesome responsibility awaits you.

The Divine reaches out to you every day in hundreds of ways.

Perhaps in this book, or through thousands of other books, through poems, movies, even television. Seek those books that appeal to your soul.

If not this one then find another, do not stop reaching for your truth.

Keep seeking.

There is a message tailored just for you at your level of spiritual growth and awareness.

The abundance of the Divine Truth has created a message so that every eye may see and every ear may hear.

The TRUTH is all around us in hundreds of subtle ways.

Let those who have eyes to see, realize the TRUTH revealed.

Prologue

In whichever direction you turn your gaze you will find One Eternal Indivisible Being manifested. Yet it is not all that easy to detect this Presence, because He interpenetrates everything....... The Unmanifest reveals Himself through the world of manifestation -
Anandamayi Ma (Indian Saint)

A Personal Reflection on the Power of Creation

Man unites himself with the world in the process of creation - Erich Fromm (German born philosopher / psychoanalyst)

Once I had a very strange experience.

One day as I sat down for meditation, I found a quiet space within in mind that I had not seen before. As I withdrew to the deepest part of my mind – I found myself letting go of all thought.

In so doing, I saw my mind enclosed in a black metal box.

As soon as my consciousness entered this space I immediately started creating within this box.

I made the box larger – and it expanded to give me more space and more space and I continued infinitely until its boundaries were infinite, as endless as the universe.

After some time in this state I saw the beauty of the Divine Mind in all creation. As my ideas flowed out into my personal universe in a box, ever expanding so, I realized is the Divine Mind doing likewise. The thought erupted in my mind, were our minds joined?

Not wishing blackness anymore, notwithstanding that it was so expansive and all fulfilling, I wished light and I illuminated it!

Now there was light! And stars, and I could see galaxies whirling and suns blazing in infinite space, and I was one with it.

After some time passed spent marveling at this universe in a box, I got the notion to shrink it. I returned the box to blackness all around me and I shrunk it to the size it was originally. Now it was no longer infinite and it was once more darkness.

However I proceed to experience myself shrinking so small that I experienced myself as a minute speck, a particle of energy, infinitely small - and the box, without changing size, once again appeared to me to be infinite in its size.

There I was in infinite darkness, and as small as I was, I started to create the universe in a box again. The box expanded infinitely. It was effortless and I created another radiant, glowing universe in the process.

It was then that the revelation of this material came to me - not as a sequence of mind images, but rather as a total understanding of the whole picture in one moment of time.

Thus began a magical journey to the most exciting destination of all, into the Mind of God.

I invite you to share the wonder with me and to marvel at the intricate turns in the road. Come with me as I take you through the pages of this book on the holiest journey of your life. For the more serious traveler, there are exercises and meditations. You can choose to do them or not, the choice is always yours. The journey may transform your life, as it did mine, and then again it may not. But it will not leave you unaffected.

<u>Chapter One</u>

*The inability of science to solve life is absolute. This fact would be
truly frightening were it not for faith. The mystery of life is certainly
the most persistent problem ever placed before the thought of man. -
Guglielmo Marconi (Italian Physicist)*

The Journey Begins

You must realize that the Divine current that flows and functions in every living being is the One Universal Entity. When you desire to enter the mansion of God, you are confronted by two closed doors...the desire to praise yourself and the desire to defame others. The doors are bolted by envy, and there is also a huge lock of egoism preventing entry. So if you are earnest, you have to resort to the key of love and open the lock; then remove the bolt and throw the doors wide open. Your education must train you in this difficult operation - Sathya Sai Baba (Indian Guru)

My whole existence is an illusion!

All that I see - All that I experience is an illusion.

All is illusion.

Chapter Two - Truth and Fear a Radical Statement

"Nothing is good nor bad. Thinking makes it so" - William Shakespeare (English playwright)

The Truth Unfolded

*There is one spectacle grander than the sea, that is the sky; there is
one spectacle grander than the sky, that is the interior of the soul -
Victor Hugo (French poet)*

Everything I experience is simply an illusion!

If at first this idea appears radical - it should - as it did to me. This
is the first radical statement.

The fact is, TRUTH is always confronting.

Anything that challenges our basic belief structure, especially
about ourselves, as radically as this statement does, is bound to raise
FEAR and disbelief.

This book then, is not a novel. It is a journey.

Each chapter will take you on a step of discovery and wonder into
the greatest unexplored realm of all - the human mind, and the Power
that created your mind!

At this point let us take the important first step on our journey.

Please return to the opening chapter. As brief as it is, pause for a
few moments to contemplate the statement, "My whole existence is
an illusion".

Consider your feelings with regards to the opening statement as it
applies to you. Consider how you would feel if you realized right now
that your entire life is just an illusion. Think about your feelings
regarding this statement. What thoughts and feelings does this bring
up for you? Be open and honest. If you find the idea preposterous,
fearful, truthful, confronting etc. examine your thoughts, especially
the very first, most immediate reaction you had to this statement the
instant you read it.

It would be a good idea, before you go any further, to write down
your thoughts honestly and to insert it in the book on the opening
chapter or perhaps to start a journal, which you will be asked to do
later on in this book. You may even wish to write in the book itself on
the opening page as permanent record of your growth.

Once you have completed this book, you are going to review both
the opening chapter, as well as your initial thoughts about it. Until
then do not revisit this page or your notes about it again.

When we return, review how your understanding of this opening chapter has changed. Explore how your understanding of yourself has changed. Note your new understanding and feelings alongside your original feelings and compare them, so that in future you will always have a point of reference to return to if you should choose to continue your journey.

Hopefully, you will have made the shift in consciousness that this, our life journey on earth, is intended to bring about, for indeed this is the journey of your lifetime.

Our conditioned and automatic response to the unknown is denial. Denial is separation of us from Truth. Our thoughts concerning separation are one of the major causes of all human suffering and misery.

Denial of change is a lot easier than confronting fear. Fear is only fear because of the challenge of the unknown. The unknown is always frightening and intimidating, the familiar on the other hand is always comforting and reassuring.

Change, even if it will eventually lead to freedom and happiness is usually resisted because the thought of change in itself is frightening. This is one reason so many people stay stuck in situations that no longer work for them.

For example, people stay stuck in relationships and jobs and other life situations that no longer work. They try to justify this staying stuck by saying that it is for the good of the kids, and they find many reasons why they should persevere in an unworkable situation or relationship.

We find this particularly in abusive relationships. The abused partner will often stay in a dreadful relationship and endure all kinds of abuse. The rationale is usually that they hope that the abusive partner will change, or that their partner is not always abusive. Indeed they will justify and endure all manner of personal anguish in order to avoid change.

Factually most people would rather resist change and be stuck in the pain of the familiar.

At some level the thought is that they can cope with the pain, it is a known quantity. Change brings up all manner of fear of the unknown. The thinking seems to be 'rather the devil you know, than the saint you don't know'.

In pain we experience a certain comfort of the familiar, whereas the unknown is shunned even when it represents joy and relief from our pain.

Being in the familiar is far easier to handle.

Most people have some level of pain and "stuckness" in their lives. The pain and suffering has certain predictability to it. To some it becomes a crutch. Suffering becomes their sense of self-identity. It becomes how they define themselves as a human being.

This is common in people who seem to always have ailments and health problems. They identify themselves by their aches and pains. They enjoy the attention their suffering draws from others. It gives them something to focus on. They are the kind of people who, when you ask them how they are doing, they actually tell you, often taking great pride in listing their misfortunes and ills!

They are often addicted to the attention and care the doctor gives them.

Love and Joy, however enticing, when unfamiliar, is shunned. If you ask anyone what they most desire from life, they will reply happiness, frequently their actions belie their words.

The purpose of this book is to take you painlessly, through change to joy. To help you find your life purpose. The journey we are about to take will illuminate your place in the world and open doors to unlimited possibilities. Here is the first step towards manifesting your life purpose and for you to create the life and happiness that is yours for the asking.

To do so, you must persevere beyond denial, beyond pain and into joy.

The Universe has a way of bringing to us lessons and teachers at the appropriate time in our lives when we are ready to receive the gift being offered.

I believe that you would not have been guided to read this book if you were not already seeking a more meaningful life. Because nothing in life occurs by accident, know then that:

"THE TRUTH SHALL MAKE YOU FREE." - John 8:32

Whilst reading this book I ask you to persevere in the reading beyond any initial denial and skepticism.

Many of the core ideas you will find to be repetitive throughout the book. Often these ideas are repeated for the purpose of leading you into another dimension of the root idea. I call them root ideas because they are firmly anchored in a fundamental Truth. Like a root, they grow and develop into various directions of thought. Each idea that proceeds from the original root, therefore, may start off with the original statement being repeated.

A further reason for repetition is that Universal Truths are immutable and eternal.

Using repetition reinforces the idea in the mind of the reader.

Truths may be so simple, or alternatively so profound, that in the casual reading, one may miss the point.

Universal ideas - not necessarily original ideas - presented here, are designed to break the barriers that are blocking your human evolution as a conscious being.

Many of the concepts herein can also be found in writings on psychology, philosophy, religion, in sacred texts and metaphysics, this should not deter you.

This book is easy to understand.

The Truth should never be difficult.

TRUTH is TRUTH. There can be no separate truths for one person that do not apply to another. TRUTH is found in all cultures, and all religions, it is pure humanism, and whether spoken by Buddha, Moses, Jesus, Mohammed, Krishna, Babaji, or even by you and I, there is only one TRUTH.

What is more we are all messengers and teachers. Indeed we all should strive to be so, for when we help another, we help ourselves. All teachers learn in the process of teaching.

(It is not a prerequisite to be a saint in order to teach, though some may say it will not hurt if you are!)

TRUTH needs to be stated and restated over and over again in as many different ways as possible and repeatedly throughout human history.

Everyone will eventually hear it in the form, style and language that is most understandable to them and in terms that appeal most to their intellect.

Simplicity is the key. You do not need to be a master of esoteric metaphysics, although if this is the route that appeals to you, so be it.

1. *The first rule of Truth is: There are no rules greater than love and humanism.*

This is the fundamental nature of the Divine. If God can be said to have human traits then it is that He emanates total and complete love and compassion for all humanity. His love is beyond the bounds of human judgment and is given to all equally and without reservation or withhold.

Any group or organization that claims to exclusively know the Truth separates itself from all other points of view. Separation creates Fear. And Fear creates Hatred. Hatred leads to a need for defense and attack.

Why does the message of TRUTH need to get out? It doesn't. Therefore:

2. *The second rule of Truth is that nothing has to be anything.*

The Universe has no demands or preconditions for Its love for you, or pre-conditions for your being here on earth or rules on how you should behave.

Humans have free choice. This being so, no limitations are placed on you. No judgment will be made of you. You can choose to be ignorant, unhappy, unfulfilled, poor, sick, rich, abundant joyful, healthy, you can have whatever you want in your life. It is your choice. You can have it! The Universe always gives you what you want and you always get what you want.

This may seem absurd to some but this concept will be explained later in depth.

This leads to the third rule of Truth.

3. *The Third rule of Truth is that the Universe always gives us what we want.*

The interconnectedness of all life throughout creation provides us with very powerful methods of creating our hearts desire. In short you actually can have whatever you want out of life. Indeed you already do. Your life today is the product of your thoughts and feeling about yourself that you had in your past right up until today. There are powerful ways of changing what you no longer wish to have in your life. I deal with this later in this book as well.

Just know that in every moment you are sending out thoughts and judgments about life and yourself that are creating your present experience.

Thinking that life needs to be a struggle, miserable, painful with suffering, will make it so.

Far be it for the Universe to give us less than what we think about. We always get what we want out of life.

Your perception of life is simply your own thoughts mirrored back at you.

4. *The fourth rule of Truth is that the Universe is unlimited.*

When you choose TRUTH, you have Enlightenment Joy, Love, Bliss and everything your heart desires, for the Universe is truly abundant and unlimited and there is no shortage of anything.

The Universe is designed to give you exactly what you most deeply think about. Your deepest thoughts create the reality of your life. The trick is in knowing what your deepest thoughts are.

Usually our thoughts represent suppressed fears that control our lives and influence all our further thoughts about life and especially about ourselves. These thoughts are formed from the moment of our birth, some would even say from the moment of our conception. Still others would suggest that some of our thoughts are even formed in past lives.

Your deepest and unconscious thoughts control who you are and how you experience yourself. They create your reality. Unless you understand what it is that makes you who we are, you cannot have conscious awareness. You will be limited by your thoughts and fears and an illusion of who you think we are, not who you really are.

Knowing the Truth, the Truth shall set you free.

Therefore let us proceed and seek Truth.

—

The University of President Street

Everywhere, we learn only from those whom we love - Goethe
(German poet)

Fortunately, I was introduced to a technique of self-fulfillment that enables one to reach all levels of ones consciousness. It is called Rebirthing. Rebirthing is an ancient yoga breathing method recently re-discovered and introduced in the West by Leonard Orr in the 1970's.

Within eighteen months one can achieve levels of awareness and personal understanding about the power of ones thoughts that eighteen years of therapy could not unravel.

The process is so powerful, that effectively it is like being given a second chance in life. Hence we talk of being reborn. Not in the religious sense, but in the sense of becoming a realized human being. Which in the end I suppose is a religious sense!

"Offering the inhaling breath into the exhaling breath, and offering the exhaling breath into the inhaling breath, the yogi neutralizes both breaths; thus he releases prana (energy) from the heart and brings life force under his control" - Bhagavad Gita IV:29

When we look at our lives we may be tempted to ask why we do not already have all the "good stuff" that we think we need.

The answer is simple, however it requires a change in your perception of the world and of how you perceive yourself.

(There is that confronting word again; CHANGE). You can be complacent living with the familiar or be brave and go beyond the FEAR that CHANGE represents to most people.

In most corporate environments, the hardest challenge facing management is to effect change. The natural instinct of the majority of people is to resist change. The mark of a truly good manager is to inspire employees to see the benefits of change, and to be willing to go beyond the status quo and into the unknown. A good leader can inspire people to reach beyond themselves and to follow a vision.

I would like to share a personal story of change in the corporate world and to a lesser extent, yet a far more radical extent, a change of human society.

I had a business "guru" when I was a young man his name is Mathew Etzine. Mathew is a slight man with a wry sense of humor and an ambling gate that belies the energy of his mind. His eyes had a Zen like twinkle and his unkempt casual dress and gray hair gave him a certain appearance not dissimilar to Albert Einstein.

He was much older than I, and he came into my life at a time when I was just starting out in business, when I really had more guts than brains!

This was to be a great lesson of how the Universe provides that which we most need at the time we need it, although it has taken me twenty years since then to recognize it as the third rule of Truth (The Universe always gives us what we want).

As fate would have it, (I do not believe in fate today - only Divine manifestation) Mathew had his own business on President Street, right across the street from me. We would meet almost every day and we would sometimes spend hours chatting on the sidewalk or outside the parking garage below his building, before ending up in either one of our offices. Mathew referred to our meetings as the University of President Street. He was one of the most open-minded thinkers I had ever met.

My wholesale company grew from a staff of three including myself into a staff of about fifty and a business turning over several millions a year.

Mathew taught me certain lessons that I never forgot. Embrace change. All is nothing. Do not be attached to anything. The whole world is in a state of change so go with the flow and not against it. The minute something works, start planning to change it because it won't last forever. The world is never constant. Everything changes. If someone resists change, then they are not working for you but against you. The only thing that is certain is that tomorrow will be different from today. Mathew was a student of life, a philosopher, a Jew, a Buddhist, a black, a white and as he would no doubt say: he is nothing and everything, and most of all he is simply another human being. A Humanist.

11

I inculcated in my staff from the inception that I expected from each of them one positive change a day in the company.

At the end of the year we would have 365 changes, and the company would be a totally different entity to what it was a year ago!

We embraced a culture of change, rooting out the stale, looking at what no longer worked for us and incrementally we changed that which no longer served us. My staff was eager to come forward and have their ideas recognized and implemented. They were always acknowledged for thinking and being creative, no matter if their ideas were used or not. I would often walk into a room and ask what can we change today? Needless to say, the staff knew their work environment best, and we made improvements at all levels, from health insurance, to the arrangement of office furniture. No one was considered too insignificant that we would not respect his or her opinion.

We took on social programs, such as training programs for the under educated staff members and subsidized education loans for the children of staff and we promoted people based strictly on their ability and potential. Some people, who had never been out of their hometown, were even sent overseas to the Far East for technical training.

The members of our company formed an employee choir that sang at our multicultural staff parties!

Our work environment was very dynamic. There were Christians of several denominations, Jews, Muslims and Hindus. There were Swiss, British, Italians, Indians, Blacks and Whites. I don't think that any two people shared the same ethnic or cultural background. Our diversity was a sense of pride in our company.

During periods of national labor unrest all commuter trains and taxis were on strike. Our staff elected to sleep in the office so as not to shut down!

This took place at a time when all non- whites were considered inferior citizens. Black people were not allowed to be managers over white people and they were only allowed menial manual labor positions. Social mixing was not allowed across the color line. Few blacks traveled out of the country indeed they needed a passport simply to travel within the country from one district to another!

We had multicultural office events, promoted people based on their ability, we educated those who were willing to go on private courses, we sent people overseas to train as technicians, and we helped some of their children go to schools outside of the country.

We were our own conscience. What we achieved was a minor miracle within the social context of the time. We took the road that was morally correct and not the path dictated by either society or the segregationist government.

For, you see, this was during the height of segregation during the apartheid era in South Africa.

Thank you Mathew!

—

The Self as Creator

Every production must resemble its author - Miguel de Cervantes
(Spanish Novelist)

We all create our own environment, especially in our personal lives, all the time, whether consciously or, for the most part, with respect to 99% of the population, unconsciously.

The collective consciousness of mankind created and continues to create, the world as we experience it.

It also creates its own consciousness.

This dichotomy means that we create our own physical reality via our conscious and unconscious thought. This in turn produces conditions, which becomes our perception of reality. It is this endless cycle of illusion creating illusion that we desperately need to understand as a prelude to manifesting our destiny as human beings. We also need to understand our planetary destiny.

Once you understand how you manifest your thoughts and create reality, then you can ascend beyond the limits of this cycle of illusion into a new reality and a new empowerment of yourself.

You will go beyond fear, illusion and hatred and into Truth.

Chapter Three - Truth and Fear. A Second Radical Statement

"Where there is hatred, there is no religion" - Babaji (Indian Saint and avatar)

All the World's a Stage

We read the world wrong and say that it deceives us. - Rabindranath Tagore (Bengali poet)

Human beings have manifested and continue still to create, everything on earth since the beginning of our time on this planet, - we create the beauty as well as the horrors of our human existence. It grows more complex as we evolve.

Yet it is all an illusion! It does not exist in TRUE reality!

This second radical statement basically is stating that we are in a real life movie.

We are the unsuspecting actors, audience and film in the projector. Daily we create the life script in which we act - every creative action constructs the movie -that in turn creates further scripts in an endless cycle of illusion.

These scripts, imprinted in our minds, are labeled "Experience" and "Reality".

These scripts are also a delusion. We inherit preprogrammed responses based on our culture, beliefs and code of ethics. We also create and embellish the scripts based on our individual perception of reality.

Every person brings a unique mix of influences and experiences, either inherited or self created, into their personal lives.

In addition to personal scripts on the individual level, there are millions of different group and national scripts.

These millions of scripts define us as individuals. They also define our societies, our institutions and national identities.

Our personal scripts are determined by our birth, parents, families, nationalities, cultural associations, work, social groups and so on.

The script permutation that forms each individual's experience is endless and ever changing.

As we grow we continue to add to our script, based on our perceived experiences, and we use this as the basis for defining who we are as individuals.

Scripts are the blueprints that determine how we should act out our life patterns and reactions to current and future events. We perpetuate and embellish the script, endlessly throughout our lives.

We are continually extending our script from generation to generation.

This process is carried out on thousands of levels varying with whom we associate with and how we define the multitude of groups with which we interact.

Nations define themselves and redefine themselves continuously based on the group consciousness script.

In the script process, we are both the creator of our script and hence our reality, as well as the end product of that reality.

All this creating, defining, reacting and acting of the script is only really experienced by the individual in the mind of that individual.

The mind is the seat of all our experiences and creative endeavors.

What we perceive as reality is created by us with the script that we have produced about ourselves. We only experience this perception of reality in our minds. We create and act out our life story invention in an endless cycle of mental games.

Consequently we are the authors of our life script, the stage actor, the film imprinted with the story, and the projector casting out the image and light of our lives.

In the final analysis, physical reality is non- existent outside of our own mind!

These self-created scripts represent only our individualized version of reality. In the physical world no two people share the same script. Each creates their screenplay separately and independent of anyone else. Every experience of reality is purely subjective to each individual alone. This is their persona. It is also the means that their ego uses to define who they think they are.

All physical realities necessarily being self-created and subjective are not real in an empirical sense.

Reality, as I have stated, does not exist for any two people in the same form. Each interprets life according to their own script and experience, and will ultimately add new experiences to their personal script adding their own unique embellishments.

Each person has their own illusion and ego interpreting events according to their point of view.

Therefore the physical world cannot be said to be real when reality changes to suit the experience of each person!

For true reality to exist it must be true for all people.

Beyond the self-created illusion, lies TRUTH, awaiting us.

When we cease the mind games and cease creating illusion we will find reality.

—

Truth and Fear

We call first truths those we discover after all the others - Albert Camus (French Philosopher)

What on earth is this all about?

If everything we believe to be real is an illusion, what is the TRUTH?

Where is reality?

What is reality?

How do we find the TRUTH?

For to find TRUTH we must! This is our true Life Purpose!

TRUTH is the only real choice we, as human beings have. Yet at a conscious level most of us are unaware of the TRUTH.

In TRUTH we are free of the Illusion. Free to discover our greatness and Divinity and manifest happier and healthier lives.

Failing to understand the TRUTH and its role in life dooms us to live in illusion. This may result in an endless repetition of patterns of behavior in our lives that is unfulfilling.

Illusions are as unstable as the minds that create them. By not having stability in our lives, we lack trust and live in fear.

These are some of the consequences that FEAR produces

VIOLENCE
CONFUSION
HELPLESSNESS
ADDICTIONS
FAILURE
ILLNESS

All negative human conditions are a product of FEAR.

Why TRUTH and FEAR?

You will only ever experience two fundamental emotions - each of which is the opposite of the other: TRUTH and FEAR.

Every emotion and thought thereafter is created from these two root emotions. Every thought you have and everything you ever experience will be entrenched in FEAR and hence illusion, or TRUTH and therefore enlightenment and love.

The Creator is unconditional and represents total LOVE, and does not experience FEAR.

Since God creates the true reality, devoid of FEAR, fear in the Divine reality does not exist.

FEAR then, is a strictly a creation of the human mind.

FEAR being a human creation is hence an ILLUSION.

Enlightened, self realized beings experience a world of joy and love. This world is constant and REAL and it is waiting for all beings to experience it.

At each moment of each day you have the freedom to choose to experience life and all situations from a place of LOVE or from a place of FEAR.

All your reactions to the world, your experiences, emotions and personal relationships stem from these two fundamental and opposing levels of consciousness - TRUTH and FEAR.

In the very moment that you experience, you instinctively know whether you are coming from a loving or a fearful mindset.

Your knowing how these two forces work is imperative to your understanding of yourself as a creative human being.

The balance of FEAR and TRUTH in your life affects every relationship you have.

In particular this is true of your relationship with yourself!

You cannot have a fulfilling relationship with another if you do not first have a good relationship with yourself.

In knowing the forces working within these two simple emotions - FEAR and TRUTH, lies the very secret of creation and life itself!

The balance and proportion of these two principles, FEAR and TRUTH, affect all aspects of life.

Addictions, death, illness, marriage, child rearing, success, wealth, war, peace, work, personal happiness, national destiny, politics, love, law, religion, - every human experience imaginable requires our understanding of the power of FEAR and TRUTH.

How one harnesses this power inherent within these opposite forces is the key to a successful life!

The power of TRUTH creates the experience of LOVE - JOY - PEACE - WISDOM - DIVINITY - ABUNDANCE - and all positive aspects of life for which our higher self longs, and which the Divine wills us to have. This is True Reality.

Happiness is our right! We are entitled to it. We must demand it for ourselves.

Fear reflects the negative aspects of life, including HELL (Hell is not a place outside of ourselves, as some would have you believe. Hell is a state of consciousness that is very real to those caught in the illusion of hell. Inasmuch as all our experience of Self and the world is experienced in the mind, one can create a living hell that is very real to that person experiencing the darkness).

That which is of the LIGHT comes from TRUTH and that which is of the DARKNESS comes from FEAR.

By this yardstick you may measure all things and all situations, whether personal or societal.

Every experience and emotion contains a level of FEAR or TRUTH. We create the FEAR; the other is a Divine state of being.

Enlightened beings, such as saints, differ from us in their perception of TRUTH and FEAR and in their conscious decision to live in TRUTH and LOVE and to thereby deny the illusion of FEAR and ego.

In so doing they choose the light and deny the darkness.

The balance between TRUTH and FEAR determines the quality of ones life. Your thoughts, emotions and reactions relating to both TRUTH and FEAR shape your experience of reality and whom you think you are as a person.

People apply the labels "good" or "bad" to everything in their lives, depending on whether that experience came from a place of FEAR or TRUTH in their minds. This reinforces the mistaken belief that good and bad just somehow "happen" to people. This thinking leads people to believe that they are powerless to change events.

Indeed people believe that they are not even responsible for what happens to them.

The most negative statement imaginable is "shit happens".

Nothing "happens" that we have not consciously or unconsciously manifested in our lives.

This line of thought is so prevalent in our society that not only is it applicable to individuals, but it applies as well to nations and corporations and all spheres of human activity.

—

Good and Bad

*The only good is knowledge and the only evil is ignorance - Socrates
(Greek philosopher)*

Unless one has a level of self-awareness - most people characterize their experiences as being either "good" or "bad" as if they bore no responsibility for anything that manifests in their lives.

Habitually people categorize their days, their conversations, their job, their relationships, in fact all that they experience, in either positive or negative terms as being "good" or "bad".

This habit is ingrained from birth resulting in the cop out of people not being held accountable for their own lives.

Understand that the concepts of "good and "bad" are purely subjective and are *not* empirical statements. In other words "good and bad" are a personal judgment of how things are.

In terms of the Universe, things just "are". They are neither good nor bad. Mankind passes judgment. God does not judge. God merely observes. God "IS".

The universe "IS". Neither good nor bad, everything merely IS.

When Moses asked God on Mount Sinai, "Who are You?" God does not reply I am the King of Kings, or the Judge of Judges. God states His TRUE nature in the response, "I Am That I Am". This is the essence of God, "I Am That." "I Am." In other words, there is nothing that I am not. I am All that Is.

The definition of "good" or "bad" is a human relative concept that we use to make judgment on a situation.

In TRUTH God does not judge, therefore, there is no judgment. When you are the All That Is, The Almighty, you are in every human experience for better or for worse. However in "Being," God is neither judging nor punishing or rewarding. God is simply Being. God Is.

To tie together these ideas, you need to allow for the concept of a Universal Being (God). You need to consider that there is no "external" God.

It, She or He is within us. I mostly use the term "He" for the sake of convenience.

22

God creates and exists in all things. God energy is within all things in the universe including us. Were He not then we could not exist, because if He were outside of us then He could not be God He would be something less. To be God He must be in everything. That is the meaning of Universal.

This being so, we are all "of God". God does not play favorites. He does not grant favors to one person and not another. He treats us all equally and impartially with total forgiveness and compassion. We can learn to tap into our Divine relationship with God in order to manifest what we want in our lives. We all have equal access to God, we are all loved equally, deserve His grace equally, and we are all equal in His sight. No person is more deserving or less deserving than the next.

Wayne Dyer is a very erudite and well-read man, and a lovely human being. I have had the pleasure of attending his lectures on many occasions. Wayne once analyzed the nature of God something like this:

"(If) God energy would not include all things (then) to be Universal and to recognize anything as being outside Itself would be to deny its very being.
So, the nature of universal intelligence is an absence of individual personality...Though you have been conditioned to believe that you are an individual, you are actually a part of the grand Universal nature that is infinite in its possibilities.... Lacking individuality, it cannot be in conflict with your desires. Being universal, it cannot be simply be shut off from you."
- Dr. Wayne W. Dyer.

All creation is Divine and the Creator has created perfection in everything equally, including you!

God has not made any mistakes. There are no good bits of creation and other less good or bad bits. All is formed in perfection.

(My youngest son, who was a seven-year-old at the time, asked me why did God have to create mosquitoes. Try explaining to a seven-year-old that a mosquito is perfect. That is one tough audience to convince!)

Everything is simply in a state of being, or "IS-ness," neither good nor bad. However, insofar as human beings choose to label things, that which is of the LIGHT and LOVE and TRUTH is good and Divinely manifested.

This is the natural state of Creation and the state that the Universe wills us to be.

The rest of the gunk is our own stuff that we create. We can choose to give it up whenever we get tired of playing in the dirt. Or we can choose to play in it forever. It does not matter. It's our choice.

Chapter Four - Truth and Fear. A Third Radical Statement

Wisdom is the greatest cleanser - Sri Yukteswar (Indian saint)

Jeffrey M. Solomon

God Without Strings Attached

God is clever, but not dishonest - Albert Einstein (German born physicist)

"God is completely without Judgment."
This is the third radical statement.

I am certain that by now many readers may feel that this is a very radical statement. It certainly challenges our culture and the belief system that most of us were raised with.

In Western culture we are taught from childhood that wrath and punishment are the inescapable consequences of an unappeased and vengeful God. Thousands of generations have been raised to believe in a God of Divine judgment, and the reward or punishment of the hereafter.

Nothing could be further from the TRUTH!

The Supreme Being is incapable of hate, anger, disappointment or negative projection.

FEAR, which is a negative and human creation, is the domain of human beings alone.

The light of TRUTH must abolish FEAR within us.

This is a very important concept to follow and I shall go into depth explaining it in the course of this book. The concept of our relationship to the Divine and the Universe may turn on its head many of the beliefs and teachings you grew up with. If those teachings were totally truthful and fulfilling you would have no need of this book and would currently be in a state of perfect love and bliss. Are you?

"God is first and foremost Unconditional Love"
Unconditional love means without having conditions, restrictions, qualification or prerequisites in order to be loved. The ability of the Father to forgive the child its errors is Unlimited.

His patience too, is without limit.

That which He has created in perfection, including us, cannot be deemed defective. We are never judged nor punished by Him for what we perceive as our imperfection, for Him to do so would be to judge His own creation as imperfect.

In doing so He would be judging His creation, and by extension Himself, a failure!

This is impossible and anathema for the unconditional love the Divine has for all His creation.

—

All is One

My own mind is my own church - Thomas Paine (English born political philosopher)

"God is Universal."
Nothing exists which is outside of God. The very word "Universal" implies oneness. There cannot be two universes. "Uni" means one.

Nothing can exist outside of the One, (the Oneness of all is the Universe) all aspects of creation are part of the One, which is God.

This is a very important concept for you to grasp.

It means that we are one and the same as our Creator.

We are eternally a part of He that is the Oneness manifest.

To see us as separate from the Universe, and hence from God is the Great Illusion!

To see us as separate from each other is the Great Illusion!

To see us as separate from the animals, the earth, the stars the Universe, is the Great Illusion!

Many problems in our culture stem from the misguided notion that Divine anger and punishment will be handed down by a deity waiting for us to screw up so that he can zap us with a lightning bolt, and perhaps a plague thrown in for good measure.

We are taught that whereas God is a loving God when we are good, He is a Fearful God when we sin. We are erroneously taught that when we die it's Upstairs for the Goodies and Downstairs for the Baddies.

The toll in mental suffering is staggering. Guilty conscience stricken people fearing that they are eternally doomed is an enormous wrong on mankind. It is a result of this wrongful thinking, as you shall see.

First, resolve to forgive yourself for all the self-hate you have. God is not capable of hate. He does not judge you. Therefore in the eyes of God you are already forgiven even before you perform an act that you believe requires forgiveness!

Think of God not just as a Father or Mother but also as a Universal Master and Friend sustaining you and nurturing you along with all creation.

To the ancients God is both male and female: The ying and the yang.

The Divine in Her unlimited love and compassion gave you a wonderful gift called "Free Will" that you may have all manner of choices and experiences without limitation or fear. So do not engage in recrimination or self-judgment. Resolve to forgive yourself for all the guilt that you carry, for God has already forgiven you. Practice self-forgiveness and self-love.

This is the first step towards enlightenment.

It sometimes helps when we see God as female, in order to fully appreciate the nurturing aspect and love associated with God. In very ancient times, society was less male oriented and many cultures worshipped the female qualities of God. Hence we have Mother Earth, the ultimate nurturer. This is the source of all life, given freely and equally to all.

At some point in time the male figure superseded the female form and this became the god of the Old Testament. This god is a warrior figure, a vengeful, and wrathful god requiring strict laws and total obedience.

As the Old Testament progresses towards more current times, the nature of God changes. He becomes a more remote figure, less involved in direct communication, retribution and the personal intervention in the affairs of man.

Some would argue that since God gave mankind the gift of free will, we have since fallen and have become sinners.

Consider this: What Father, or Mother would give his or her children freedom of choice in order that they may experience all the wonders that life has to offer, and when they make the wrong choice they are punished! Where then is freedom of choice?

This concept is a machination from the mind of a madman!

It is inconceivable that we be punished for not making the choice that God would have us make!

If we truly were sinful beings, incapable of making correct decisions, this would also mean that God is defective for He has created us imperfectly. He then punishes His creation for being imperfect! In other words, God has no control over His creation. Not only that, but God has messed up big time. Clearly this is ridiculous

29

and we should no longer be at the effect of religious dogma and religious institutions that teach this gospel.

If you choose to see yourself as a sinner, you are accusing God of being deficient, for having created you imperfectly!

Believing that God will punish you, you see God not as the Divine, compassionate and an absolute loving Father or Mother that God is, but rather you experience God as a vengeful and wrathful deity threatening you with damnation and hellfire for your transgressions!

This insane scenario is indeed the creation of the mind of a madman. However, the madman is not God.

It is the creation of mankind alone.

This is the illusion of guilt that our belief system has imposed on us

Guilt and punishment are powerful devices used by those institutions intent on control and the subjugation of their congregation.

It is also the result of the wrongful and frequently intentional misinterpretation of scripture. As long as clergy are seen as the keepers of a complex system of so called "Divine" laws and are considered the interpreters of Divine will, then they will keep the faithful dependent on them for salvation. Thus they create for themselves job security and social standing, and land, buildings, and cash flow becomes the major priority. Churches generate enormous income from the faithful.

Relying on only one set of scriptures is also a source of divisiveness. This promotes egalitarianism and limits an open mind to the wonderful diversity of human spirituality and culture.

That is why in the tours Sharda and I lead to sacred places, we embrace the diversity of beliefs on the planet and we learn from enlightened beings of other cultures who are willing to share their traditions with earnest seekers of the truth.

In the new Millennium, we dare not allow separation engendered by close-minded individuals and by religious dogma to be a source of division and conflict between people. Our oneness and our mutual Divinity should be acknowledged. Human diversity should be celebrated rather than being the cause of conflict.

That which divides us as nations and as people is the ultimate heresy.

Indeed, the heresy of the human condition is the heresy of illusion and separation.

"There is ONE unchanging indivisible REALITY which, though unmanifest, reveals Itself in infinite multiplicity and diversity. That One - the Supreme Truth - is ever present everywhere in all circumstances. Referred to as Absolute Reality (Brahman), He is no other than God Almighty. God Almighty is nameless and formless; yet all names and forms are His. He is the Father, Mother, Guru, Friend, Creator, Preserver, Destroyer - everything. His essence is Being, Consciousness, and Bliss. Indeed, He is in everything and everything is in Him; there is nothing but Him. Try to see God in everything and everybody, including yourself. God Himself is revealed in some guise even in individuals supposed to be sinners, also in suffering seemingly unbearable" -
Anandamayi Ma (Indian Saint)

The Eternal Self

One can never consent to creep when one feels an impulse to soar. -
Helen Keller (American essayist)

Although you perceive your reality as being fact and not illusion, you can no more harm yourself in life than you can harm yourself in a dream.

This is not to deny the existence of physical pain. Identifying yourself with the physical body you inhabit is an illusion. You are not who you think you are. Your experiences, social status, appearance, race and religion are the things that you use to define yourself as a being. None of this is who you are. Who you are is defined by what is real not only in the moment or a year from now, but what is real for all time. The eternal truth is reality. That which is made by man is but dust and illusion.

Your soul is eternal; your body is perishable. Therefore, the soul is the real you. The soul takes on a body in order to have a physical experience in the physical world. This it will do hundreds, perhaps thousands of times in the course of its evolution.

Evolution of the soul is what life is about.

The path of having multiple human experiences enables the soul to evolve and grow. The physical world is a playground and a school for the soul, at the end of which it gives up its body and returns to its natural form that is spirit.

The soul is a permanent part of the Divine. Having been created as such since all eternity.

You need to understand that the soul is an aspect of God experiencing Itself. It is a Divine emanation. Do not see yourself as a soul in separation from God.

Your soul, being Divine, has the same ability to create from thought as God does. And it does so in the human form.

Your soul has total consciousness of its essence and its ability to create. In the physical form, in order to express free will, it may forget its link to Divinity. You nevertheless continue to create your world and your reality in the physical world. Frequently this is more often than not an unconscious process as far as you are concerned. Creation in the denser physical world is also slower for most of us to manifest than in the subtler world of thought and spirit. Consequently, because of the lack of immediate results between the time we have a thought and the manifestation of that thought into reality, we frequently fail to make the connection that what we are experiencing now is a result of our past thoughts about something.

Your awareness of your God identity and your ability to create is often lost in the process of your becoming a physical being so that you, in your humanity, can manifest your free will within the physical experience.

Your soul and the human body that you have taken on, are nevertheless one with God. Your spirit is as eternal as the Divine Itself, because you are the Divine.

The soul can be likened to a direct piece of God that has taken upon itself human form. Thus it is able to experience the fullness of the physical dimension. Nothing that it does while in human form can actually harm the soul. Ultimately it must be seen that the physical world is a playground for us to have all kinds of wondrous experiences in the knowledge that this world is but an illusion, a holograph in three dimensions if you will. Nothing can harm us for we are not who we think we are!

That is why that great teacher, Maher Baba, after decades of a self-imposed vow of silence, bestowed these simple words on mankind when he finally broke his silence, "Don't worry – be happy". There was even a hit reggae song using this theme, "don't worry, be happy". Consider how many young lives were touched by this sacred insight to life. It conveys a deep and fundamental truth. As I have said, the truth may come from any source at any time and always in a form that receiver is most receptive to hearing. Even in a rock and roll song. Isn't life great!

The soul is both "one with, and of, the Divine", and by extension all people are intrinsically a part of God. As a whole, mankind is God. We are one being, one source, and intelligence.

The soul is a reflection of its' Source, that is the soul is a reflection of God.

We are truly made in the image of God and we are one with all souls, and all of mankind is one.

All souls are interlinked, and because all of mankind is ultimately one soul, it is incumbent on us to treat each other kindly and with respect. The harm that you do to another, you truly do to yourself. The forgiveness you offer to another, you truly offer to yourself. The love that you bless another with is a blessing on yourself.

Your mind is linked with all people as one. When you are in your unconscious, illusion state, your mind will join with other, like-minded, beings in the manifestation of the lower thoughts of mankind. When you are present in the here and now and totally conscious of your Being, your thoughts will soar and you can raise others up unto the light of Reality.

Understanding the interrelationship of all beings, the illusion and futility of war, hate and envy will fall away. You can immediately see the smallness of thinking in the lower state of mind. How narrow and stupid are our little games of seeing competition between beings, when we are all one.

You will be motivated to help all aspects of yourself; that is to help others. This readily becomes apparent. You do not loose anything by sharing or helping another. Indeed you only ever help yourself. You will hasten the consciousness of the entire planet, and heal the differences you have created between your various soul selves.

Your job is to move from confrontation to cooperation.

There can no longer be competition only cooperation.

The total human organism is really one. It will evolve better and quicker once we drop the mindset of separation and competition, and once we resolve to help all aspects of our greater self, that is all humanity, to be the best that they can be.

Always remember that to help one soul is indeed nothing less than to help oneself!

To harm another is to harm oneself!

Your soul is also the vehicle through which the Divine directly experiences Itself. It is the means that the Divine has of having the multiple physical experiences of the billions of aspects of Itself in human form.

This means that all human experience is Divine and of God.

God cannot be injured consequently all human experiences are ultimately harmless in the greater scheme of things, as if a dream. All human experience contributes to the Universal experience of the Divine experiencing His own advent. The free will granted to human beings ensures an endless multiplicity of choices that forms infinite combinations of experiences, all of which are ultimately safe. In spite of how we, in physical bodies may immediately perceive physical experiences; we *can do no harm!*

Our job, if you will, is to express our free will by choosing to grow and to evolve as physical beings to the point whereby we can see beyond the illusion and rise above it and become our true God-selves.

As the army-recruiting slogan says, "Be all that you can be."

(The truth is sometimes found in the most unlikely places!)

In demonstrating the highest thought of what we can be, so we discover the peace, love and harmony that is our true state of being.

This is what the Divine desire is for us, and in It's infinite patience and love It can wait for us to achieve this state of Grace.

Should we fail, and if mankind destroys itself in the meantime, the Divine will simply continue with creation, for that is what God does. Perhaps in the next evolutionary cycle we may succeed. This holds true for us as individuals as well as for mankind as a whole.

We should not be so vain as to think that we are the first and only attempt at physical creation in the Universe. There have been others before us and there will doubtless be others after us.

The challenge for us is to succeed. Success is defined as achieving a state of grace on earth.

This we can do by honoring ourselves collectively and individually as Divine Beings. When we acknowledge all others as an expression of ourselves, and when we honor all creation as holy and we walk lightly upon the earth with respect, we will have succeeded.

When you acknowledge your Divinity you will also appreciate that you do not need an intermediary either in the form of a person or an institution to intercede on your behalf with God.

God is, and we are Him.

Realizing this magnificent statement about your True self should offer you much comfort and support and remove all manner of self-doubt.

When we understand this and when we teach the TRUTH, and Humanism in our schools, our children will grow up knowing that they are safe, loved and eternal beings. They will know that all nations are more than their brothers all people are one being manifesting itself in a multitude of interesting forms.

Children will grow up knowing that to help another is the highest form of self- help there is!

In conclusion, when we help another we truly help ourselves. This is our eternal quest on the path to self-realization.

<u>Chapter Five - Let's Grow!</u>

"The body is a treacherous friend. Give it its due; no more.
Pain and pleasure are transitory" - *Sri Yukteswar (Indian saint)*

Jeffrey M. Solomon

A Word on Karma

Every why hath a wherefore - William Shakespeare (English playwright)

We all need to learn specific lessons in the physical world caused by our own karma.

Karma is an Eastern word used to describe the Divine Universal Law of cause and effect.

There are four Truths that affect karma, which is balance, in the Universe.

1. As you sow, so shall you reap.
2. Truth is immutable and constant (unlike physical experience). Always seek the truth.
3. Thought is creative.
4. Forgiveness is the highest expression of your Divinity.

You need to understand the Universal Law of cause and effect or karma. Every action and thought you undertake creates karma. The imbalances that you create, in negative thought and actions, require a similar and equal amount of balancing reactions, which affect us individually and as a group.

Nations and societies also create karma that affects them.

Our actions are important. The actions that we allow our elected officials and bureaucrats to engage in, on our behalf, is also of critical importance to us.

Jesus said, "As ye sow, so shall ye reap." This is a Universal Law. This is the law of Karma.

In physics this force could be described as; "For every action there is an equal and opposite reaction". (Sir Isaac Newton - Third principle of gravity)

Opposite means that when you push out positive actions, the Universe pushes back to you with positive reactions and vice versa with negative actions. When you create positively, the positive response from the Universe will return equally to you.

These are Universal truths.

This is another Universal Truth: All TRUTH howsoever stated remains the truth.

Truth is immutable, no single person, sect or religion has an exclusive lock or monopoly on Truth.

There are millions of individuals and thousands of cultures and religions that have found a way to God. Diverse philosophies may appear to be fundamentally different from each other. To this extent nations have fought wars over such differences. When the TRUTH is expressed, a person with an open mind and with no axe to grind will comprehend the underlying homogeny of all TRUTH and all points of view.

There is no limit to the number of ways TRUTH is articulated in human traditions; consequently there is not simply just one path to the truth!

There are a million rivers leading to the ocean, each shall find its own path but the ocean of Truth remains constant. All truths lead to the same ocean (God).

Karma is wrought by our thoughts.

Dogmatism and rigidity of mind is the enemy of enlightenment and have no constructive role in achieving enlightenment. Let your mind be a reed that bends in the wind of ideas, allowing that all things in life are possible.

Having truly found God, there is no further need for prayer. When you live in God you are with God always. The need to pray diminishes, for ones every thought and action praises the Divine. You live in God.

"Need" falls away. The annihilation of need diminishes the creation of negative karma

In God realization, all desires are fulfilled. There is nothing more that you need, and your being will be complete.

Without God realization, one senses a lack of completion and a restlessness of mind. You "need" things. Once those needs are met then you need more, bigger and better. No amount of material gratification can complete our needs. Our homes are never perfect, our salaries are never adequate, our cars are never the ultimate machine that we may desire, our careers are seldom fulfilling, our relationships are uneasy.

Whatever the "need" is, we can never achieve complete fulfillment unless our soul is fulfilled.

The very fact that one may struggle in areas of ones life is a sign that you are swimming up-stream. You are resisting the ease that is the natural state of a realized being.

Struggle is the surest sign that your life is not working.

Struggle is a symptom of going against the natural order of the Universe.

This is your surest indicator that you should reevaluate what you are doing.

When you reach spiritual fulfillment, your needs disappear.

Explicitly, those things that you thought you could not live without, become unimportant. If you desire something then the "neediness" aspect of desire dissolves and one is left content to have desire without "need".

Without "need" for material possessions, you will observe them as illusions, incapable of anything other than the fleeting gratification of the senses. They provide an expedient use in the moment. You may nonetheless appreciate and enjoy material things for what they are, but you release attachment to them. You will not define your identity and self by objects and possessions as our society has taught us.

Therefore, in the space of Truth, you are able to perceive wisdom inherent in all creation and the Mind behind All That Is. No longer will your thoughts "need" to create damaging karma.

Uncontrolled thoughts equal uncontrolled lives.

"Free will" leads us into temptation when applied unconsciously.

This is the source of restlessness.

Thought is creative. Constantly dwelling on a thought such as "there is not enough" or "I am not satisfied" or harboring feelings of resentment, becomes self-manifesting.

That is; as you think, so shall you be.

Therefore:

Your thoughts create your reality. Your reality is a reflection of your mind

Being free willed, we disturb the natural harmony of the Universe by way of negative thoughts and actions that arise from "need".

Expressions of hurt, fear, jealousy, discontent and destruction are not in alignment with the natural order. Thought precedes expression that in turn precedes action.

When all three of these aspects of your nature, thought, expression and action, are in alignment, your "Trinity" is in its most powerful and expressive state.

Negative thoughts are ego driven. When expressed outwardly, negative force manifests in various unpredictable destructive ways such as violence and wars, degradation of the planet and drugs or any number of detrimental, FEAR motivated expressions.

The natural order, thus upset, must be corrected. And it is.

The capacity of souls to reincarnate should be seen in the context as an opportunity for one to learn from past actions and thus we gain the prospect to balance the cosmic scales, as it were, through the Law of Karma.

In reincarnating over many lifetimes with the purpose of evolving to higher states of consciousness, each lifetime affords you the opportunity to grow more spiritually advanced in your progression towards a state of Truth and enlightenment.

One should seize the opportunity to grow in the physical world. Here you can substantially increase your level of spiritual maturity. Consequently you will eliminate the repetitive cycle of unlearned lessons over consecutive lifetimes. On a Universal magnitude, the good that you create through attaining spiritual growth truly helps all of mankind to grow spiritually as well.

All souls are one. That which you do for yourself, you do for all of Mankind.

The Jewish Talmud states that the deeds of the father affect his children unto seven generations.

This is a period of approximately five hundred years.

The enormity of this statement can be gauged when you take into account the number of people this statement refers to.

Consider, if you will, the thousands of descendants in the USA who claim to be descended from Thomas Jefferson after two hundred and fifty years. You will appreciate the colossal number of people who can claim ancestry from you after five hundred years!

Each and every one, according to the Talmud, will be affected by your deeds today.

A broader interpretation of this is that your thoughts and actions affect everyone.

Therefore it is essential to be conscious of your thoughts and actions at all times.

Also consider another gem of wisdom from the Talmud, that to kill one person is as if one killed an entire universe!

—

Your Thoughts are your Reality

As he thinketh in his heart, so is he - Proverbs 23:7 (Bible)

Great teachers such as Moses, Jesus, Buddha, the Mahatma, Krishna and Muhammad, raised the spiritual consciousness of the entire world.

Such is the power of thought of a single enlightened individual that it can shake the world.

Each teacher above produced huge shifts of awareness for all of mankind through the power of their thought, spirit and deeds.

Such is the power of one. This is the power of TRUTH.

Their lives are of greater consequence to us than the most powerful mortals and kings.

This identical power inherent in each of these saints lies within you, today, right now.

Jesus said as much when he stated that all that He did shall you do too *and even more*.

Frequently, the good that many great teachers accomplish is misappropriated and subverted by avaricious individuals and organizations for political and selfish gain.

For example, who ever heard of a Holy war? The idea is spiritually preposterous!

This is an affront to the Divine Name. Christians, Muslims, Hindus and Jews have all embraced this concept at various times in history and some continue to do so today.

It is outrageous to wage war in the name of God or to presume that God takes sides in any conflict.

The Divine is tolerant and non-judgmental. He allows us all manner of latitude for error, knowing that ultimately the human soul is the true essence of what we are. In truth, we are eternal beings.

God knows that if we choose the illusion of suffering, our powers of creative thought will manifest every manner of horror and suffering. That is the lot of mankind.

He also knows that the illusions we create for ourselves also give rise to the opportunity for our healing. In order to have the prospect to heal, the Universe constantly presents us with opportunities to learn lessons resulting from our thoughts and deeds.

There is no problem that does not have a solution. God places the solution with the problem.

My friend Mathew says, "There are no such things as problems, there are only hidden solutions."

Do not miss the opportunities in this lifetime to balance the karmic debt.

If you do, you will have similar experiences with additional opportunities for healing in another lifetime.

Therefore should you continue with destructive behavior, the necessary lesson shall appear in various situations in this lifetime and the next, over and over again.

You need to be alert to the opportunity to heal destructive patterns. Grow every step of the way. Every situation in life is a chance to ask yourself what is being shown to you in this moment about yourself.

Remember that life is just a mirror reflecting your thoughts back at you.

Ask yourself what your highest thought could be in each moment. Know with certainty that nothing happens to you in your experience of life that does not have significant meaning.

Your job in this lifetime is to look for the meaning, without blame or anger, of what you need to learn from this experience.

God constantly presents you with opportunities to grow. Look for the lesson to be learned. Look for the hidden meaning behind challenging situations.

Ninety nine percent of people never perceive the reality of a situation and therefore they miss the opportunity to understand the lesson, to heal and to move on.

When you finally comprehend the lesson you will heal and learn, and you will advance and grow.

Remember this. Those people who appear as your greatest challenge, those who intimidate you fundamentally, are your greatest teachers.

Be grateful and not resentful for their presence in your life.

—

Everything is Fine - Even When it Is Not

Why do you hasten to remove anything which hurts your eye, while if something affects your soul you postpone the cure until next year? - Horace (Roman poet)

Books, like this, and hundreds similar, can help you to leapfrog the cycle of spiritual ignorance and help you to find the path back to your own Divinity.

Awareness is your first step towards changing your life.

As the Course in Miracles states, *"God has placed the answer together with the problem"*.

What this is telling us is that the solution to all problems is already there before you even have the problem! There is no problem for which God has not placed the solution, even before one is aware of a problem.

When my friend Mathew used to tell me, "There is no such thing as a problem, only a hidden solution", I did not grasp the true significance of this statement at the time.

This is a magnificent thought.

Please read it again.

I have carried this thought with me for thirty years and it never fails to inspire me and to intrigue me with the implications it carries within its meaning.

Take into account that the only thing that is keeping you stuck with a problem is your own lack of awareness along with the thought that you "need" something in order to have the solution. When you move from needing into acceptance and "Being", the answer will present itself to you. It's that simple.

God has no agenda regarding the time it takes you to realize this. He is in no hurry for you to "get it"; after all He created time! He has all eternity. The world, unfortunately, does not. God does have a desire or a preference that you become enlightened but He has no "needs". As desire is not the same as need, God does not interfere in your life choices, He has no "need" to. He is with you all the time in every thought and moment, creating growth opportunities for you, such as the reading of this book, a television show, a meeting with someone, or a question from a child. At every turn the Universe is

45

presenting you with possibilities to expand. Are you aware enough to recognize them?

As far as God is concerned, everything in the world is fine and "just is". And this is how you should be. If you move from a state of want and need into a state of being and trust you are expressing your God-self. As long as you "want" or "need" the Universe will align with your thoughts and create want and need. As long as you think that you "need" you will. Give up "need" and go into the present moment and just "be" and accept the world as "just is" the way God does, without judgment, and "need" and "want" fall away.

If you think you "need" something first look at what having that thing represents to you. If you think you "need" more money, you do not. What you want is the things that more money represents to you. Perhaps it represents security, or a certain lifestyle. Rather focus on what the change would mean to you and see yourself in that state of change and know that the answer is placed together with the problem. Therefore see yourself, and believe yourself to be in the state that you wish to be, without "needing" some specific event or thing to create the changed state.

Having faith that the answer is already there for you, and know with certainty that problem is already solved.

Eventually mankind will get the message and become self realized. Or perhaps we won't. If we do not, we may destroy ourselves, perhaps we will get it right at some far distant future.

God, being a patient parent, knows the truth, that we are eternal beings. Therefore, in the ultimate sense we can do ourselves no "real" harm on the playground we call earth. God is content to let us play our little games. He lets us take ourselves as seriously as we choose to, then, when we get tired of the game, we go home and clean up!

There is no need for Him to judge us - nor does he choose to. Judgment is superfluous All is well the way it is, even when it isn't. This is the Divine dichotomy!

We, however, will continue to judge ourselves. We will continue to create misery and suffering and want through the illusions that we create while in the physical world.

This is not to say that God does not care. God's greatest desire is for us to cease our stupid games and to find our way back to Him in Truth and bliss. God desires an end to our suffering. For He feels everything that we feel. Indeed God experiences every thought and feeling that each of us feels. He is One with us and we with Him.

He would choose only peace of mind and harmony for all of us. That is His desire and His gift to us. He has no wish to see us suffer. However He will not interfere, for our free will is also His gift to us.

Consequently neither will He prevent us from suffering. His gift of "free will" to us only requires that we use this gift wisely. Suffering is a lifestyle choice that we create. He will not deny our wish. We will always get exactly what we want!

If we choose to see the world as a place of FEAR and suffering, that is what we shall have.

At all times we are at choice to create our reality. Only awareness of our choices is required of us.

He that has eyes let him see!

To escape the cycle of suffering we must open our eyes and hearts to the Truth and banish illusion.

Once we realize the creative power of thought both as individuals and at a group and national level, we will realize that what we have is exactly what we think about and that which we fear most is manifest.

The Universe will deny us nothing. The Universe reflects and mirrors back to us that which is our deepest and strongest thoughts and makes it manifest.

To change the world we must first change our thoughts about it.

The reason we often fail to see our negative thoughts is because we suppress most of our feelings about ourselves and about life in general.

Fear is past anger projected into the future and anger is past fear brought into the present.

The yoga, or science of Rebirthing, entails the practice of seeing our "sponsoring" or deepest hidden thoughts and the harmonious release of these thoughts from the mind and from the cellular level in our bodies.

Sharda and I call this Life Alive. Life Alive is way of being alive and conscious that we teach in seminars and that we practice.

It is beyond a mental and intellectual process. Life Alive requires one to be aware of the body as a temple in which one places only life enhancing substances.

This means being aware of the quality of air that we breathe, the quality of food and water we take in, and yes the quality of people we allow into our lives.

All things are energy and all things, like a magnet affects ones balance and harmony.

Above all of these is the breath. This is the key for the release of emotional damage, to create new life, and vitality. Vita = Life. Webster's Dictionary defines vitality as "vital principle or force. Power to live or go on living". Therefore, Life Alive!

If you desire health, bliss and harmony and love, then you have but to change your thoughts about these things, and your lack of having them.

The first step in Life Alive is to recognize the life negating thoughts and influences that you do not even know you possess and which, indeed, possess you!

One learns to release darkness and energy draining (deathist) thoughts from the body and to replace them with life-force affirming thoughts.

The yoga science of correct breathing in the Life Alive program is, for me, the most efficient way to clear old thoughts and ingrained negative patterns, and to replace them with affirmative, positive and constructive thoughts.

This is one of the techniques we practice, along with meditation and having good teachers, on the path to God and self-actualization.

—

The Created World

The questions which one asks oneself begin, at last, to illuminate the world, and become one's key to the experience of others. - James Baldwin (American author)

Let us go back and look once more at the concept of "good" and "bad". All life-negating thoughts begin with a negative thought about oneself. Therefore one needs to revisit the subject of good and bad, or, I prefer Truth and Fear, to understand the meaning and working of these opposing forces and how they affect us.

Even in regard the vilest manifestations of human behavior, "good" and "bad" is purely a human judgment about a situation or something and it is not an absolute statement of TRUTH.

This is a strange concept to follow for those raised in the Judeo-Christian ethic of reward and punishment. It is one that most people will find perplexing if not downright troubling.

Every murderer, including the perpetrators of the Holocaust, justified their actions - at least to themselves- as "good" or "necessary" for a variety of reasons, none of which, for the purposes of this discussion, are of consequence to us right now.

Similarly every victim judges the actions of the perpetrators of bad acts as "terrible" or "evil". So will all decent people of conscience, for obvious reasons.

In judging, everything depends upon the individual's point of view regarding how they, perceive and judge a particular issue. It is good to remind oneself at this juncture that;

Mankind Judges and punishes, - God, however, merely "Is ".

When people cannot comprehend the needless suffering of starving children, the poverty of the underprivileged and disasters that affect innocent people, they frequently cry out to heaven and ask, "How can a just God allow so much pain and misery on earth?"

In the extreme we may deny the existence of a Divine Force altogether.

This is natural when we perceive the world as chaotic, unfair and a dangerous place to live.

Jeffrey M. Solomon

Is it any wonder that people consider leaving this place? People want to die. People work towards their own demise by choosing death enhancing life styles.

The food chain and diet is one way to shorten ones life. Another way is to poison the air that we breathe, a stressful lifestyle is a sure killer. If that does not work fast enough we can add cigarettes, drugs and alcohol. All told, all the factors combined are a sure way to a slow and painful death.

We therefore need to look at who truly creates pain and misery and why we allow it to exist. Who creates poverty, homelessness, malnutrition and human misery, and how? Who should take responsibility for these things?

We need to ask who is responsible for the planetary degradation that results in droughts and soil erosion. Who builds houses in hurricane areas and clears trees that protect the coastline from storms? Who poisons the soil with pesticides and genetically modified foods? Who creates global warming and air pollution? Who spreads out in urban sprawl and uncontrolled breeding? Who threatens wildlife and is responsible for the mass the extinction of plant and animal life?

Who creates drugs and alcohol and cigarettes? Who produces fear and conflict and creates armies that drain economies, produce nothing beneficial, and diverts cash from the health system, schools, conservation services, and the needy? Who creates the needy?

We need to look at who.

Then look at why.

Then ask whether God is responsible for this condition or is it ourselves?

The annual military budget of the USA alone is sufficient to provide food, clothing and shelter, for every homeless person in the world! By far the single biggest national expense of all nations worldwide is military expenditure.

Health care, shelter, education and famine relief do not even come a close second.

We are responsible. Collectively we have created governments and leaders who implement such wasteful policies. We tolerate the degradation of our environment for the sake of a material lifestyle. As long as the pollution is not in our backyard we turn a blind eye to the corporations and institutions engaged in such practices. Indeed many

50

people benefit from the stock prices of corporations engaged in the awful mistreatment of the earth and the exploitation of third world peoples. Our pension funds and mutual funds invest in them even if we do not directly do so ourselves.

Because we have chosen to see ourselves as different from each other rather than as one with each other we allow fear and mistrust to govern our relationships.

We have created governments as well as institutions such as the FBI and CIA and their equivalent and through them we see ourselves as separate from other nations.

Every nation has such institutions. Some, like North Korea, cannot feed themselves, yet their fear and xenophobia is such that they have created huge armies and intelligence apparatus rather than food, medicine and education.

We also have created separate social classes within our own country, separate religious groups, separate racial groups and various other institutionalized forms of separation from each other, such as the old school tie, the social club or the right church or even charity.

Creating separation is the primary cause of FEAR. Fear leads to feelings of threat from without and a need for defense. When we do not perceive attack, we have no need for defense.

Indeed all FEAR stems first and foremost from feeling separate from God. When you no longer feel connected to your Source you truly are adrift and that is a fearful place to be.

Therefore when one is disconnected, one perceives danger and attack from all causes and from all directions and from there arise the perceptions of a need for defense.

When you are in your God-self you acknowledge your own immortality. You *know* that nothing can harm you. You also know that everyone is connected to you and to everything else. Therefore the Divinity is an energy that runs in all things, and we cannot judge it, nor do we need to be fearful of it.

There is a saying that I cannot remember accurately but it goes something like this.

When the Nazis came for the Communists I did not protest for I was not a Communist.

Then they came for the Jews and I did not protest for I was not a Jew.

They took the homosexuals and Gypsies and I did not protest for I was neither.

When they came for the Catholics and I did not protest for I was not Catholic.

Then they came for me and there was no one left to protest.

In separation, we fail to see the oneness of mankind, by choosing not to feel the pain of others.

If you turn a blind eye to discrimination you reinforce your separateness.

When we are not directly affected by discrimination, we tend to ignore the injustice and we fail to see that we have a unique, special responsibility to each other and the oneness of all life.

Apathy allowed the Nazi rise to power in Germany.

We choose separation so that we can look the other way at poverty, especially when it affects other cultures and nations.

We tend to view other nations as "foreign" to our culture and therefore as lesser.

We emphasize differences rather than commonalties.

We emphasize our individualism and our separateness.

We choose to see difference and diversity, not as the miracle and wonder of life expressing itself in multiple forms, but rather we perceive diversity as a threat to our way of life.

We dehumanize others, be it for military advantage as in the case of our perception of Russia, China, Iraq and Iran, or as economic as in the case of Mexican immigrants.

All nations have allowed their governments and military to reflect their basest mindset and to thrive as a xenophobic, fearful demagogues.

You and I empower them.

Governments act out and mirror our collective societal fears.

This justifies their existence to the taxpayers and politicians.

A nation is simply a people's vision of life reflected back at them.

We have replaced Love with FEAR and separation in our governments and institutions because FEAR has replaced love within us.

A deeper explanation of this is that we create our world experience through our thoughts, words and deeds.

We must therefore assume responsibility for all those conditions that arise and result from our fear of the physical world.

It is always best to accept all people and all things without judgment.

When we judge others, we set ourselves apart from them.

The greatest FEAR experienced by mankind is when we feel separate from God.

This separation hides from us who we truly are.

From this illusion stems all other Fears and feelings of hopelessness.

We are encouraged by the clergy be it Christian, Muslim or Jew, to see God as separate from ourselves.

Christians believe that if you do not accept Jesus as your savior then you cannot go to heaven, so it is their job to convert all nations to Christianity. There is great competition, and much hostility, even amongst churches, as to whose Christian theology is correct.

Muslims are taught that all non-believers are infidels. Infidels, especially Christians and Jews are not to be trusted. In the past when the Muslims conquered other nations an infidel had to either convert to Islam or be killed.

Jews are taught that they are the chosen people and that a Jew must give special consideration to another Jew before that of a non-Jew. Jews, unlike most faiths, discourage conversion to their ranks.

The competition amongst organized religion for the minds and souls of the flock is intense.

The faithful are encouraged to perceive that it is a matter of "our God" versus "their God".

We see God as a being who can be cajoled for favors, and railed against when things go wrong. When we do this we are obviously in the illusion created by our ego and we are clearly not in our higher self.

Seeing God as separate, is denying that He is universal and in all things.

When we see God as He truly is, in all things, then we must also see Him in everyone and everything. This naturally includes us.

Judging anything as good or bad therefore must by definition, set that thing apart from us.

Our ego does this, for it wants to see the world in terms of good and bad, and consequently as separate from us.

In so doing, our ego justifies to itself that our perception of danger and the need for self-preservation or defense is warranted.

Ego selves blame others, even God, for pain, suffering, guilt and misfortune, for it is not in the nature of ego to willingly accept responsibility.

The accumulated result of thinking this way is the world in which we live and which *we* have created. God did not create that which we ourselves have made.

God's world does not contain the insanity and chaos of the world that we perceive.

To see the world differently we need to change our perception.

All conflicts between neighbors and nations must be seen as an illusion. There is no justification for fear or attack.

People must realize that every person is their brother and sister. Our very children and our parents are parts of us as is all of humanity. There can be no separation between people save as our insane vision creates such imaginary barriers. As long as we perceive separation there will be competition for land and resources between the haves and have-nots. The result is conflict and thoughts of attack and defense.

It is essential to see the unity of life on our fragile planet. The interconnectedness and holiness of everything should be respected. Earth itself is a great mother being which accepts our presence and provides for us. It is our sustainer.

Only the mind of a madman perceives the world as a hostile place that challenges him and which needs to be conquered. It is a perversion to damage the delicate lungs of the earth, through the wanton destruction of the rain forests. That which breathes life into our own bodies and cleans toxins from the atmosphere is slashed and burned to create grazing land for MacDonald's hamburgers. Corrupt third world governments at the expense of threatened animal and plant species allow uncontrolled logging.

Polluting the life giving arteries of fresh water rivers and lakes are a self-destructive activity that agribusiness and industry engage in. In the next century the scarcest resource on earth will be fresh water.

Already large areas of the earth are dying. Desertification is growing at the rate of thousands of acres a day.

Urban sprawl drains wetlands, which filter out the poisons we spew in obscene quantities over farmlands. We thus kill the liver of the earth that detoxifies the planetary system for the sake of another mall and a parking lot.

The farming of animals instead of grain increases the desertification the planet. Animal farming takes an enormous toll on the resources of the plane that is quite staggering. It is beyond the comprehension of most people. I deal with this subject separately in the chapter "The Price of a Cow" and I urge you to read it seriously.

There is abundance enough for all of mankind if only we adjust our way of thinking. Corporations should not be in wasteful competition for the resources of our little planet. And waste does not come from faceless entities called "corporations". Corporations are you and me and the next-door neighbor. They are your friends you meet in church and on the golf course and at the school PTA meetings. They are the husbands of the soccer moms, and the mothers of your children's friends. These are the people who decide the policies and the use of resources for the industries where they work and which they control. They affect the lives of every person on earth. And so do you.

The leaders of this small life raft of life, floating in the vast blackness of cold space, alone and throbbing with life must be nurturing and protective. We cannot spew trash all over our home and smoke and pollute in the little house that we all share. We will get sick and our earth will get sick and die.

We must beat the swords into plowshares and teach a curriculum in our schools that our sages knew well, that of honoring the earth. Homes must be built economically. We do not need 10000 square foot of space for a single average family along with the power and resources and land that it consumes. When you have a home of 10000 square feet, your neighbor will certainly desire a larger one. We must break the cycle of consumerism for the sake of the future generations.

Our sages tell us, that which we do affects the world even unto seven generations!

We do not even consider the legacy we are leaving to our children, let alone the inheritance of future generations.

Without a doubt we are a dangerous and primitive species, little deserving of the grace and infinite love with which we are truly blessed. We appear to be petulant and ungrateful, seeing lack amidst plenty, attack amidst love and we curse in the face of blessing.

To truly honor the will of our infinitely benevolent and Divine Creator, all peoples of this earth must change their thoughts and the way in which they think.

It begins with you. Now.

—

Judgment

Don't judge any man until you have walked two moons in his moccasins - Native American Proverb

The new Millennium is demanding of us a change in our thought process. Our perceptions must change. The energy we put into our lives and living must change focus.

We cannot blame God for our wrongful perception. No longer can we blame God for the ills of the world and accuse Him for the cruelty which our minds, ever fearful of attack, perceive to be all around us.

How then can one figure out the meaning of a world filled with the misery of the starving, and the plight of helpless children?

Mankind alone bears the responsibility for the abuse of the gift of life and the desertification of the planet, and the greenhouse conditions that have created havoc with the climate. Hundreds of years ago the desolate Sahara Desert which stretches across a part of Africa almost as large as the USA was once fertile and abundant. Elephant and giraffe roamed the plains. One can still see the primitive rock etchings of animals and hunters in the barren wastelands.

Today the trees that brought the rains are felled, the grass grazed barren by the flocks of ancient farmers. The soil is blown away and the rain no longer falls. The people are poor, malnourished and the children are starving.

Realistically the earth can sustain a population of a billion people. The population of the world today is four billion and the fresh water resources of the planet are overwhelmed.

If we think that this cannot happen in the USA we are wrong. Farmland is rapidly disappearing under urban malls. Land is worth more to property speculators than as a wheat field.

The topsoil, a mixture of toxic pesticides and chemical fertilizers, is running off into the Gulf of Mexico.

Early explorers of the Americas reported schools of fish so plentiful that they had only to lower a bucket into the sea and haul up fish. Today the fish are gone. The herring are no more, the Atlantic salmon is endangered, and the manatees are almost gone. The fish have been strip mined by factory ships and gill nets.

Such is the human hand in the poverty that faces four fifths of mankind.

Metaphysically speaking, how do we understand the plight of the seemingly helpless victims?

Why does a soul choose to incarnate in such difficult circumstances? Is God a cruel God?

What can we do, should we simply ignore the condition of our brothers and sisters?

The answer simplistically is one should not ignore their plight - nor, however, can one judge it.

The Course In Miracles states that there are no victims.

In order to begin to understand the complexity of the human situation, we need to be enlightened in the TRUTH and have a whole new perception of reality as it applies to ourselves.

What we must understand is that things in the physical world are never what they appear to be, nor are appearances necessarily real.

Reality cannot be perceived if ones perspective is devoid of enlightenment or open-minded thought. Even with enlightenment, only the greatest teachers are capable of taking into consideration the complex metaphysical factors at play that are beyond the comprehension of most of us.

Consider for a moment: Is the soul of the starving child reaping the reward of a past life? Is this life the karmic debt for past life consequences?

This is too easy and simplistic. I would not brand every unfortunate soul as getting his or her just comeuppance in this life. A starving infant may have been a saint or a sinner - One cannot judge nor comprehend the illusion presented by the physical world. Suffice to say that nothing is, as it appears to be.

Perhaps the soul of that child is highly evolved. Could it be that by prior contract to its present incarnation, it is taking on a difficult life experience to accelerate its karmic development?

In the process thereby, it may attain enlightenment sooner.

Furthermore, what if that soul was taking on the karma of society or even that of the world? In its pain ands suffering, it could be that it was one of millions of souls taking on the burden for the rest of us and is thereby helping to alleviate the potential for a great karmic debt on earth?

Did all the souls who perished on earth in World War II and particularly those who suffered so tragically in the Holocaust, need to commute some past life karma?

Consider the possibility that, in their taking on the awesome burden of being Holocaust victims, the victims of the Holocaust saved the entire world!

They caused the German war machine to divide its efforts and resources between the war effort and the holocaust victims' own extermination. In the process of the Final Solution, the resources required in the massive extermination effort, their incarceration in camps, and their mass transportation by rail and road, the administration and finally their deaths consumed much of Nazi Germany's limited war resources. The unbelievable effort required to accomplish the "final solution" and the manpower required of Hitler's Reich were diverted from the German war effort against the Allies into the mass extermination of the Jewish nation and other minorities. Thus were sown the seeds of defeat of the Nazi war effort.

Does history owe these dear souls a debt of eternal gratitude? I believe so.

We cannot truly judge the great cosmic plan.

We can never know all the possibilities of even a single human life. The cause of suffering is multi-faceted and linked to hundreds of combinations and events related to past lifetimes, present and future lifetimes, personal soul evolution, plus the evolution of the world and the universe.

What I wish to emphasize is that things in the physical world are never what it superficially appears to be. Appearances are not real. And reality can never be perceived from a mind that is unenlightened.

Our mind will always create our own interpretation of the world.

Until you learn to escape the illusion you will forever be ignorant of the true purpose of your own soul!

Prior judgment or pre-judgment is nearly always wrong.

What one must do is, help your fellow brothers and sisters from a space of unconditional love, with detachment from judgment, and with kindness and acceptance. Do not assign blame on the Divine. God is not Judging and God is certainly not punishing anyone.

Be aware that you may judge a person as the "poorest, most unfortunate" human being. This is always your judgment - not God's.

That individual could be a saint or teacher helping you to learn non-judgment, tolerance and humility.

Those who confront and challenge you most are really your greatest teachers. Often they are people you dislike because they force you to look at your responses and thoughts about them. You should be grateful for their presence in your life and seek the lesson being presented to you as an opportunity to grow.

People who confront you and bring up your fears are doing precisely what you need in order to be made aware of your character flaws. These are the people you need to pay the closest attention to.

Never equate spiritual development with only the fortunate and the materially successful amongst us.

Babaji, one of the great teachers of all time could be found bathing the feet of beggars in the streets of India.

Jesus ministered to the untouchable lepers of His day and healed their wounds.

These Divine beings saw not the outward physical circumstances of the person but the great soul that is a reflection of their true self. In other words they see every person as a manifestation of the Divine. The soul of every person is a both part of you as well as an aspect of God.

This is the lesson:

Judge not lest ye yourself be judged.

—

The Guru and the Motor Accident

If I had but two loaves of bread, I would sell one and buy hyacinths,
for they would feed my soul - Koran

Maheshwara Haidakhan Baba, known as Babaji (the simple father) is the most highly self-realized being. He is known as the yogi Christ of the East for his teachings and countless miracles and healings.

In the Himalayan foothills in the district of Nanital, is Haidakhan, a simple Indian village that is the site of one of the holiest places on earth, Mount Kailash. It is here that God is said to manifest and to take on a divine physical presence.

In 1970 a youth was found by local villagers in a cave at the base of Mount Kailash, on the banks of the River Ganga (Ganges). He was in a state of deep meditation. His body was of light so pure, so bright, that the villagers could not look upon Him.

Over a period of forty five days, while sitting in constant meditation at the peak of Mount Kailash the body took on a more earthly countenance and the energy which radiated from it toned down so that the villagers could approach Him.

They saw a beautiful youth of magnetic countenance and indeterminate age, perhaps about eighteen years old.

The wisdom and presence of this youth attracted the attention of the local authorities. He had no mother or father, no birth records and no schooling and yet He could quote the sacred texts by heart. He knew the families and biographies of all the people who met Him for the first time.

People were attracted to Him from all over India, including government ministers and high officials.

Soon Westerners from all parts of Europe and the USA were experiencing strange haunting dreams of a man whom they did not know. They were compelled by visions of this person calling them to India. Some of the people were doctors, some were psychologists, others were drug addicts and some were rock stars.

Unknown to one another, they began seeking this strange and compelling figure of their dreams. Their quest found them trekking to India through the Himalayan foothills to the remote village of

61

Haidakhan to find this haunting figure. Not knowing exactly where they were going, their individual stories are miracles of circumstances and chance happenings that brought them all to Haidakhan.

There, at the ashram (spiritual community or hermitage) in Haidakhan that Babaji had built, Babaji gave his darshan (holy sight - blessing) to all who came and He performed teachings and healings.*

Babaji, was known to take on and commute the karma of his devotees to save them from intense suffering.

One day after the fire ceremony in the sacred Dhuni (fire pit) at Babaji's temple, Babaji was taken violently ill. He started to vomit black bile. His devotees were extremely concerned, they had never seen him like this. He was considered to be Divine and hence above mortal illness.

On this occasion, a busload of devotees returning from Babaji's ashram in Haidakhan had gone off the road. The bus fell twenty feet down a mountain ravine.

Miraculously, no one was injured.

Back in the ashram, Babaji knew instantly of this event and He informed His concerned devotees of the accident. He told them that His illness was the result of His passing the accident victims karma through his body. He explained that even though He was able to Divinely commute the karma of the victims, His mortal body was not beyond the Universal law of karma.

In order for them not to be injured, He took on their karmic debt and His illness was a result of that.

Babaji, was also known to appear as a poor beggar in disguise and to wander the streets of the city.

He washed the feet of holy men, and pilgrims alike even though he was considered a Mahavatar, or Supreme Being. This lesson in humility was to demonstrate to others that one never knew how the real Supreme Being would appear or where he would appear and those random acts of kindness are the duty of everyone.

The question is, would you recognize God if he knocked on your front door?

———

* On our tours to sacred sites and power places we take groups to Babaji's ashrams in India. This is part of an ongoing spiritual awareness program run by Sharda Collard and myself. It is one of the most intense experiences one can have.

<u>Shastriji the Teacher</u>

Happiness is not a possession to be prized, it is a quality of thought, a state of mind – Daphne Du Maurier (French writer)

In my own personal situation, I first heard of Babaji over lunch with Sharda Collard and Sondra Ray.

Sondra is a close friend of ours and is considered to be the mother of rebirthing. She is also an author of several self-help and relationships books and is the founder of the Loving Relationships Training.

Sondra first told me about this remarkable guru named Babaji whom she had spent time with in the Himalayan foothills. When she related the litany of miracles and the amazing first hand experiences she had with Babaji, I was certain that I was dealing with a crazy person, to state it politely.

She related how strange letters would arrive from India at a time when she had retreated into seclusion in Bali to write one of her many books. No one knew where she was and yet letters arrived calling her to India to seek a saint that she had never heard of.

Sondra said that no one gets to Haidakhan without Babaji's blessing and she related to me how many had tried and for multiple reasons they never made it. Flights were delayed, transport broke down, illness caused them to turn back etc.

At that time I was an "A" type personality businessman and I was extremely skeptical of people who professed miraculous encounters, psychic experiences and especially religious revelation. At that time of my life I would welcome Jehovah's Witnesses and Mormons at the door so that I could rip their theology apart. I was the one that found every argument to prove that Jesus was a fake. Babaji as far I was concerned was another cult among many. I was too "together" to get into this stuff!

My partner to be, Sharda, brought Babaji into my life. As I became more aware, little miracles would occur. It felt as if a new awareness and expansiveness was opening my mind. I found that I could intuit information about things of which I had no knowledge.

In Haidakhan, at Babaji's ashram, prior to his passing, Babaji had instituted a devotion to the Divine Mother. This is the recognition of the female energy of God along side that of the male energy.

What Sharda and I did not know at the time, and as we later came to find out, the future of energy workers is going to be enhanced by couples working together in harmony and balance. The ying and the yang if you will, working together in harmony.

We were instructed that this is what Babaji was showing the world by the institution of the male aarti (prayer ritual) alongside that of the female aarti, namely that the time of all male or all female energy being dominant would no longer work in the new paradigm.

The need for mutual recognition of the interdependence of the two energies creates a force in which the sum of the whole is greater than the independent parts.

Within that year, I traveled to Haidakhan in India with my twelve-year-old son, Micha, to join Sharda who was leading a group with Sondra, to India.

I had originally asked my daughter, Morgan, who is older than Micha, to come with me but she did not want to go, and Micha jumped at the opportunity to go instead. You only get to Haidakhan if you are meant to.

This is how we found ourselves in a beautiful Babaji ashram in the foothills of the Himalayas, pristine, serene and simple.

We were blessed many times in so many ways whilst there. One of the things that stand out in my memory is Babaji's small bedroom. Before morning aarti that is at about 630am, Babaji's original attendant, Man Singh, goes to clean and pray in Babaji's bedroom. The room is tiny and barely can hold four people. So a line forms at about 430am of devotees who wait for Man Singh to finish, after which he puts chandan (a colored paste) on their foreheads It is said this opens or raises the mind to greater awareness.

Three other people are usually allowed into the room prior to chandan to meditate or simply be in the very powerful energy of the room as Man Singh does his devotions to Babaji. This is the equivalent of being in the holy of holies.

Some people have been going to Haidakhan for years and have never had this experience. Just like getting to Haidakhan, unless you are meant to be there, you never get there.

We were privileged to be in the room each day during our brief stay there.

From there we traveled to Rajahstan, to the home of Sri Vishnu Dutt known as Shastriji, (the title denoting a great teacher or sage) a wise teacher in his 90's who had been Babaji's priest.

It is extremely rare for anyone to be invited to Shastriji's home, and for a newcomer it is almost unheard of. Nevertheless there we were.

(The Indian government of Rajahstan subsequently has honored Shastriji as their greatest Indian poet of the past 100 years, having written over 60 books on medicine, philosophy and poetry).

Shastriji has also been given the gift of psychic ability by Babaji, who called Shastriji the purest man on the planet.

When we arrived at his home, Shastriji met us. Micha immediately told me that he felt deeply drawn to Shastriji and he felt as if he knew him. Shastriji asked me what my son had said and I told him. He chuckled as if it was an inside joke that he had been keeping to himself. Then he told Micha that he (Shastriji) had a son in his youth by a previous wife. Both the son and his wife had subsequently died and he told Micha matter-of-factly that Micha's soul was the reincarnation of that son!

Shastriji said that the reason we were there at his house in the first place was for completion. That was why Micha had accompanied me on this trip, and not his older sister.

Shastriji told Sharda and myself that we are very unique insofar as we are two beings sharing one soul. This he said is a very rare occurrence. Although neither of us realized the significance of this at the time, we have subsequently been guided to an awareness that it is our duty to meld the two energies, the male and the female, into one.

Together, the power of one is greater than the individual two in separation.

The love and energy emanating from the home of Shastriji put us into a state of bliss that lasted for weeks.

—

Power, People and Time

If the doors of perception were cleansed everything would appear to man as it is, infinite. - William Blake (English poet)

Never disparage anyone who appears less than oneself.

Similarly do not unnecessarily hold in high regard people in positions of power, influence and wealth simply on those accounts alone. (Consider, for example, the behavior of the recent presidents of the USA in the past twenty years, to say nothing of the leaders of countries such as China, Iran, Iraq, Paraguay, South Africa, Cambodia, Uganda, Yugoslavia, and Russia etc.). Do not dismiss as worthless those who are less fortunate and of humble circumstances.

Power people are frequently extremely poor models of humility and compassion. They have yet to learn how to handle their positions in an enlightened way as an example to mankind. From such people you can learn nothing but greed, avarice and FEAR.

People in powerful positions are frequently stuck in a mindset of fear of material loss such as the loss of assets, prestige, reputation, position and rank. Frequently they are paranoid, avaricious, deceitful and manipulative.

Rising to power because of an intense insecurity, power people need to continually accumulate more power or wealth to allay the insecurity. It is common to find that people, while outwardly appearing calm and effective, are seething with self -doubt and anxiety. Often their personal lives are a disaster and they have difficulty relating to anything outside of their ambition.

Defining themselves by what they have achieved materially they lack a true sense of self worth. They may be distrustful, fearing that people are out to take advantage of them.

The fact that some people are in a position of power and affluence is not necessarily an indication of Divine karmic reward! It may be that they are being given an opportunity to transcend their ego and to be of service to the world. How power is used is indicative of character rather than simply having power. As such you should base your respect for individuals.

The challenge for power people is to realize with humility the blessings that they have in this life and to use it for the good of others in charity and in championing worthwhile causes.

They should give away their wealth in large charitable amounts and use the power they have to do as much good work as they can.

If corporate executives gain their wealth and power through the exploitation of labor, as in the case of some corporations, such as Nike, then the karmic debt will be heavy.

Michael Jordan, at $25,000,000 per year, (at the time of writing) earns more as a corporate spokesman for Nike than all 35,000 Vietnamese workers in a Nike factory combined.

Working 6 days a week 8 hours a day for $47.00 per month, it takes a Vietnamese Nike (and Reebok) factory worker, twenty minutes of labor to be able to afford to buy a single egg! *

*The 35,000 mostly Vietnamese women earn an average of $47.00 per month that would make the annual payroll about $19,740,00. $5,000,000, less than Michael Jordan earns as Nike corporate spokesperson! This is about 50% less than the lowest paid workers in other foreign companies earn. In one plant, effective July 1 1999, the minimum monthly wage has dropped to $40.00. Nikes Manager of Corporate Responsibility, Chris Helzer, defends this position because both Michael Jordan and the 35,000 employees are being paid what the market dictates!

The workers sit for eight hours on wooden stools hunched over sewing machines, doing repetitive work and are frequently abused by the Korean managers, who do not even speak Vietnamese, and who were imported by Nike into Vietnam.

---

* Nike and Reebok employees work in hot factories with toxic chemical, glue and solvents to make the $120.00 pair of sneakers that you see in the shopping malls. The cost of the rubber sole and the few pennies worth of pieces of fabric used in the shoe probably cost more than the labor component. The athletic shoe industry, led by Nike, has to be one of the biggest rip- offs of the American public and is without a doubt, in my opinion, a model of corporate shame and greed.

The lives of thousands of workers plus their children and families could be measurably improved through a more enlightened attitude by the corporate world.

In the USA Today of October 4 1999, the newspaper cites a reduction in the use of Toluene, by Nike, a highly toxic solvent that affects the lungs and central nervous system. The risk in the use of these cancer causing solvents has been known for years, yet was not stopped until 1995. Because there was a public outcry in the USA about the physical beatings and abuse of workers by the mostly Korean managers in Nike plants, the use of such petroleum based solvents has subsequently been reduced and ventilation in the plants has been improved. USA Today makes no mention of the health of those workers who have worked for years with these poisons, nor Nike's plans to address this issue. For years Nike refused journalists admission to its plants unless they could be certain of a favorable report. An independent environmental monitor from UCLA Berkley, named Dara O'Rourke, declared the plants much improved but noted that they still exposed workers to heat, noise and hazardous chemicals.

One cannot imagine what they were like before the public outcry!

Michael could conceivably take some of those millions and do something worthwhile with them even if the corporations will not, that would be the highest thought. If he did he would shame the corporate world. The effect of his generosity would undoubtedly have a multiplier effect through other exploitive corporations. He could start a worldwide consciousness movement highlighting the plight of exploited workers and he could enlist companies to do better in the field of social responsibility.

Corporations should use their power and influence to spread the wealth and raise the living standards of their workers, create educational opportunities and housing and medical benefits for the people they employ in poor countries, and be a light in the community in which they operate.

They will create educated and loyal employees who will in turn become future, loyal customers for their products.

Universal principle: *The more one gives the more the Universe will give back to you.*

Be cautious of emulating the behavior of materially successful people for the sake of greed. Emulate instead, the behavior of spiritually successful people, for in doing that one can be most effective, especially if one is wealthy or powerful.

Prejudging anything or labeling someone or something as good or bad, blocks one off to all possibilities of seeing what truly is - and in so doing you shut down your mind to what could be!

This is of particular relevance to anyone who denies the existence of a Universal Intelligence.

Denial of what is, or even of God, matters not at all, least of all to God.

Your opinions and preferences do not affect the Divine.

If you choose to deny the existence of a Supreme Intelligence, it does not matter.

Whether you believe in God or not, or whatever form you choose to worship Him in it makes no difference.

There is no such thing as blasphemy.

Knowing that everyone of us is an aspect of God I can imagine God seeing the humor in an atheist denying his own existence.

In infinite patience He waits. It does not matter if you reincarnate a hundred lifetimes or a thousand lifetimes eventually you will get it. "It" being conscious awareness of the Divine relationship between the All That Is and all that is.

"It" also means being aware that you are a human being. The mere fact of your being is an expression of what you are. How you choose to be is more important than what you do.

If you can be the highest expression of life in every moment, appreciating your life and the sense of wonder in being alive and sentient then you are expressing yourself in being.

God experiences Himself through your being. Therefore the highest form of meditation and prayer is when you acknowledge your being. Doing so will result in appreciating the 'being" of others and honoring that higher part of others, which is ultimately the God within us all.

Stemming from a sense of being requires you to be aware of yourself at all times. You need to be an observer of your own life and to see the ebb and flow of events as a great journey you have chosen to have.

Being the observer of your own life also means seeing the Divinity in your every interaction with others. Awareness of the meaning of every interaction as more than a casual happenstance will elevate you beyond the mundane into true Reality. Observing your

Self creates the opportunity for you to detach from the moment and to be in touch with your higher self or the God within you. Beyond this you can also view yourself observing yourself in ever-higher levels of consciousness.

The "now" is the moment of creation.

Being in the 'now" or the present moment as an aware observer is where Reality exists. You are constantly defining yourself with your every thought and action. Being present and conscious in the present moment is to be part of your own creation. Creating and defining yourself is truly all you are ever doing, and that occurs right now, not in the past or in the future, but now. Reality is here and now. The future represents only future concerns and worries not yet manifest. Yet if you realize that the present moment was the future at some time in the past, then all your past worries were for nothing. Right now you can make choices that redefine what you are, for the better.

Unconsciousness is also an option you can choose if you wish, as is worry and resignation and helplessness.

You can choose whatever you want to believe right now.

You have freedom of choice to do so. This is your free will expressing itself. Indeed, God has no problem experiencing Himself from the viewpoint of an atheist! You can choose to believe that God does not exist or that this is the only life there is, or that the present universe is the only creation there ever was or that when you die that is the end of your existence.

God has no preference how you choose to believe, or what you believe. Everything is perfect the way it is. Every experience of every human "being" human is a unique God experience. The sum total of all life expressing itself, in all its forms is what God is.

This is what God does for a living, so to speak. God creates continuously, which is what you are doing when you are "being" rather than doing. In your being you are defining yourself anew in every moment. This is the exact moment of creation!

The sum total of all humans "being" is the expression of one life form, humanity, in its totality. There is no one way of being that is better than another way of being in the sense that a Christian being cannot be said to better or preferable than, say, a Muslim being.

All is one. Oneness is the true sense of who we are being. When we separate ourselves from life we are no longer being but doing. God does not do. God is. He has no preferences, neither hating nor loving one person or nation more nor less. He accepts all in love.

Love is the essence of being.

Separation requires an act of doing away with the natural state of being. Acceptance of all expressions of life, and seeing life as a unity, is an act of being.

This is one definition of what is meant by "Turning the other cheek". No action on the part of another should affect your being and hence your love.

"Forgive them Father for they know not what they do" is a high expression of being. By refusing to be affected by the acts of others and by not being willing to see others as anything less than expressions of Divinity is a high state of being. This is all the more so if those others are unconscious of what they do and of who they are, and their intention is to hurt you.

In the act of "doing' you create hurt and you crucify yourself.

In the act of "being" you elevate and glorify your Being.

Your awareness of being the eternal soul that you are must extend beyond this present incarnation of yourself and beyond this cycle of creation.

This present incarnation of the Universe is one of many cycles of the creation and destruction of the eternal Universe.

Indeed the Universe is in a constant state of creation or becoming.

Following this will be a period of destruction that will last billions of years. Destruction is merely another aspect of creation. Nothing dies it simply changes form, it is still becoming something else even in the destruction of its present form.

The ever-expanding Universe, physicists say, will ultimately peak and then contract. When it contracts, according to current theories, all matter will condense into a super dense ball of minute proportions. Out of this minute super-dense matter will arise another "big bang" and the process of creation will continue.

A newer theory is that the Universe is ever expanding. If it continues to expand infinitely, the solid matter will become so dispersed that it will effectively disappear in the vastness of the infinite all.

Time and space is so vast that it is beyond our ability to conceive of eternity or infinity.

Earth is a relatively young planet, the sun a relatively young star, both being several billions of years young. Human existence on planet earth is only a couple of million years old. (Scientists cannot agree on this. Some would say only a couple of hundred thousand years). Either estimate is insignificant. Either estimate is a mere tick of the cosmic clock.

To put the subject of human existence in perspective; If we were to draw a Universal time line representing the age of the universe in periods across the page like this, and we filled a page with periods, mankind would be one period at the end of the page.....................
....●

Restated, on a four-mile highway, life on earth would be the last twelve inches and human life would be the width of a pencil line drawn across the road.

The world is estimated to be about 15 billion years old, a young planet in a young galaxy.

Our species, homo erectus may be about 200,000 years old. In terms of time, our existence is not even a blip in time.

The arrogance of the human ego, creates the illusion and overstates our importance in regards to the whole of creation! Our religious philosophies certainly propagate this myth.

I think that we are more like a planetary joke. I can visualize the representative from earth at an interplanetary convention introducing himself to some highly evolved galactic being who responds "Earth who?"

In ancient Hindu Veda texts the rishis, (enlightened beings who wrote the ancient Vedic texts), calculate one day of Gods creation as being 4,300,560,000 years long. This is one day of God (Brahma). In this context, perhaps we can agree that the world was indeed created in six days, six God days or about 26 billion earth years.

According to the ancient rishis the total age of the Universe is 314,159,000,000,000 years (314 trillion years) or one Age of Brahma.

There have been countless ages of Brahma.

That should put the human ego in its place once and for all!

—

__Negativity__

Whoever is happy will make others happy too. - Anne Frank (German -Jewish Diarist)

Consider once more the concept of "good" and "bad"

Bear in mind that I use good and bad in terms of the common usage and understanding of these terms and not as a judgment though God knows I am guilty of judgment, (He really does know).

When you have a positive experience, your emotions and feelings tell you that you are experiencing sensations such as JOY - LOVE - HAPPINESS - WELL-BEING - LIGHT - HARMONY - and a sense that TRUTH and JUSTICE has entered your life in this moment.

With a negative experience, you may feel FRUSTRATION - ANGER - HATE - VIOLENCE - HELPLESSNESS - CONFUSION - VICTIMIZED - and a sense that SEPARATION - UNCERTAINTY - INJUSTICE and FEAR has moved into your life in that moment.

If you are a person who experiences and sees a joyful side to every situation and shrugs off adversity, that is wonderful. You should expand on that ability and focus on bringing even more LIGHT into your life. The world needs more people like you!

Generally people internalize most of their feelings. Life is experienced as a mixture of emotions, ups and downs, or "good and bad". Most people hold back on expressing their feelings - suppressing what they truly feel. They do this for a great variety of reasons. Many lives are lived in quiet frustration, moments of anger and days of feeling just plain blah - neither up or down.

Frequently people have a feeling that life is unfair. They may feel that too many people have too much and that somehow they are not getting a fair share. Perhaps they lack a good relationship. Possibly their work is unsatisfying or they cannot find steady employment. Nothing in their life seems to work right. Many people have periods in their lives when such a state of existence seems to be all that life is about. They live their lives uncomplainingly always hoping that the future will be brighter, they plan for the day when their kids are grown up and they can start living again, or they have some similar vague expectation of better times laying ahead in some future time and place.

The great news is that negative states of mind are curable. Negativity itself is curable.

It is curable at the individual level as well as at the national and global levels. The cure process is the same in all cases. Negative states of being are a human manifestation. Negativity is a self- created state of mind and therefore it is an illusion. If we change our thoughts about our condition, we change the condition itself. Some people have a great deal invested in their pain and unhappiness, especially if it brings them attention from others. If their thoughts reveal a strong attachment to being in a negative state, no amount of affirmations to the contrary will change the negative condition. Only when a true willingness to change is present, will change occur. It is much like an addict or an alcoholic, people get addicted to misery.

The process of cure entails willingly moving to a state of healing, first mentally and then physically. One must become self-empowered. To do this you must learn to reclaim your power and to move to a perception and understanding of TRUTH and reality.

In the first instance, know that today is the future that you dreamed of yesterday and which you thought would be better.

Reality does not exist anywhere except in the moment of now. To change your reality you can only do it now.

Your creative ability is always working in the present moment. NOW is the moment that you are creating your tomorrow. Certainly your dreams may be realized today, tomorrow or a year from now, conceivably even a decade from now. The thoughts that you allow into your consciousness in the present moment will manifest. You have no control over the time and manner of your manifestation however you can change your life when you change your thoughts. Indeed creation is the only thing you actually do in Reality. You manifest your own being from moment to moment. If your thoughts about yourself reflects grandeur and love and joy that is what you shall become. On the other hand if your thoughts are ones of "need" or ones of "lack" and insufficiency this too you will create in you life.

As a child of God, indeed as a living aspect of God, your vision of yourself must reflect nothing less than the Glory and Beauty and Righteousness of the Being that you truly are!

You can do it. You must strive towards achieving enlightenment and give up the life and the thoughts that no longer work or serve you in your life. Truth is light. This is the eternal state of Reality.

(Anything else is just not a light)!

Not only are you able to create light, you must do it. Happiness is your natural state of being! Any other state is unnatural - an ILLUSION for which you, being in your ego, are responsible for sustaining.

Ego can be described as a state in which you are effectively telling God that you know better than He what is good for you. So you separate yourself from God and you live in Fear.

You must realize that you and God are both dwelling/sharing your body. You are never alone but you can choose to experience yourself as separate and alone by creating that illusion if you wish.

As long as you live in separation you will create chaos. It cannot be otherwise. All the choices you make, that you imagine are for your own good, are made in ignorance.

I have stated before, you cannot know all the factors behind a given situation, it is beyond your ability to know this. Therefore any decision you make without God and all thoughts that you hold about something are bound to be wrong.

If we cannot trust ourselves to make the correct choices, how can we trust ourselves to act in our own best interests or to find happiness on our own?

There is a better way. We must learn to conquer our egos and ask God to take over our life. Surrender to God and say, "Okay God, I've messed up. My life is not working as it should work. I AM willing to have You take over. Please take over my life for the highest good of all concerned. Help me overcome my ego. I surrender to you. Amen. (or OM)"

Practice this surrender every morning and evening. Each time you have a situation where you need to make a decision or where your ego gets involved, mentally remove yourself from the situation and the outcome. Remind yourself that you have now invited God to take over and say, "God I admit that I do not know what is in my own best interests. You take over this situation. I surrender to you for the highest good. Amen"

Being in God space and God time means that you can align your thoughts with the universe and detach yourself from all emotional involvement regarding the outcome of events, and trust that your highest good will manifest from the situation. It means giving up control to a Higher Force. It means forgiving yourself for hurting yourself all these years.

In this way you can create an effective and meaningful life. However you do need to examine your concepts of happiness and see whether it is ego driven or whether it reflects a spiritual dimension as well. That also means your being of service to all aspects of your being. All aspects of your being include all people on earth, for the God within you is the God within them as well. Seeing everything as a reflection of God will unite you with the wonder and Glory of the All for you are God manifesting Yourself in everything around you!

What is your idea of Nirvana? Is it really the two cars, the 2.5 kids and the white picket fence house in suburbia?

Chapter Six - The Creators of Reality

If a Tree Were to Fall in a Forest and No-one Was There to Hear it,
Would it Make a Sound?
- Bishop Berkeley *

---

* You may be interested to know a piece of interesting synchronicity. I have used quotations such as the one above about trees falling, as a vehicle to create interest and to get you thinking about the *many varied sources of wisdom in this world.*

Whereas I knew this quotation, I had no idea whom to attribute it to, nor could I find the source in my references.

I was resigned to leaving this statement as the only unaccredited quotation in this book.

For seven months I had a Berkshire Hathaway annual report next to my bed in the event that I might one day read it. Knowing that wisdom can appear from any source, even from a roadside billboard, on a whim, I picked up the report to see if anything of metaphysical interest lay therein. There on page 14, under Accounting - Part one, was a reference by the Chairman of Berkshire Hathaway, Warren Buffett, to the above quote along with the name of the author! Thank you Warren for showing that wisdom is everywhere and when we seek we shall always find.

Creation

In order to create there must be a dynamic force, and what force is more potent than love?
- Igor Stravinsky (Russian born composer)

What is the sound of one hand clapping?

It is easy to hate these Zen questions!

Their purpose, however, is to get you meditating on the meaning of life, creation and particularly about how we each create our own perceptions of reality.

Reality for every human being is experienced in the mind. There can be no argument about that.

Consider for a moment that in order to think and experience and create, our minds generate electrical impulses. These are impulses of energy.

The energy is CREATION manifesting. Every thought is Creative.

Thought is the energy of CREATION.

Here then is a simple explanation of how the world is created. I say is - not was - because you are not finished yet. In fact you are still busy creating even as you read this.

In case you feel that the responsibility of creation is a little burdensome, you may be pleased to know that you do have a little assistance, from the other six billion souls on this planet.

Whenever your five physical senses, experience anything such as- sight - sounds -touch - taste - smell - your mind reacts and stores the experiences via energy impulses in your brain.

This wonderful hard disk storage called memory has amazing capabilities.

You are capable of retrieving a memory over and over with the intensity of the original experience.

Not only that, but you can edit, alt, delete the event any way you wish and visualize many different outcomes - and this too, you are able to experience as if the experience were real.

When you dream, you experience entire worlds and events. These may appear completely real and sometimes terrifying.

Our minds have awesome powers to create. And so they should when we consider in *Whose* image *we* are created!

When we create we experience reality in the form of mental energy!

In the final analysis - energy is the basis for our perception. Energy is the form of our reality. Energy is indeed the very "stuff" of which we, ourselves, are formed.

Our entire reality consciousness and experience is energy based.

It is important for you to understand this energy structure in order to know yourself as a being of energy.

If you could see your body at a subatomic level, you would be astounded!

Matter is composed of atoms. You have seen diagrams of atoms. The center of the atom is the nucleus. Around the nucleus are electrons. The electrons spin around the nucleus at a tremendous rate. They are held in orbit by the magnetism or gravity of the nucleus. The space between the center of the atom, that is the nucleus, and the electrons swirling around it is enormous.

If the nucleus of an atom were the size of a tennis ball and set in the center of a football field, its electrons would be in an orbit that circled the sidelines. In between would be empty space!

Your body, from your bones to your brain cells, including all the molecules in your body is composed of atoms. Atoms that are comprised mostly empty space.

Consider this image the next time you think of yourself as being a "solid" citizen!

If you could shrink to subatomic size, human bodies would appear to you much like a galaxy of stars in outer space. There would be bright lights, which are the atoms, blazing in a dark sky of emptiness.

The atoms would sparkle like suns, with electrons flying through black space in vast orbits around the suns. We would appear to be a huge mass of suns in the boundless black void of space. We would appear to be very different from the "solid" being that our physical senses would have us believe we are.

Our real bodies do consist of vast spaces of empty void. Our bodies truly are less solid matter and consist largely of empty space.

Why then do we not see ourselves as we truly are?

Is seeing believing? Or is it not?

Our senses cannot see reality, only the illusion. We cannot trust our senses for information about what truly is.

Consequently our egos are constantly re-forming our life experiences into patterns that affirm our illusionary sensory experiences. In this way we create what we perceive as being right. In so doing the ego self challenges the creation of God.

Let us explore the process of experience.

Awareness and experience are created solely of energy within the brain - some may call this awareness "mind". Curiously the very atoms that comprise who we are physically also are pure energy. These atoms are exactly the same as those found in a rock, or a tree, or a glass of water and even in a ray of sunshine.

The ultimate source of all energy is God.

This is the same source energy as is found in the core of an atom. All matter is composed of atoms. When astronomers listen with radio telescopes to what they call the background hum of the Universe, it sounds like Ommmmmmmmmmmm.

The entire Universe is comprised of this energy. This eternal unifying energy that is in all things is the same as that which flows through you too. All is One

Energy cannot be broken down or destroyed for it is the Source of True Reality.

It is eternal.

The sheerest form of energy that we can physically see is light.

This is not to say that light is the ultimate form of energy. It is just the finest aspect that we can see or measure. Energy can be in the form of visible light such as the spectrum of sunlight or invisible light such as x-rays and gamma rays, radio waves, short waves and microwaves.

Beyond the vibration of light is the spirit or astral spectrum. Beyond this there are other, finer levels of energy.

Energy becomes more gross (dense) as it descends from the high spiritual planes down through the astral and physical planes. It becomes light then gas, liquid, simple cell, plant, animal matter and culminates in mineral form such as rock and metal.

All things are universally bound by the same originating conscious energy.

This has tremendous implications in our appreciation of the process of creation.

When scientists split an atom it releases energy - the ultimate "stuff" of the universe.

It is the stuff of solid rock as well as the stuff of subtle thought processes and everything in between.

Our sensory experiences including our awareness of self and our sense of reality comes down, in the final analysis to just one thing - ENERGY.

When you consider how you create your reality out of thoughts, and when you truly understand what the ramifications of this process are, a great revelation materializes.

The secret of our being, known to great spiritual masters, is revealed in the language of modern day physics. The grand Unifying Theory of the Universe is coming closer to reality as the distinction between spiritual thought and quantum physics draws inexorably closer.

The nature of TRUTH is such, that all shall be revealed unto each generation in terms of their ability to understand and in the language best suited to their understanding, whether it be in the language of nuclear physics or ancient texts!

In Biblical days the revelation of this knowledge was presented very differently than in the present Nuclear Age. Yet the message is unchanged.

So it is through all ages, all cultures, and at all levels of understanding. Yet all Truth remains the same Truth, presented in the language, myth and legends appropriate to the time.

The level of consciousness of the person receiving this knowledge is also a major factor affecting how much and how deeply they can receive it.

The rishis (sages) of ancient India received this knowledge thousands of years ago in a manner far advanced and very different than that of the public at large. It was through the practice of yoga that they taught others. A person can be trained to rise to a higher level of awareness and understanding by a sage or a guru who has already mastered higher levels of consciousness. Yet no one will rise above the level that they are capable of understanding. Some may be content with myths and legends. Others with Bible stories. The levels that one can ascend to are many, yet each will ascend only as far as they are willing to trust and have faith.

In Europe during the Middle Ages, enlightenment had to be through Christ Consciousness. If not one was a heretic or was accused of witchcraft! Even those who attained enlightenment had to tread carefully for fear of antagonizing the Church. There was a fine line between enlightenment and heresy, a line that many fundamental religions, in their intolerance maintain even today.

The Church still considers Christ Consciousness as a prerequisite to enlightenment.

Their failure to acknowledge that God is not confined to one sect or belief system has created separation of thought. This separation in itself is a limiting factor in the spiritual advancement of mankind.

God does not have one faith that He favors above all others. Indeed God does not need our prayers and our liturgy or our churches.

Christ consciousness is fine as long as you remember that to achieve this method of awareness one does not have to be a Christian nor even to have any knowledge of Christ. Indeed anyone who has ascended to this level of consciousness will already acknowledge the perfection in All That Is regardless of race, religion, sex or creed.

The Hindus, Buddhists, Jews, Muslims and most shaman tribal cultures all achieve grace through their own systems of belief. Hindus, who are possibly the most tolerant of all major religions, probably have the highest number of spiritually enlightened beings on earth.

When one thinks, you engage in the act of creation by calling energy into creation. Your thoughts are creative and shape your reality. You are inextricably linked to the energy that is the fabric of the Universe and which you call into creation by the mere act of thinking.

This is how God, with whom we are one, creates.

Contemplate the Divine Source of Universal energy. While doing so keep in mind that you create energy which is the building blocks of atoms, and atoms are the building blocks of all matter. Your mind is one with God in the process of creation.

The following concepts are important in order to understand the nature of your being.

I will summarize them for you:

The mind is the source of the creative process. The mind creates from pure thought energy.

This energy, is the basic underlying indestructible force in the universe and the building block of all matter and all creation.

God Creates with the same energy as our thoughts.

All thought originates at the inception with God.

We call on this God energy when we manifest and create,

We co-create with God for we are "of God"

The energy, which we create in our mind and all the atoms of every object in the universe, is one and the same "stuff". All is created from mind, whether our mind or God's mind.

There is nothing that exists on earth, in our solar system, nor in the far- flung galaxies, that is not of thought.

Creation is the process of the transformation of Awareness into Thought. Thought into Word (the Creative Word). Words into action.

Human beings dream, meditate and create thoughts. These thoughts are as real as those that we experience from those originating "outside of our minds".[*]

The Universal Creator and we engage in exactly the same process of creation. This is the meaning of being created in the image of God. It is not a physical image but rather a spiritual image. As I have already stated we are indeed aspects or parts of the One, manifesting in all Its Glory and Diversity.

The process of creation begins with awareness or Mindfulness transforming into thought - and from thought into word and then into creation.

As thought energy coalesces, the particles of energy condense into very fine and invisible form. At the highest level, the vibration of this energy is extremely subtle. As it descends through the many layers, or dimensions of creation, it takes on an increasingly denser form.

In spiritual terms, we know of these layers or levels in many terms. Some refer to them as "planes" of existence, such as the Astral plane, the Buddhic Plane, the Atmic Plane etc.

---

[*] This is an intentional contradiction - but I use it for the purpose of expressing this concept.

In truth all realities are in our mind alone, we experience our perceptions of the world and ourselves nowhere else but in our minds

In Kabala it is represented by the Tree of Life and the manifestation of the Word into matter is the Shechinah or Divine Light.

As Divine thought descends through the many spiritual levels to the physical realm, it culminates in the density that is the form of the physical world. In this plane of existence, energy is hardest to move. The illusion is strongest and our distance or our removal from the Divine Emanation or Godhead is at its greatest.

The goal of spiritual realization is to develop an awareness of these other levels while we exist on the physical plane. The higher we can ascend, the closer we draw to our Source. This is what our soul desires. This is what our ego would suppress.

Ego, being an expression of the physical world, keeps us separate from God. It is that which we need to overcome in order to be self-realized beings. We must overcome our over identification with the physical aspect of what we think we are. Our looks, or our social standing, memberships, occupation or anything else does not define who we are in the physical world. This is what the ego identifies us as being. This is the illusion of what we think we are.

A Kahuna (Teacher / Master) in Hawaii by the name of Pua Mahoe has a wonderful definition of ego which she shared with me, **E**dging **G**od **O**ut.

In spirit, the ego disappears, the more so the higher we go. Our physical lives constitute a struggle between the ego, which is most powerful on the physical level and hence ILLUSION and our souls which are finer and of the spirit and hence TRUTH.

The tool which ego uses to keep us stuck in illusion is FEAR. The more that one fears to let go of the ego, the more you are stuck in denial and suppression. Fear is the hardest challenge we face. I have seen apparently fearless men who will fight a man twice their size, bungee jump from a bridge, fall apart when they confront their own egos. This is the ultimate challenge, and no amount of physical derringdo can prepare one for the subtlety of confronting oneself.

THE TRUTH SHALL SET YOU FREE!

"So shall my word be that goeth forth out of my mouth: it shall not return unto me void, but it shall accomplish that which I please, and it

shall prosper in the thing whereto I sent it" (God's revelation to Isaiah) Isaiah 55:11 - 12

—

You Are What You Think

When a vision begins to form everything changes, including the air around me. I no longer seem to be in the same atmosphere. I feel a peacefulness and a love that are indescribable. I stand alone, and nothing can touch me. - Jeane Dixon (Modern American Prophet)

You carry a vision of reality fashioned by your thoughts and your belief system.

Although you have created your reality, you react to this self-created reality as if it were separate from yourself. It is as if you had no part in its creation and therefore you are at its mercy and fickle whims.

By perceiving the world as separate, one reacts to life rather than realizing that it is something you are responsible for creating in the first instance.

By reacting to what is erroneously perceived as reality, you separate yourself from living and you treat your life as if it were beyond your control.

This behavior creates a cycle of reactive actions and deeds that produce specific consequences that, in turn, elicit further reactions ad infinitum. Finally your life feels as if it is spinning out of control in a series of reactions and counter reactions until you feel that events are controlling you.

Have you ever watched a dog chase it's tail? Once it gives up the illusion that its tail is separate from itself, it releases all attachment to trying to catch its tail, it is able to lie down quietly and chew on it's tail from one end to the other to it's heart content!

We are like this dog. As long as we give power to the illusion that life is outside of us we have a need to control life and catch it by the tail. All we are doing is chasing an illusion.

I have never met anyone who has successfully caught an illusion.

We can never gain satisfaction while chasing an fantasy. The minute one gets what they think they want their goals change.

There is always someone who has more of what we would have and the goal is always just beyond the horizon.

This is called living in the future. The future does not exist and cannot make you happy. All the futures you ever dreamed of are right here, now in the present!

If you obtain what you think you want or need you only satisfy your ego for a brief time before a new set of wants and needs arises. At best one can only achieve momentary satisfaction before the restlessness sets in again.

If what you have, is important to you to the extent that you become attached to it, you also carry the fear of losing it as well.

True satisfaction cannot be achieved through the attainment of material goals, because the material world itself is not real.

It is not real because that which is eternal and therefore real nourishes our higher self, that is our soul. True reality is the attainment of enlightenment and unification with God. Once we have that, all other wants and needs fall away. Indeed the less attachment you have to the physical world, the wealthier you are. True freedom lies in being unattached to that which has no value.

Nothing created by man of the physical world can be said to have true value.

The pharaohs built pyramids, empires, and monuments and then buried enormous wealth with them, along with food, servants, boats, magic charms, gold, and clothes. What is become of all this? It is as if it never existed. Scattered to dust.

So what importance would you place on your house, your clothes, your car, your money? These things carry no value even in your lifetime. All they do is burden you with taxes, responsibility, and insurance and tie you down so that you are never free and you are always in fear of loss. The benefit of material possessions is ephemeral and should be seen as such. In them you gain no lasting joy.

The entire material world is an expression of our thoughts.

The united power of many people produces the physical world and brings it into being.

The structure of the world as we comprehend it could crumple in a second if collectively we changed our thoughts about it!

The illusion of "reality," that which we call life, cannot exist independently of ourselves. As we create reality so do we sustain it and we can destroy it. It has no independent existence outside our

87

collective thoughts about it - and it evolves in accordance with our state of mind.

Physical reality, therefore, is the reflection of the collective human experience. It exists on many levels. From the individual perception of reality it develops, changing as it extends through the - family level - religious group level - racial level - socio economic level - community level - city level - state level - national level and world level.

In summary, the world is the reflected consciousness of all levels of human thought from the smallest unit of a single individual to the billions of people who are constantly manifesting their reality in all manners of ways.

Thought, being energy may lead to the creation of new processes or the production of a new product. Some thoughts are destructive, others not. Some reflect anger or love and some may be directed either inwardly or outwardly.

Every thought, however, manifests in energy and some will become "reality", that is they will lead to action and hence to creation.

A simplistic viewpoint would be that a thought about food might lead one to cooking or driving to purchase a meal. A thought about a cure for a disease may lead to research and a new medical breakthrough. A thought about love may lead to an expression of love - as will a thought about anger.

Not all thoughts result in direct physical action. Where does this thought energy go?

Thought works at so many levels of existence apart from the physical world. Your subconscious thoughts affect your world- view, your life situation and your relationships at every level.

When your thoughts are in agreement with the minds of others, they are further empowered.

The world is the amalgamated thoughts of billions of individuals engaged in a process of thought and energy release.

Depending on the intent and the force behind the energy of a thought, it may pass without intention.

On the other hand concentrated and sustained thought may lead to physical manifestation.

Sustained thought by a multitude of people is very powerful. Consequently we must be very careful and responsible about the thoughts we hold and nurture, the beliefs we hold on to, and whom we choose to align our thinking with. We must be particularly careful when we align our minds with negative thinkers, bigots, politicians and hate mongers - all of whom have FEAR based thought structures. The cost frequently can lead to unforeseen consequences.

When groups gather in prayer it may result in a positive and uplifting experience. When groups gather to spread hate and fear, then riots, chaos and, frequently, war are the result.

It is easy to see that every man-made object - whether a piece of art, music, or a scientific breakthrough is the product of an idea brought into manifestation.

Mankind also produces ideas beyond those of having to take an idea and to transform it into a tangible object.

These are the subtle ideas like those of philosophy, ideology, and the treatment of the environment, community, health, wealth, security and self-esteem.

In quantum physics, the smallest reducible component of an atom is pure energy. Like light it is neither particle nor wave, but it exists in whatever form the observer causes it to exist!

I will deal with this in greater detail in a later chapter.

Observed light displays a unique and puzzling dichotomy.

It will be perceived by the scientific observer to be a stream of energy like a fine laser beam.

However, with a separate set of observations, light is seen to oscillate and flow in a series of waves consisting of cycles with peaks and valleys.

The presence of an observer changes the results of the observation of light energy.

The bed you lie on, the chair, the floor beneath your feet, the food you eat and even your own body appears solid in appearance, this, too, is an illusion. Everything is made of atoms.

All solid matter, as I have previously stated, when viewed at the sub atomic level, consists almost entirely of empty space. Solid, is indeed a misnomer! An illusion!

Since the ultimate "stuff" of creation is energy and energy arises from thought, are we then the creators of thought or that which is created by thought?

If we were inanimate objects incapable of thought we would be created.

However, here is another dichotomy. Like the duality of light waves, we have our own duality. We are thought beings, and that means that we are light beings. Therefore we are the creators!

Simultaneously we are the products of a Greater thought process, and so we are also the created.

That which is the creator is also the created from a higher thought form.

Are we also the products of what we create? Are we responsible for what we create?

We exist in a state in which we have created a catch 22 situation. We think that we are the product of our environment and not the creator of it.

Even as we create our ideas about the world, in that same moment we are also subservient to the world that we have created. We have also imbued our creation with a dichotomy of its own! Not only do we create the world in which we live, we perceive our world as having an existence of its own and therefore separate from ourselves. We create it and we also think that because we see ourselves as separate from it, we need to react to it!

We believe this to be true because:

What we think about manifests and therefore it is!
This is the Great Illusion!

You probably do not see yourself as a creator, nor do you consciously realize that the act of thinking is and of itself a creative process.

Thinking that you are the sum of the product of your environment, the result of your genes, or society, or race, etc. creates the result - and therefore you are what you think you are.

You do not have to be at the mercy of circumstance, but you are because you think you are.

And as you think, so are you.

I know that this is a very difficult concept to follow, particularly if this is the first time you are being exposed to it, but persevere. You will get a better grasp of this idea as you read further.

When you believe strongly enough that you have no control over your environment and your life you will not.

Your thoughts reflect and therefore create what you think about. It does not matter if you are conscious of your thoughts or not. As long as you hold a thought somewhere in your mind or subconscious you are going to create that thought materializing. Your thought structures become a part of your personal experience that you hold to be true and self-evident.

You may deny holding a particular thought. When you find yourself being ill it is unlikely that you will attribute your illness to anything that you think about.

However you must accept responsibility that at some level of your mind you are putting out the energy or thought that creates your illness. Illness is the opposite of being well, or well being. The process of well being is being in the state of wellness. That implies being well at the physical level and the mental level.

Thought precedes all states of physical activity. Therefore being in a condition of un-wellness or illness must first be preceded by a thought, usually unconscious, that creates the physical condition of illness.

If someone has a string of unsuccessful relationships or businesses failures, it seems unreasonable to say that someone would intentionally create failure or bring unhappiness upon themselves.

However, at a deep level that person is harboring a thought that they are a failure, or that they are undeserving of love or success, or that nothing ever works for them, or any one of hundreds of other similar life sabotaging thoughts.

Self- sabotaging thoughts are common in every person. They could result in defeat and loss on the one hand or, perversely, just the opposite effect on the other hand. They could be very successful.

Being terrified of loss, a person may overcompensate and become a super achiever, extremely egotistical, outwardly very self confident and very successful, or anything in between. Either way, neither the overachiever nor the underachiever will experience any greater sense of joy than the other as long as the negative thought principle exists.

This pattern of having limiting thoughts about one-self is called a "Personal Lie".

A Personal Lie is a limiting thought that you have about yourself and which you hold to be a truth that you have duly empowered.

Personal Lies originate from many self limiting thoughts you may have, and often can be traced back to your birth trauma, early infancy, childhood, life traumas and even past life traumas.

You are usually never aware that you even have these self-limiting thoughts unless you have had intensive psychotherapy or have been through a rebirthing program.

The limiting thought behind a Personal Lie is indeed an ILLUSION which originates in FEAR and hence it is not of the TRUTH.

Everyone has Personal Lies, which, through processing can be identified, and eventually one can eliminate them.

Until one is trained to recognize the limiting forces behind the Personal Lies embedded within, and you have eliminated them from your thought process, you will be bound to live a lie and to be the victim of your own unconscious thoughts. As you already know, your thoughts, even your unconscious ones, create your reality.

When you understand the Truth, the Truth shall set you free!

Am I a butterfly dreaming that he is a man, or am I a man dreaming he is a butterfly?

This is the well-known paradox of existence that we have created for ourselves.

Once we realize that we have created the dream itself - then neither the man nor the butterfly exists - only the thought that created the dream is real - only the energy of creation is real - all else is simply illusion.

To be aware one must beware.

That is to beware of the impulse to give energy to that which is self-defeating in life.

Being aware implies two things. First "being ness" and secondly awareness.

In 'being ness', you are in your true self. To experience "being" you must withdraw from thoughts of separation and "be" in the moment of now. Be the observer of yourself. Detach from your involvement in the illusion and be the silent observer of your own life. Even as you are experiencing, be aware of yourself having the experience. In a state of "being" the awareness will follow. Be totally present as the observer of your own life in the moment of now.

Have trust and faith that all that happens is for the greatest good. Respond by doing that which will create the finest vision you can have about yourself. That is, with love, forgiveness and compassion.

When one learns to change the thoughts about whom one Truly is, you will experience yourself as the greatest person in the finest vision of the Greatest Soul in the Universe. You will forgive yourself for all the past abuse and past incorrect thoughts you had about yourself. You will release your anger with forgiveness. You will acknowledge your Divinity and the beauty of your soul and you will create TRUTH, in your life.

Staying stuck in ILLUSION, one cannot recognize the Truth. You cannot grasp the Truth if you deny your divinity and your oneness with the True Source from which you arise. Your creative mind is an eternal part of the Source of all Creative Energy. Choosing separation of Self from the creative moment of now is the source of all fears.

When you choose to live in a state of fear this sustains the illusion of the physical world and the illusion reaffirms itself. This is ego. The ego would deny your enlightenment. Enlightenment means awareness and consequently the death of ego, the loss of the little self, and the merging of oneself into a Greater Consciousness in which the "I" is no longer important.

You need to recognize that you are not bound to the physical world, this is the created world of illusion. You are the creator of the your physical experience. You are therefore in it but not of it.

In the physical world the error you made is that you have vested your creation with a life of its own - a life which you have made indistinguishable from your own.

Humans are like drug addicts - they depend on the "reality" fix to confirm their own existence.

So no matter how difficult they may find their life in this creation of theirs - people are committed to the illusion with a life and death urgency - they cannot imagine any other existence outside of this experience that they call life.

They trust their illusions over God - the real source of Truth and Reality.

No wonder people live in fear - the fear of letting go. The fear of DEATH sustains them in life in this world.

—

Death the Sustainer

Death destroys a man, the idea of Death saves him - E.M.Forster -
(English Writer)

Mankind constantly recreates the physical universe.

A person's identity is intimately tied to the illusion of who they think they are in the physical world. People hold on to a vision of a solid earth, nationalities, leaders, families, friends, cars, businesses and the face they see in the mirror. These are all devices people use to define themselves and their place in the world. All of this is an illusion!

The ultimate mistake is to think that your body, by which you define yourself, really is who you are.

You cannot begin to imagine who you really are! You hide your magnificence behind a million distractions that you create in order avoid seeing that you are a holy being. And in your holiness lies salvation, peace, calm and contentment.

To let go of the body is to deny the ego and to go through the illusion of death - and death is our greatest fear. We have so tied our identity, via our ego, to the physical world.

Fear is the source of the ILLUSION that people hold on to regarding the permanence of the physical world.

Fear of the death of the ego becomes the great Sustainer of life.

Death is the ultimate test of our faith in what we believe to be real. To face death - and the prospect of the end of ego and illusion, and to willingly give up all attachments to the physical world, is a frightening prospect for most people. People spend a lifetime investing in their physical existence and making the ego's perception of themselves the means by which they define themselves. This definition of who we think we are, and the prospect of releasing this perception through death, confronts us with the ultimate challenge to our entire belief system...the perceived end of self!

The prospect of release, or death, is difficult to face if you are not completely detached from the illusion. It is the fear of death and the lack of faith, that is the certainty of knowing yourself as a spiritual being, as an energy being, and an eternal being - that holds us captive.

It is hard to give up the drug of illusion and to accept responsibility for the life one has created. People choose instead to live in fear and denial of their Divinity, preferring instead to cling to the self-created illusion of themselves, that is an image far less than what they really are!

Most people will do anything they can to sustain this Grand Illusion. Fearing loss of their self- identity, ego prevents them from seeing anything that contradicts their existing concept of the world. Instead of being greater than we are - we live in the illusion of being much less than what we truly are. Hence we are all become victims of circumstance - the created - not the Creator.

You may correctly conclude that in order to sustain this belief system of being the hapless victims of life's vicissitudes, people need to live in denial, suppression and avoidance of what is real.

Death - is what keeps us alive - or more precisely it is the fear of death that drives our life urge.

Many churches promulgate the concept of original sin. This is the concept that mankind is inherently sinful from birth and therefore we are in need of Divine forgiveness for the sin of being human. This erroneous philosophy, was created by men of the church as an instrument of control over fellow man, and has lead to generations of people spending their entire lives in abject terror of life itself. The belief that one is an unredeemed sinner and that one is consequently destined to suffer in life and possibly in the hereafter as well is the cause of untold human misery. This belief, that we are the victims of the very thing that makes us what we are, our humanity, is an insane concept in the extreme.

The belief that one must suffer in life and in death is enough to make anyone God fearing, and, more to the point, *Death fearing!* [*]

Please, if you hold the belief that you are a sinner, if you were raised to believe that you are wicked and undeserving of Divine grace, please understand the error of this mindset.

[*] *Christianity has made of death a terror which was unknown to the gay calmness of the Pagan - Ouida (English novelist)*
"Man dies when he wants, as he wants, of what he chooses" - Jean Anouilh (French Playwright)

The most merciful and loving Father forgives you even before you can "sin".

Know that there is no sin in God's world, where all is good, and God forgives you your thought that you have sinned and that you should be punished, even before such thought arose in your mind!

Only you, alone, can create the illusion of hell, even in the spirit world. God is unconditional in His love. Unconditional means love without conditions. Unconditional love is the only love that exists in the kingdom of God. There is no other. Know then that it is safe for you to let go of your fear and guilt and to forgive yourself for having such thoughts. You deserve to be forever in a space of love and peace, confident that your very existence is an expression of God's will, and as such you can do no wrong. Resolve to forgive yourself now!

As long as you believe that you were born to die, your premise for living is the fear of death!

Death is really only the loss of the ego. One releases in that moment the illusion of identity that you used all your life as a means to define yourself in the physical body. In Death one detaches from the loved ones and the family you have created, as well as the home you manifested, the foods you thought you needed etc. You become aware of a greater and more sublime truth. The relationships you had will be seen to be far grander than you imagined them to be, and the true nature of your life's purpose will become apparent to you.

Finally, you will be amazed at how narrowly you defined yourself in the physical realm.

The astral or spirit world is very sublime. In it the powers of manifestation are remarkable and instantaneous. You can see the Divine plan of your life and the reason you took on this incarnation as well as the reason you had the relationships and experiences that you did.

Because people do not trust the reality of God during their physical lives, preferring instead to embrace the illusion that they have created, death allows us to release the illusion voluntarily.

However, it is common, even in death, for some souls to continue to cling to the past life illusions until it has gone through the transition and accepted its death and is willing to move on. Until such time it can sustain the illusion and may even become earthbound and unwilling to release itself into a higher plane of existence. One could say that souls that are in denial may continue the habits of ego even after death. They may create a form of hell or purgatory for themselves with their unwillingness to release themselves from the world of illusion.

A person having achieved Divine awareness and an understanding of the nature of reality may consciously complete their mission on earth, and they can voluntarily and consciously give up the body and leave.

In the Indian tradition this is called mahasamadhi.

Samadhi, is the conscious union of ones mind with that of God. The maha-samadhi or the supreme Samadhi is the conscious leaving of the body in order to merge the soul back into the infinite from which it originated.

In the case of Paramahansa Yogananda, following a banquet in Los Angeles in honor of the Indian Ambassador, he posed for photographers then, soon after the ceremonies, he lay down and left his body. Three weeks later, the mortuary in Los Angeles reported that Yogananda's body had shown no sign of physical decay nor did it emit any odor. It remained in death as it was in life with no sign of physical disintegration.

A similar situation occurred with Babaji, in India. He finalized his business at the ashram, sent certain disciples away and lay down and left his body. Like Yogananda, after several days, there was no sign of bodily decay.

The lack of bodily decay and deathly attributes of certain saints has been recorded in all religions.

Many Indian saints are on record of having taken mahasamadhi. It could be argued that Jesus knew of his own death and chose the time and manner of it.

The person that is in communion with God while in the physical realm, and is aware of the Truth, passes over consciously and without fear. Indeed they can do so, for in their consciousness they know that they are but extensions of the Father and Mother energy.

"Verily, verily, I say unto you, the Son can do nothing for himself, but what he seeth the Father do: for what things soever He doeth, these also doeth the Son likewise" (Jesus) John 5:19

On Truth; Jesus said, *"To this end was I born, and for this cause came I into the world, that I should bear witness unto the truth. Everyone that is of the truth heareth my voice."* John 18:37

An enlightened being understands the illusion of physical existence. Enlightened beings come to this world with a mission of which they are conscious, usually from an early age.

They frequently return lifetime after lifetime, time and again, like a visitor, and with each incarnation they assist mankind, and hence the world, towards a higher consciousness. They appear to all peoples of this planet and teach in the manner best suited to the culture of their physical environment.

Therefore the saints and sages of all cultures, whether aboriginal, Christian, Buddhist, Jewish, Hindu, Animist or Moslem, should be equally honored. They all teach the same message of compassion, love and tolerance.

None teach hatred, war and separation. None teaches the need for arms, nor do they teach their followers to be prepared to defend themselves against their fellow man. None come here to increase fear but rather they are here to overcome fear.

None ask to be honored. Their message is one of humility and mutual respect without the need for ego and personal accolades and aggrandizement. Our teachers know that the shallow adulation and gifts of this life are of no meaning and are therefore worthless. They would rather you helped your fellow man than to accept anything for themselves.

The criterion for knowing if someone is a genuine saint, or a fraud or a cult leader, is the above criteria. If they fail on any of these counts, be wary of false prophets for there are many.

You, too, can release yourself from the Great Illusion and experience true reality. This experience is not limited to saints, for we are all the same Sons and Daughters of God.

You too, are capable of experiencing a shift in your consciousness towards truly enlightened creation brought into reality from a space of Love and true Divinity, connectedness and awareness.

Release the thought of yourself as a victim in life's drama, and you will also disempower the grasp of the illusion and fear's hold over you.

Once you achieve release you will no longer perpetuate the illusion and fear and you will teach your children to break the cycle and thereby pass on this legacy to future generations.

We desperately need to break the cycle of illusion and victim consciousness for the salvation of mankind.

You should now consider at this point, a meditation of reassurance in order to reconnect yourself with the Divine attributes of God within.

Take a few minutes of quiet to affirm the following to yourself:

"I am alive in this moment and I honor the power of my life urge in overcoming death. I affirm and strengthen my life urge and I am increasing in youthfulness and health each day of my life."

This is a great affirmation to use daily when you wake up in the morning.

The attributes of the Creator are:

- UNLIMITED AND UNCONDITIONAL LOVE,
- FORGIVENESS
- COMPASSION
- JOY,
- PEACE,
- HAPPINESS,
- CONFIDENCE
- LIGHT and
- WISDOM.

All these, is His will for you - and nothing less!

Therefore Love, Forgiveness, Compassion, Joy, Peace, Confidence, Happiness, Light and Wisdom are the natural state of your being and the state of all being-ness everywhere.

You do not earn this grace it is your birthright. Claim it. *Demand* of God that He grant it to you.

This is the TRUE STATE of REALITY. When we create anything that is not in accordance with the Divine State of Being - we are creating an illusion.

The attributes of the Divine are everywhere and in everything. Humans cannot possibly limit God.

Miracles are in everything, yet we refuse to see them.

If we were to see rain only once a year and it began to rain every couple of weeks, we would be amazed. It would be a miracle. Is it not already a miracle that we get rain regularly? Can we not rejoice in the wonder of it?

If flowers never bloomed, and then one day they did, we would proclaim a miracle. Can we not see the miracle in the bloom anyway?

Familiarity blinds us to the miracles all around us everywhere, everyday. We need to practice seeing with new eyes. We do not truly see that which is right under our noses!

The harmony and balance of the seasons, birth and creation, even the heavens above us are miracles, given without end and sustained by a loving, caring Creator.

We cannot limit God's presence to a certain place. A place absent of God, as I have said, cannot exist because nothingness must be where the mind of God is not - and nothingness does not exist. God is omnipresent.

Inasmuch as we cannot limit God we also cannot limit His unconditional Love, Forgiveness, Compassion, Joy, Peace, Happiness, Light and Wisdom, which are the very emanations of His Being.

If, for example, you do not experience Love, it is not because Love does not exist.

You have shut out Love and replaced it with the Illusion of FEAR.

When you recognize that, then everything will flow in your life. All the love, peace and abundance that is yours to have and is exactly what God desires for you, will be yours.

For the sake of all mankind give up the investment you have in every negative thought, emotion, feeling, attitude and judgment. Stop denying God and stop denying your own eternal Divinity.

"You must realize that the Divine current that flows and functions in every living being is the One Universal Entity. When you desire to enter the mansion of God, you are confronted with two closed doors; the desire to praise yourself and the desire to defame others (ego). The doors are bolted by envy, and there is the huge lock of egoism preventing entry. So if you are in earnest, you have to resort to the key of love and open the lock; then remove the bolt and throw the

Jeffrey M. Solomon

> _doors wide open. Your education must train you in this difficult operation" - Sathya Sai Baba_

Spend some time thinking of how you can start living your life as a conscious and joyous being by eliminating your negative thought patterns. It is worth taking thirty minutes every morning meditating on how you are going to do this.

—

Fear - The Self Fulfilling Prophecy

*Fear is a disease. It blocks the flow of energy. It spreads. It destroys.
If it is not stopped it kills. - Paul Williams - (From Das Energi, the
only book ever published by Elektra Records)*

Fear is an imagined state in which you believe that you can be threatened.

In this state you experience anxiety, fear of loss, and all sorts of unimaginable (I should say imagined) terrors. You foresee the worst possible outcomes for yourself should you lose this creation called fear, and your attachment to it.

Thoughts relating to fear are as powerful a creative force as anything you can imagine. Fear is very powerful.

The fear of losing ones attachment to the illusion of ones life motivates almost every driving principal of survival. One perceives all forms of threats to ones security and to ones physical sense of identity.

Fear may be related to all manner of physical concerns such as job security, health, environment, political, safety, emotional, etc. This fear psychology merges with the group fears experienced by other people in your family, community and social group. The group fear then is able to merge with the energy of national and a global fear.

The fear progression builds to a critical energy mass that grows and feeds upon itself and becomes a self-actualizing process.

FEAR becomes a self-fulfilling manifestation that forms an ILLUSION OF REALITY. When you manifest fear or anxiety, it validates the thoughts you have about your own vulnerability in a cycle of cause and effect. Consequently you perpetuate this belief in FEAR in a never-ending cycle!

When the first inkling of something being amiss begins to permeate the consciousness, fear thoughts are mirrored back to you, confirmed if you will. This sparks a further round of collective thought that is used to validate your fears. Anyone who has experienced a stock market run will be familiar with the conception and self-realization of panic thoughts.

Over and again, fear thoughts, like compound interest, are reinvested in mass illusion and the illusion itself becomes self-fulfilled!

Among our greatest fears, one stands out; the loss of our own life. What we fear most, we manifest.

Consequently it is no accident that governments and industries, which reflect the national mindset, have created weapons of mass destruction, biological and chemical agents, pollution, destruction of the eco-system and so on.

We have even manifested previously unknown diseases (AIDS).

Franklin D. Roosevelt wrote: "The fourth (essential human freedom) is freedom from fear - which, translated into world terms, means a world- wide reduction in armaments to such a point and in such a thorough fashion that no nation will be in a position to commit an act of physical aggression against any neighbor - anywhere in the world."

Every threat to your physical existence ultimately manifests in fear as you empower it.

In this manner you animate your fears. The power you give to the thought increases until the thought has power over you. When it materializes, that becomes the proof and validation of the fear and thus a threat to your safety. Thereby you prove yourself right every time.

That which we fear most will manifest. Only we have the power to manifest our fears. Only we have the means to disempower our fears.

How great and terrible is the power of the ego to create the seeds of destruction - that keep us in fear that we cling ever more desperately to the Great Illusion!

In your personal life, because you fear the loss of those things that provide you with a sense of what you are, you may create the exact situation needed to create such loss happening. In this way you validate your original fear.

Should misfortune befall you, it corroborates the accuracy of your belief system and it empowers the cycle of fear over again.

As an example, consider the dynamics of an abusive relationship.

Some people have one abusive or failed relationship after the next. They create an endless pattern of anxiety, manifestation of fear thoughts and confirmation of the thing they most fear.

Seldom does one ask the simple question: "What is my thought surrounding this circumstance, that I have created this happening in my life?"

Being responsible for what you attract in your life is the first step in your liberation.

An individual who is unable to create a successful relationship may have the idea that there are no decent prospects to be found, and may entertain thoughts such as, 'all guys are bums / all women are gold diggers there are no good ones. Such judgment projects the blame outwards to some vague notion that somehow life is not fair or that one is getting short-changed.

What is missing from this type of thinking is the awareness that people are personally responsible for attracting exactly the type of partners into their lives that will actually serve to prove their negative beliefs about relationships!

People never admit to creating their own defeat. However, remember, that what you think is what you get.

Most of us are prone to some degree of self-delusion. The level at which these feelings operate can be ingrained so deep that we are usually not aware of them. Indeed were one to be confronted with the suggestion that we have self-sabotaging thoughts we would deny it vigorously and we would be indignant if anyone suggested that this reflects what we truly believe about our self.

Unless you have undergone deep therapy or had a spiritual awakening, your Personal Lie (that which you hold to be true about yourself - but which in reality is false) governs all that you do and think.

At the deepest subconscious level Personal Lies probably evolved in early childhood, at birth or even earlier. Personal Lies are buried so deep in our psyche that without therapy, one may never know what they are or even that they are there.

In the course of rebirthing people, Personal Lies similar to those below, surfaced in one form or another in most individuals. Needless to say, no one had prior cognition or awareness of having such thoughts about themselves. However once they acknowledged the pattern and effect of the Personal Lie in their lives, it was an epiphany, and healing could commence almost immediately.

How many of these statements would you acknowledge applied to you?

I am a failure
I don't deserve love.
I deserve to die
I should never have been born
Whenever I feel joy I get hurt
Whenever I get too close to someone I hurt him or her.
If I succeed I will die
I always hurt the ones I love
I am a loser
I am not wanted
My parents wanted a boy / girl
I should have been aborted.
If I have joy I will hurt others
I do not want to be seen

There is an entire catalog of Personal Lies. The above is just an example of feelings that even well adjusted people may have.

Few are aware that at the core of their being such thoughts not only exist - but they are extremely powerful and that every thought and feeling they have about life stems from this root thought, this Personal Lie. Most people (I would dare say all people) have such negative thoughts in one form or another!

The consequence of a Personal Lie is the Death Urge.

The Death Urge is the result of a thought, "I don't deserve to live" or some variation of this, but it expresses in a desire not to continue living.

The death urge creates the belief that you are aging and that you cannot continue to live as if you were still eighteen years old. It is to blame for thoughts which one may express in comments such as "I'm not as young as I used to be" or "I'm too old for that" or "When I was young I used to..." or "Act your age" or "I'm dying to....." etc.

As you now know, the power of thought is creative. What do you imagine often-repeated thoughts such as these are doing? These are actually personal affirmations about yourself.

What are you creating by embracing such thoughts? Can you create a vibrant, healthy body and mind when you are harboring such thoughts about yourself?

All Personal Lies and Death Urges are totally avoidable and illusionary - yet they are very real in their ability to govern and affect our lives!

Our thoughts create our leaders. Thought creates our type of government. Frequently they are destructive and corrupt. This is in part a reflection of our own minds. We validate their corrupt behavior by avowing that all politicians are corrupt. How often have you heard that remark?

If our thought is that politicians are inherently corrupt, and if thought is creative, what are we going to get?

Corrupt leaders of course!

We always confirm the perfection of our creation!

What a paradox!

What is equally frightening is how we think about our children and the youth of today. Consider the following statement; "Kids today are so.... lazy / immoral / dumb / irresponsible / ill mannered / lack values / dishonest / stupid / ignorant / promiscuous / rude."

Then we are surprised when they turn out this way. Consider what we are creating with such thoughts about kids?

Our children and our leaders are a reflection of our minds.

We give away our authority to the illusion that we are too weak, and helpless to do anything about corrupt leaders.

We affirm that we are powerless to effect change in our lives every time we state, "What can I do? I'm just one person. I'm nothing. It's the guys with the bucks who control everything."

How fragile our existence is, we are so helpless, - and therein is a great lie! Nothing could be further from the TRUTH.

People cling to the lie - and the illusion that everything is beyond their control. They fear losing the lie that they have created, for the lie validates their thought about something. No one likes to admit being wrong about such fundamental issues as their own lives and relationships!

Ones ego goes to great lengths to sustain personal belief systems rather than to admit that what they perceive is really a total illusion.

That which think you about - you create - and it will manifest.

Maintaining a belief system that one has spent a lifetime in creating and validating, produces a very powerful incentive for the individual to continue to reinforce in order to stand vindicated in what they believe to be true!

Your ego has won and once again you have proved that you know better than God.

Thinking of life as separate from yourself, you will experience everything that happens to you as something beyond your control and you will accept no responsibility for having created it. Naturally, when your thoughts of separation manifest, you will be correct. You always get what you think, so you are never wrong. But all you are right about is the illusion you have manifested and reality will have eluded you.

Your ego will always try and convince you of the validity of your thoughts since you created it, that it must be right!

Now it is time to un-create it!

—

<u>Separation</u>

When you are in touch with God, you will see all your desires mysteriously fulfilled... He has given you everything; but only when you forsake all His gifts, preferring Him, will He surrender Himself. When you show God that you are willing to sacrifice everything to know Him, He will come to you. - Paramahansa Yogananda (Indian Saint)

Inasmuch as you cannot disown your own thoughts because they are a part of who you are, more so than even your arm or your leg, so then are you a part of and one with your Creator.

This is a very powerful Truth:

YOU CANNOT FOR ONE INSTANT BE SEPARATE FROM GOD!
To see yourself otherwise is your illusion!

Here is a second powerful Truth:

ALL PEOPLE, ALL LIFE, ALL EXISTENCE IS ONE AND THE SAME!
Believing in separation from another person, or to see yourself as separate from anything at all, is an illusion!

Consider this carefully and mull it over in your mind a few times:

To believe yourself to be separate from God, you must also deny that you exist at all!

Inasmuch as your thoughts have no existence without you, so must you exist as a thought within the mind of God.

The world and all creation exists as one in the mind of God. Therefore when you think that you are separate from God, you also deny that you are part of the universe as a whole.

This is one of the mind tricks that the ego plays with our consciousness.

Consider the meaning of the word universe. "Uni" means one. Therefore there can only be one, all encompassing <u>uni</u>verse. If you were truly separate from all that exists around you, that would imply that there is someplace where God is not. That someplace would be you!

If there were somewhere that God is not, then that somewhere would not be part of the uni-verse. Therefore that somewhere would not exist!

The importance of this concept is fundamental in changing ones point of view of reality and ones place in the world. Everything that exists is of the same energy emanating from the one and only Source. To express it in quantum physics terms, all matter is united oneness and that is in the commonality of its source that is energy.

There is no separation between us as people, and there is no separation between us and the universe, and everything within it. To see this any other way one must deny ones own existence, and therefore the existence of the universe.

What then of your notion of reality? What do we make of your perception of physical reality?

You are created of energy - every atom of your being is made of energy.

The process of thought requires energy and indeed thought is energy in motion.

In thinking, you engage your mind in the same creative process as the Creator in whose mind you exist. Indeed your entire consciousness is only a thought. So it is with God. All creation is held in the thought of Him who sustains His conscious thoughts.

And inasmuch as your thoughts are undeniably inseparably a part of you, so you are part of the Divine in whose thoughts you exist.

Are you not then one and the same as the Divine?

Are our thoughts any less than we, who think them?

Are Gods thoughts any less than God Himself?

Our thoughts are His thoughts and His are ours.

Consciousness may indeed be described as the level to which we are able to tap into the thoughts of our Creator.

The greater our ability to rise into a higher thought, the greater is our conscious awareness.

We are indeed one with God, of God, and inseparable from God.

Another thought on the nature of what we are is that we exist as long as God exists. We are eternal and immortal beings.

I will repeat this for it is very important that you consciously embrace this idea, *like our creator, we are eternal beings.*

Neither the mind of God, nor the energy formed from His thoughts, i.e.: ourselves can ever be destroyed!

To see ourselves as less than the Divine beings that we are is to see ourselves as cut off and separate from God. Separation is the Grand Illusion we create for ourselves.

Separation is what you engage in when you listen to your ego and you do not embrace the reality of your Divinity and oneness with God.

A mind that is going through feelings of separation from God is stuck in death feelings, or has its death urge working.

Indeed in the spiritual awakening of ones consciousness, one works to shed the effects of the ego that keeps one stuck in the illusion of separation from the world.

This process of transcending the ego frequently brings up ones death urge. For to shed the ego is to die a living death and to transcend to a different state of awareness that can be frightening to some people. That is why in the yoga practices, the teacher, or guru, leads the student through a series of practices designed to ease the path to enlightenment.

Even when you are not enlightened, when you have not transcended your ego, you are no less a divine being co-creating with God in the conception of the world.

When thought energy goes out from yourself, i.e. when you think, you in point of fact become a partner together with the Divine, in creating the world.

You are one being with God, therefore your thoughts cannot be separate from His.

Seeing the power of your thoughts any other way engages you in separation and Illusion.

Your thoughts are very powerful. Therefore it is desirable that all thoughts be done with awareness and good intention of the results that they produce.

Contemplate what happens with the energy produced by the thoughts generated every second of the day by the billions of people on the Earth.

I visualize energy as a form of psychic steam. This steam emanates from the Universal Source and from each one of us. Like moisture in the atmosphere, it is light, airy and is invisible, until it attracts other drops of energy and it starts to coalesce. Then, like clouds in the sky, energy unites and commences to manifest as a tangible accumulation.

The mass of mankind's thoughts propagates into the universe. When sufficient power is behind the thoughts and emotions, then the sum of the energy coalesces and actualizes into the physical plane.

The process of creation can be described as Awareness actualizing into Thought, from Thought to Intention and Word, and finally there is Creation. All of this is just the transmutation of Energy.

Every action ever taken is based on this sequence of events.

Every great invention and created work has followed this process.

The implications of this human mind connectedness are enormous. It must of necessity affect how we perceive ourselves, our relationships, our place in the universe and our relationship to God!

Jesus, the Mahatma, Moses, Buddha, Krishna and innumerable saints and sages all had total awareness of their connectedness to the All that Is. Mental and spiritual power comes with Divine enlightenment. Aligning with the Divine you can manifest and create from the power of the mind alone. The sages knew that their relationship to God was that of the "Son of God". They knew this to be true for all of mankind.

They understood that all is "of" the Divine, therefore inasmuch as God could be compared to the sea, we are vessels filled from that sea. Although we are not the sea, we are of the sea and indistinguishable from it. When we return to the sea we merge seamlessly with it, compared to oil that separates from the sea. The merging is enlightenment. Enlightenment may be described as awareness of and becoming one with the Source.

The title that Jesus adopted, "Son of God" applies to every one of us.

In TRUTH we are all of us God.

Human beings exist in a strange duality. The Real world of the spiritual dimension, that is eternal and defines who we truly are, plus the physical world which is the ego-self created illusion of what we think is real.

It is meaningless to base your judgment of self on externally perceived underpinnings such as, your appearance, your job, your religion, your social standing, education, accomplishments and so on. None of these is a reflection of what you truly are.

All physical measurements of self worth lack permanence and abiding substance.

People spend most of their waking hours reinforcing that their sensory perception of the world is correct. We already have established how limited our senses are. However the need for reassurance is a very compelling human drive. For the ego, physical reassurance is a survival imperative.

In the short term a new car, a face-lift, a job promotion etc. can create the illusion of approval or assurance of self worth that people are constantly seeking, but physical gratification is fleeting. Soon, the ego needs further assurance, so people constantly search for the next new thing to provide them with a sense of fulfillment. But this is always a fleeting sensation.

When our beliefs are challenged, we may feel compelled to defend them because we imagine that our very sense of self is under attack. Self-justification is a very powerful imperative to the unenlightened. The ego's addiction to perceiving attack and hence its ostensible need for defense for what it imagines is it's survival is incredibly strong.

The perception of being attacked and the need for defense, are separatist thoughts. Attack and defense lead to feelings of separation, fear, mistrust and attack and counter-attack.

Where nations are concerned, the outcome is war.

"Whether you worship Christ, Krishna, Kali or Allah, you actually worship the one Light that is also in you, since It pervades all things. Everything originates in Light, everything in its essence is Light" - Anandamayi Ma (Indian Saint)

Indian Saints

Since I received the Guru's grace, I see only God wherever I look...Whatever I see in this world is only God - Ekanath Maharaj (Indian mystic)

With enlightenment that proceeds from knowledge God realization becomes not only possible, it is desirable.

All human kind has the ability to attain the God realization of the ascended Masters.

Jesus said "All that I do shall you do - and more". The lesson is that Jesus was here to show us, by example, the way. The way is to be like Him and to attain ascension and holiness in our lifetimes.

Today in India, there are many saints who work "biblical" miracles. In a country that is tolerant of religious sainthood, "expect a miracle" is not a phrase but a working model of daily life that numerous acolytes, apprenticed to self- realized masters are striving to achieve. Perhaps the most famous living saint, although by no means the only one, is Sai Baba. He will live until age 93, by his own statement, and then he will choose "mahasamadhi" (the conscious departure of the soul from the body) to ascend from his body. (Not die). He reputedly performs miracles everyday as a matter of course.

Carolyn Myss, the well-known author, has written about receiving "vabuti" a sacred ash from Sai Baba at a time when she was seriously ill in hospital. According to Carolyn, she had no previous connection to Sai Baba, but one day found herself wishing that she had a magic cure in the form of Sai Baba's vabuti that she had heard about, the ash that he reputedly materializes out of pure thought energy from his hands. Within a day or two, Carolyn mysteriously received a package in the mail containing vabuti! She was cured within a short while after taking it!

Sai Baba is about 65 years of age and has a large Ashram in Southern India..

Another great teacher is Shri Mahaprabhuji Haidakhan Baba, (The Great Lord and Father of Haidakhan) known as "Wale Baba" the Simple Father or simply as "Babaji"

Paramahansa Yogananda has extensively written about Babaji in the book "Autobiography of a Yogi". Babaji is also regarded as the

Christ of the East. He reputedly returns to earth periodically in times of need, the most recent occasion by manifesting a body for Himself (not by being born of parents) out of pure thought energy. Babaji also leaves at will, (mahasamadhi), when he chooses. He was last here in the physical world, in 1984 and he has promised to return again. Babaji regularly appears to His devotees both in their dreams and sometimes in actual physical form to guide them at crucial points in their lives. There are numerous books and documentations of Babaji's miraculous appearances to devotees, frequently noting him appearing in more than one place simultaneously.

Babaji is one of the greatest masters of Kriya Yoga, being one of only 18 Siddha Yogis in the past thousand years. Babaji established a lineage of Kriya Yoga practitioners that dates back to the legendary Patanjali. His devotees and Kriya practitioners who received direct instruction from him include, Sri Lahiri Mahasaya, Sri Yukteswar in the last century and Yogananda Paramahansa this century.

The videos and books on Babaji are wonderful to see and there are many web sites devoted to both Sri Babaji and Shri Sai Baba.

Westerners tend to be dismissive of such stories of saints and miracles. But that is part of our un-consciousness, our seeing the Universe as being limited to what our own inadequate senses are able to perceive.

People frequently ask why we do not see miracles in the world today as they did in Biblical days. Remember that thought is creative. If people are cynical and are closed to the idea of miracles, the Universe will show them exactly what they want - no miracles!

We are entitled to miracles. In the wonderful book "A Course in Miracles" the Divinely inspired writings tell us that we deserve miracles, we must ask for miracles, in fact we must demand miracles, it is our right!

You want miracles? Then expect miracles!

As Dr. Wayne Dyer said, "When you believe it, you will see it".

———

Jeffrey M. Solomon

Magic in Mexico

Men talk about Bible miracles because there is no miracle in their lives. Cease to gnaw that crust. There is ripe fruit over your head. - Henry David Thoreau (American Essayist)

You are what you think.
"Reality" is merely your own mind reflected back at you.
Through the process of creative thought, mankind acts in accordance with the Universal Laws of cause and effect. We are continuously involved in the process of creation, whether you are conscious of it or not. We cannot stop thinking and therefore we never cease creating!

The creative thought process done with intention is REAL creation. I am not referring to self- delusion, although delusion is one of the prime results of the manifestation process, albeit an unconscious one.

Creation involves the transference of thought energy from the mind into substance and substance into reality!

This is the act of actually fabricating reality and bringing it into existence with the power of ones thoughts.

My daughter, Morgan, a teenager, is totally rooted in the world of MTV and fashion. She is the poster child for the "material girl. Nevertheless she is incredible at manifesting her desires.

She is not consciously aware of creating in the sense of her understanding of how her intention creates her results, however her powers of manifestation are amazing!

One of the hats that I wear is that of owner of a travel business. We do tours to power places in the world, conduct seminars and training's and study with spiritually developed beings.

Recently on a trip from the USA to Mexico with the family, I was upgraded by the airline to first class. This little upgrade perk is sometimes extended to people in the industry as a courtesy by airlines, and at their discretion.

Morgan was quite miffed that she was not upgraded and she was determined that she would be upgraded on the return flight from Mexico.

116

I told her that an upgrade for her was out of the question as one had to not only be a bona fide travel agent but you had to have an IATAN identity card (the International Airlines Travel Agent Network) to prove it.

She was very determined, and against my better judgment on our return flight, she persuaded me to ask the station manager at the airport for an upgrade for her. He cheerfully explained that he could not allow this and that in any event we should have made all the necessary upgrade requests back in the USA with our airline sales representative prior to commencing travel.

Then in a sudden turn of mind he said, "what the heck, I will do this just this one time" and although my three kids were not eligible, all four of us were upgraded!

You could have bowled me over with a feather. The kids, needless to say were delighted!

This was not the first instance of creative thought on this journey, but one of many occurrences of what I feel was Divine intervention on this trip. Mexico is a very magical country.

When we arrived in Mexico we drove from Mexico City through the Mexican valley via small towns en route. Our final destination before returning to Mexico City being Ixtapa, a charming resort city north of Acapulco on the Pacific west coast.

My three kids who were aged 7, 13 and 15 at the time and I departed from the silver city of Taxco that was our final in-land city before we headed westbound to Ixtapa on the beautiful beaches of the Pacific Ocean. I had a rudimentary map photocopied from a guidebook that showed the principle cities and major highways, but it was not a real touring map.

I guess that after a lifetime of travel one gets a little blasé about trip preparation and things like that. I have a pretty good sense of direction. I have crossed the desert from Jordan to Israel, driven across India, and so on so, all without maps, so what did I need to be concerned about on a little vacation trip in Mexico?

I figured that that the map I had was adequate enough for our needs. All we had to do was to head south towards Acapulco and at some point on Highway 95 we would hit a town called Iguala where we would detour north on highway 51 for a short while and then the highway turns south west to Ixtapa. Piece of cake, right? Was I ever wrong!

We left highway 95 just as the map indicated and we headed north on highway 51 from Iguala. Just as planned, we were heading in the direction of Ixtapa on the coast by the shortest route. We would make Ixtapa in about three hours. After about twenty miles I started to get a very uneasy feeling in my body. Just being on this road felt very wrong and uncomfortable to me and I told the kids that I was heading back to Iguala to recheck the route.

In rural Mexico it is extremely hard to find an English speaking person, and we did not speak Spanish, so finding someone who could give us directions was going to be a challenge! Usually if someone does not speak English if you just mention the name of the place you are going to, and if you look helpless enough, you can usually figure out by a person's gestures which direction you should be heading.

I have learned from my travels that it is also a good idea to stop and ask at least three different people for directions, just to confirm that what we understood was indeed correct!

After the standard three- person check, I realized that I being directed to head towards Acapulco.

I figured that perhaps I had taken the wrong highway turnoff on to Highway 51. The Ixtapa turnoff, I figured, must be a little further down the road. So I headed south and I looked in vain for a sign indicating a turnoff to Highway 51 to Ixtapa.

We never did see highway 51 again, nor did we see any other turnoff to Ixtapa.

By now we were miles off course. We prayed for guidance, we said our mantras and sang songs to the Divinity for guidance. In spite of this we eventually found ourselves in Acapulco, 300 miles south of Ixtapa. We were so completely off course and by now it was night-time and it was dark, and we were hundreds of miles out of our way! By nine o'clock at night we found ourselves hopelessly lost in Acapulco, a huge city built on the slopes of a mountain and we were without a map and we had a major language barrier. The road we were on twisted and turned under mountain bridges and over passes. The four-lane road split and split again going off in all directions, under bridges, over passes and around mountains. I this point I just surrendered. I told God that I had no idea why I was here, or even where "here" was, but there must be a purpose for being where we were and I resolved to surrender to the flow of whatever happens!

For some reason my thoughts had created us being here, but why I had yet to discover.

At a traffic light, a taxi suddenly pulled up next to me and caught my eye. It was quite literally a rolling discotheque on wheels! It had the mandatory thumping boom box music accompanied by strobe lights inside the cab that were flashing and flickering, and purple neon trim beaming from the roof and the license plate casting an eerie glow all around. You could not avoid seeing this vehicle from a mile away and if you missed seeing it, you sure as heck could hear it! I have never seen such a remarkable vehicle before or since.

I waved to attract the driver's attention and after he turned down the volume of the stereo and I managed to ask him for directions. Realizing that I was a hopeless "gringo" and that I could not understand the complicated route he was yelling to me in Spanish across the traffic, the taxi driver gave the universal motion to "follow me" and follow him I did. One could not lose him! His car shined in the traffic, a searchlight for stranded tourists, blinking and booming for lost wayfarers in the dark. After some miles of twists and turns through lines of traffic, he put us on the loan coastal road heading north to Ixtapa. Then he turned back with a disco honk on his musical horn and just as quickly he was gone.

What a guide we had manifested! Like Moses, with a pillar of fire to guide the way at night!

A further two hours of driving passed on this unlit and ill-maintained coastal road that curved through hills, down valleys and past small, impoverished villages. It was not long before I was getting too exhausted to continue. My driving any further would be impossible without my being a danger to us and to others. We needed a hotel, but where would we find one? There was nothing but dusty villages and only remotest possibility existed of anything resembling decent lodgings appearing in such an isolated and poverty- stricken area. All we could do was trust and pray.

Such were my thoughts when out of the darkness a large sign appeared in the headlights. A resort lay ahead! I swung off the road to find that I had come across a small but very charming private resort in the midst of a coconut plantation. It was clean and modern with, and, as I found out in the morning, it had a beautiful sculpted garden that was overgrown with bougainvillea, mango and avocado trees. There were pools set in this delightful garden setting. It had a petting zoo with rabbits, a deer, some assorted geese and turkeys as well as a caged jaguar.

At breakfast the following morning, I met our host and owner, Jose. Jose spoke perfect English. Over coffee Jose proceeded to inform me that he only has a 5% occupancy rate at his resort. The resort is a labor of love for him more than it is a commercial proposition. He subsidizes it from the income from the coconut plantation. Jose was very congenial and I think that he welcomed our presence and the diversion that we brought to his morning routine.

I related to Jose the story of our journey that had culminated in our being here at his resort. I told him how our three hours journey from Taxco to Ixtapa had taken us the entire day and that we still were not there. I explained how I had started down Highway 51 when I had decided on a whim to turn back near and as a result we were now 300 miles off course.

Instead of sympathizing with my plight as I expected Jose to do, things got really interesting. Jose informed me that we were extremely fortunate that we had turned around at Iguala when we did. He told me to avoid that route at all costs. Jose explained that Highway 51 though a direct route to Ixtapa, it is overrun by rebel bandits and drug dealers. They apparently hijack cars and rape and murder their victims. The local police are also apparently involved with the bandits so there is no rule of law!

Jose told me that just two weeks before we arrived, a foreign diplomat was murdered and robbed on that very same road and his car was stolen! "No one", according to Jose, "ever takes that route to Ixtapa"!

We had unconsciously manifested a safe three hundred-mile detour plus a disco cabby/ pillar of light in the dark, and a great and friendly place to shelter for the night! All in all not bad going for one day's work!

Later after we took our leave of Jose we set off for Ixtapa and arrived there just before noon. We started our hotel search by going from one hotel to another following a long row of hotels in the "hotel zone", a strip of resorts extending for several miles along the beach front. Being the Easter vacation week, the room rates were over $200.00 per night for a decent four or five star hotel. But price, as it turned out, was not the issue. Indeed price was purely academic. Every hotel that we tried was completely full.

We drove around fruitlessly in the heat from one hotel to the next until we had seen almost every hotel on the beach. The kids were getting miserable and hungry. All they really wanted was to hit the beach.

We stopped at one resort to try and find accommodation and when I was unsuccessful I asked for a list of all the hotels in Ixtapa along with their phone numbers from the concierge. I then proceeded to call all the hotels on the list.

I was getting to the end of the list when my seven-year-old son, Alexander, spontaneously channeled Babaji. I should not have been by this time but I was amazed. He had never shown any inclination towards channeling anything before and he did not even know what channeling is anyway.

"Daddy," he said, Babaji just said to me that we must have the very best hotel in Ixtapa and not to waste our time with the other hotels! I had no better ideas of my own so I checked my Mexico guide-book. I found that there was one hotel in Ixtapa, the Westin las Brisas, set on a cliff overlooking a beautiful private bay that is the highest rated hotel in Ixtapa. It is above a five star rating, it is a Grand Tourismo or GT, meaning it is in a special luxury category all of its own.

"OK" I said to Alex, and I proceeded, with much trepidation, to call them, afraid of what exorbitant nightly rate I might be quoted from this hotel whose luxury rating was off the map! Even *if* they had rooms, could I afford it?

I got through to reservations and they told me they did indeed have rooms! Well, I figured one down and one to go. The next step is to ask the price. I held my breath. Give me the bad news. I braced myself and I waited for the rate.

The voice on the phone came back, "For a travel agent the rate will be $125.00 per night"!

Wow! Nirvana! This was the best deal at the best hotel in town!

So, thank you Babaji for coming through Alexander.

We had the best accommodations in Ixtapa at a really great room rate.

The "Mexico miracles" did not end in Ixtapa. There is more to tell.

Before our return journey to Mexico City and finally back to the USA, I checked with several sources at the hotel and I asked whether we absolutely needed to return to Mexico City via Acapulco. I was told again and again not to take the direct route. (The old three persons check).

We headed back via Acapulco and arrived on the outskirts of Mexico City on a Saturday night.

In the mountains, 50 miles south of Mexico City, our rental car decided to die! As we were going through the mountain passes approaching the valley that cradles Mexico City, the car spluttered and lost power. I downshifted to second gear and we coughed along at twenty miles per hour the car slowly fading and losing speed. Soon we were crawling along on the right shoulder of the road, coaxing the car for every last mile I could squeeze out of it. Streams of traffic hurtled past us on the highway, oblivious to what is no doubt a common sight on these roads, a dying car. The kids and I all started praying spontaneously. Morgan, the biggest skeptic in the world, who challenges me at every turn, was determined not be stuck, and in desperation she started chanting a power mantra, Om Namaha Shivaya.

Several minutes later the car sputtered as if to finally give up and die. We looked around desperately aware that we had a flight home to catch and that we were in the middle of nowhere. Suddenly and abruptly the engine sputtered and sputtered again, this time a little stronger. Slowly the dying motor coughed and inched its way back to life. A little at a time the power crept up, the rev counter needle fluttered higher on the dashboard gauge and the motor pulled harder. Was it going to last or was this a last gasp? Without warning the engine fired. It caught. The motor roared.

We pulled off the shoulder of the road and into the slow lane and soon we were in the mainstream traffic lane and headed to Mexico City!

We did not realize that one final hurdle still lay ahead of us.

Mexico City is the largest or second largest city in the world, depending on whether you ask a Mexican or the Japanese from Tokyo.

It takes an hour and a half if the traffic is reasonable, to drive from the south of Mexico City to the airport in the north. The road is not a freeway in the conventional sense, it is more like a six- lane road through the city that forks and winds before some lanes split and split again. Much like Acapulco, there are underpasses, overpasses, traffic lights and multiple cross- roads wheeling off in different directions at every intersection. Airport signs are few and far between. To get around Mexico City every driver carries a map. This is not a city designed on a square grid like most cities in the USA. In Mexico City you need to know which city zone you are in and which city zone you want to go to. Then you need to know which Avenida or avenue you want in order to get to your destination. This is a city of medieval design. I did not have a city map. Any resident of Mexico City will tell you, drive in Mexico City without a city map and you are pretty much on your own, and by the way, good luck!

So there we were. In Mexico City and the Saturday night traffic was something unbelievable.

I had expected to find a modern ring road around the city, as one would have in the United States, and which would be sign-posted "Aeroporto" or with some other significant airport indicator such as a picture of an airplane. Perhaps there is one. However, nothing indicated its existence to me, and with no Spanish language ability beyond Aeroporto or a picture of an airplane to guide me, the airport road could have hit me in the face and I would not have recognized it!

Having driven for nine hours from Ixtapa via Acapulco, through mountain roads and then finding myself in Mexico Cities' famous traffic on a Saturday night, getting to the airport was turning into a daunting task. Additionally, a nearby volcano was active and the air quality was sulfurous. Already the worlds most air polluted city, the air that night was worse than usual. This was my idea of Dante's Inferno on wheels!

Being a dark, bumper-to-bumper traffic congested Saturday night, I was also running low on gas. Knowing that I had to return the rental car with a full tank of gas, I decided to pull into a gas station. Once there I found the gas station attendant and I proceeded to ask the attendant for directions to the airport. He replied, "Right ahead senor, over the hill, about one kilometer". Less than one mile! We were right there within a stone's throw of the airport!

When I returned the car to the car rental agency at the airport the assistant at the desk confirmed to me that we were extremely fortunate to have found our way to the airport. He told me that lifelong residents of Mexico City regularly get lost and no one drives without a map of the city with them in their vehicle.

So why was there no map in the rental car I wondered?

These are small examples of the miracles that one can manifest, and indeed we do create in our own lives, everyday.

The difference between seeing a miracle and seeing a coincidence is one of perception.

The conscious person perceives that the difference is also one of intention prior to receiving a miracle and gratitude afterwards.

—

If All the World's a Stage, You are the Illusionist

As far as the laws of mathematics refer to reality, they are not certain, and as far as they are certain, they do not refer to reality - Albert Einstein (German born physicist)

The world currently finds itself in a state of mass illusion.

People consider certain events in their lives as a threat to their well being. They see these events as emanating from circumstances and people exterior to themselves. Threats are perceived to exist everywhere. The world appears to be an uncontrollable series of chaotic events with which they struggle every waking moment to control. This is a world of turmoil, hostility and fear.

By failing to accept responsibility for that which they have created in their lives, individuals must inevitably become the hapless victims of their own handiwork.

This is the experience of events controlling you. People become victim to their thoughts that their lives are out of control. Feelings of individual helplessness are prevalent. An air of desperation and indeed resignation abounds when one feels unable to direct the course of ones own life, let alone the feeling of powerlessness in being able to influence national and international events.

In this low state of consciousness it is common for people to lay the culpability on circumstances beyond themselves rather than their accepting responsibility for having created everything that happens in their life.

Even when we create unconsciously, that, which we think, becomes real to us. I have said this before and it is important to be reminded of this.

The process of unconscious thoughts multiplied, leads to the creation of a universal illusion on a grand scale. The illusion is that of seeing oneself as the CREATED not the CREATOR.

The consequence of this way of thinking leads one to thoughts of victim consciousness.

We shall try to uncover the mystery of the experience of TRUTH and REALITY through a series of simple self discovery exercises and meditations.

With this in mind, you can engage in a simple visualization exercise right now.

Relax quietly. Visualize a busy intersection with which you may be familiar. Imagine that you have a video camera and that you are filming the passing traffic. You are fixed in one spot at the side of the road and you are looking straight ahead through the camera's viewfinder. You are only able to see in the single direction that you are facing.

Take time to imagine the scene that you are viewing through the fixed lens of your video camera. See vehicles appearing from one corner of your field of vision and see them moving into the center of your screen. Then imagine them passing out of sight in the opposite corner of your screen. Spend a few moments with this view. Now consider some alternative ways you could be viewing this scene with your video camera. Again, try to spend a few moments with each scene. Try to imagine that you are zooming in and out and notice the change of image in your viewfinder. Now try to see the traffic out of focus. Next see the traffic in freeze frame, passing one frame at a time. Try the fast forward and slow motion settings for a different perspective.

If you have a normal imagination, you will have no difficulty in visualizing these different scenarios.

In the few minutes that you have just spent in imagination, you have just created new perspectives of reality.

However consider where, in these past few minutes you saw the images?

You saw them in your mind of course.

So even when you actually view a real tape, where do you see the images?

You see and experience it in your mind.

Therefore there are at least three realities to be considered here. The actual time of filming the event and the stored memories of your mind and those events recorded on the tape.

Nevertheless you experience all three of these memories only in your mind.

When you film you may be aware that your video camera is filming one frame at a time. Electro-magnetic images are recorded on the film. These images are captured on the tape one frame at a time.

Each frame is a single, unmoving image. When you play the tape back, the speed of playback and the slight variations between each succeeding still frame creates an image of movement. There is no actual movement on the tape, only the illusion of movement.

Notwithstanding that the recorded images exist on a strip of tape, they are meaningless until they are viewed by someone on a screen.

So although we view a screen and we fall into the illusion that the action is happening on the screen, the fact is that the screen itself does not contain anything!

The screen is merely a reflection of what exists on the tape.

The image on the screen also does not have meaning unless someone is there to view it. It certainly has no permanence.

Only in your mind is it given life, meaning and permanence.

Yet we never consider that fact when we watch the tape.

Once again we create a reality to suit what our senses perceive and tell us is happening.

Ultimately the absolute screen is your mind. Here alone is where true perception occurs. However, like the tape, we never give a thought about where perception or reality exists.

If our senses perceive events outside of ourselves, we do not question the reality of this. We content ourselves with the illusion of reality.

A good movie can transcend reality. People can be totally transformed and absorbed in the illusion created by a good thriller.

They frequently shriek, squirm, feel anxious, laugh and cry during a good movie, which in that instant, in their minds, the movie becomes their reality!

When you see a good movie you may loose all awareness of existence outside of the movie.

You are able to forget where you are, and you forget your problems as you lose yourself in the drama and you lose track of time.

In that moment you have created a new reality for yourself wherein all else ceases to exist. This is analogous to a dream state wherein only the present experience exists as real

This movie version of reality is also not that different from real life as you experience it.

Only in life your emotional commitment to the illusion is much greater, especially as you have the starring role! Therefore it is natural for one to try to control the outcome of every scene and to script every event to suit ones fancy.

By analogy think of your brain as a recorder.

Regard your five senses, your eyes, ears, nose, touch, and taste as parts of that recorder.

The recorder parts, that is your senses, in and of themselves are dumb, just like a movie camera or the image on a screen. Your mind is still necessary to give life meaning and permanence to experience.

The question you should consider is whether you experience life and a movie any differently in the moment that you are experiencing them?

Both experiences are purely mental, neither could exist outside of your mind. Indeed your mind is the only place that experience of any sort can meaningfully exist.

Furthermore, inasmuch as the movie is a record of the past so are your life experiences.

Even as you experience something, in the very brief time it takes for your brain to process the information, categorize and analyze it, it is by definition, already past history. You can never ever experience physical life 100% in the present moment through the senses.

In this sense one is always responding to events which are past.

All incoming information is of necessity, past by the time you perceive it.

This is not due to any fault on your behalf it is merely a fact of the physical senses operating in a physical world in which time and space determine the outcome of physical experience.

The exception to this is your thoughts that arise spontaneously in the present moment.

Awareness precedes any ability to measure it. The instinct to duck, the impulse to swerve, the flash of inspiration, all of these exist outside of time and space and require no pre-cognition. They arise in a space of awareness outside of time.

In meditation, the objective is to be able to access the here and now.

This is the space of the eternal becoming, the merging of awareness and being-ness, the infinite moment of now.

As limited as our senses are, they are the only physical means that we have to record and to inform us about the material world around us.

Our minds interpret subjectively and choose *how* to create a sense of understanding and how to respond to the signals being fed it by our senses. We interpret, and categorize these experiences according to a multitude of devices such as what we think we are (ego), the programming we have undergone by our educational, cultural and parental models, and what we have learned from our life experience.

I use the words *create* because the mind is very interpretive of its experiences.

Your interpretation of something will determine your experience of it. Your interpretation is dependent on your judgment together with the overwhelming need of your ego to justify that your perception is both correct and within the parameters of your belief structure.

Your sense of self is dependent on your always having consistent results to your physical experiences. People who do not are frequently labeled as schizophrenic. That is to say that if your interpretation of what is real extends beyond the accepted bounds of normality you may be regarded as mentally ill.

Judgment is formed by culture, life experiences, conditioning, expectations, level of fear and love plus thousands of emotions that make each of us unique.

The sensory images are imprinted, interpreted and stored in your mind without which your experience would be non-existent. In other words you could not experience anything without your mind to receive and interpret your experience.

All experience, whatever you think, feel, see and are aware of about yourself, your loved ones, your world, exists only in your mind. This is important to understand.

The mind is where reality dwells. Reality outside of your mind does not exist.

Without mind, you have no sense of self, nor a sense of anything beyond yourself.

Your senses are merely the apparatus and collectors of information and your mind is the interpreter of experience.

Only your mind has experiences and contains consciousness of both the external world and self- awareness.

Therefore any sense you have of reality existing outside of yourself, in spite of what your senses tell you, is an ILLUSION.

Therefore in referring back to the exercise that we did at the beginning of this section, reality exists within. Reality is edited by the ego and it is constantly being edited to fit your individual world-view and so it is ever changing. You are the creator of your reality. That reality is unlike any other person's reality. Consequently that which we perceive to be reality is indeed just illusion.

—

Seeing

The light of the body is the eye: therefore when thy eye is single, thy whole body is full of light.. Luke 11:34 (Bible)

Sight is perhaps the single most important of the five senses as a source of information about the world.

Obviously, without the brain, the eyes would be useless. Without mind, the brain would be useless. If the eye functions and if the brain or the optic nerve does not, the eye is blind.

We know that seeing is really an eye brain/mind combination.

What does the brain see and how is this similar to the function of a movie as described in the previous section?

Light is energy. Light is reflected from an object to the eye. What the eye actually sees is the light reflected off an object. Just as we see the moon at night because the sunlight is reflected off it, so we see everything as reflected light.

Remove the light source and all visible objects become invisible.

Light travels from an object to the eye and then to the brain. Here it is received as a series of still images similar to those captured on a movie film.

We, however, perceive these images as continuously connected. The fact is that like the images on film that we discussed earlier, the object being observed is really reflecting a subtle and imperceptible state of continuous change.

The light that is reflected off something in that one millisecond is not the same light reflected off the object seconds earlier.

That is why when you see stop frame photography, that is photography that shoots an object such as a plant over several days and then is speeded up. You can see the seed germinate and grow, then the stem pushes through the earth and finally a flower appears and then the plant dies all in the space of one minute.

The camera captures and records light. The light emanating from the subject, in this case a plant is different in each frame of the film.

You can never step into the same river twice because the river is constantly flowing. So it is with the light that flows of all we see.

The constant stream of reflected light off an object every instant could be considered as separate information packets, like film frames

131

of information. If you could move at the speed of light so that you could keep up with a light beam reflecting off an object, time would stand still. If you were viewing a beautiful sunset and you could hitch a ride with one of the light beam images of the sunset, you could watch that sunset forever and never see it turn to night. You would be forever with the sunset. Similarly with the plant in the example above, if you could hitch your britches to a light beam that flower would bloom for eternity.

Therefore, in some manner and in some form, time ceases to exist at the speed of light and all that ever is and ever was and ever will be exists simultaneously in an eternal now.

Back on earth and reality, you cannot move that fast and so time passes you by and dusk turns to night, flowers bloom and fade, exactly consistent with your physical experience and therefore also consistent with your interpretation of reality.

Flies live in a greatly accelerated time frame compared to us humans. They perceive our movements as very slow. Hence when you try to swat a fly, its perception of your hand moving is very different to how you see your hand moving. A fly will observe your hand as moving in slow motion and so in the fly's accelerated world, the fly can easily escape your hand.

Many creatures live in time frames that are radically different from human beings. Birds, while not as quick to take wing as a fly, will react extremely rapidly to danger.

A slug by comparison sees the world moving in a blur of motion and does not readily distinguish the movement of fast approaching danger.

Perception is indeed linked to time. Time is relative to the perceiver.

Anyone who has seen Claude Monet's wonderful paintings of water lilies and cathedrals will understand the concept of the ever-changing nature of perception.

Monet set up several easels in front of his subjects such as his famous multiple paintings of water lilies and cathedrals. As the light changed each hour during the course of the day, he would quit painting on one canvas and start on the next. Set side by side the series of identical paintings reflect the same scene but are vastly different from each other as the light and shadows change.

Each fraction of a second, your eyes receive a batch of photons and electrons reflecting off the objects that you perceive.

Thousands of separate images, like individual movie frames, are received and projected on to your brain. You have the ability to recall these images from memory by using the energy of thought and memory.

Such memory images may be recalled in a variety of different memory recall patterns.

You may remember images as a series of frame by frame flashbacks, like slow motion with even an occasional rewind. Or you may recall one still frame fixed in your memory.

Finally you may recollect a continuous series of action frames like a movie.

And like a movie, you can replay the recorded scene from memory one frame at a time or in a stream of action, you can also choose to review memory in slow motion, rewind, fast forward, freeze frame, and even edit.

When you recall an event from memory, you frequently edit it, change it and distort it to suit your particular frame of reference.

You will often change events and create an unlimited number of new "realities". You may edit out background, zoom in on a particular aspect of a memorized scene, hold it still and examine it and so on.

Our minds do anything they choose with the images they store even in the very moment of perception.

We create our reality in so many different ways.

Most people have mentally reviewed a past event, and have, with the benefit of hindsight indulged in the mental game of "I should have said..." Regret about missed opportunities to have expressed our self differently is one very common form of memory editing.

You may immediately be familiar with the feeling of editing the storyline of an unpleasant event to reflect a more satisfactory, albeit imaginary, outcome.

Perception of reality is therefore highly subjective at all times. Should one compare notes from a group of witnesses to an event, there are differences in reports based on each individual's perception. The perception and processing of information in each mind is subject to personal creative subtleties.

The mind creates every moment. Whether it is in the creative, receive or playback mode, and sometimes in more than one mode at a time, it never shuts down in a healthy person, even during sleep.

In order to experience, you have to create reality, and in creating, you create according to your own perception of reality.

This is a strange dichotomy. We create our reality and our reality creates what we perceive.

There is no way we could possibly experience anything otherwise.

Whatever the mind is engaged in, everything that we experience, must of necessity only exist in the mind, and exist only as energy to be expressed through the creative process of the mind responding to the created.

All reality exists only as an expression of mind.

All such creation is ultimately illusion.

Following this chapter is a series of simple exercises intended to expand self awareness and heighten perception and consciousness. You may, if you wish, continue reading the chapters beyond these exercises while simultaneously implementing the Daily Visualizations presented herewith.

<u>Chapter Seven - Mind Awareness</u>

We are helpless without God's support. No effort is complete without prayer, without a definite recognition that the best human endeavor is of no effect if it has not Gods blessing behind it - Mahatma Gandhi (Indian politician philosopher)

<u>Visualization Exercise I</u>

I want, by understanding myself, to understand others. I want to be all that I am capable of becoming. - Katherine Mansfield (New Zealand born writer)

Over the coming chapters we will indulge in a series of visualization exercises. The purpose of the exercises is to help to put you in touch with your higher consciousness. It would be very helpful if you could find a quite spot at home. Find a place where you can sit undisturbed and at peace with yourself. You deserve some time alone with your thoughts. Tell your family that this time is your private time and that you should not be disturbed.

Keep a journal of your feelings, thoughts and impressions as you progress.

Remember to date it and if need be to write in the time as well.

HINT: Get some small business card size cards or Post It Notes and write reminders to yourself of the daily exercise. Keep them in your pocket or stick them in front of your computer, on your car dashboard, and any place where you will constantly be reminded to focus on creating awareness in your daily life.

I cannot stress strongly enough the need for you to be both rigorous and diligent in the practice of the following exercises if you truly want to transform how you perceive.

The key to any spiritual practice is discipline.

I have a corner in my home and a tape player on which I play soft soothing music. I burn a large candle as the flame helps to clear the air energetically. (Cleansing by fire)

I also have a comfortable seat to relax in. I have surrounded myself with nice objects, books and sacred pictures and things that promote a feeling of connectedness and well being.

In my travels to sacred places I have collected objects, crystals, stones and items which have been blessed or worn by saints and teachers. I keep these sacred objects to remind me of my connection to holy people that I have met. It also connects me to the holy places on earth that I have been to.

This is my sanctuary that I have created.

You deserve such a place too.

The implications of the statement at the close of the preceding chapter, namely, that everything we experience must of necessity exist only within our mind and nowhere else - should be pondered for a few minutes in a quiet place.

First, clear your mind of all the busy thoughts and take twenty deep connected breaths in order to focus your mind and to get your energy flowing. Breath deeply and exhale immediately without pause at the top and bottom of your inhale and exhale. Breathe rhythmically and in strong connected breaths. Do not force your exhale. Let it flow out like a big sigh with the force of gravity. This process will strengthen your focus and will clear the energy flow through your body.

The inhaled breath is strong and it affirms your life force. The exhaled breath is the release and is gentle, uncontrolled and flows naturally.

I recommend that you do this breathing and clearing process before each exercise.

Close your eyes and focus:

Quietly reflect on the many things you experienced through your five senses today.

Think about your experiences - starting with easy to deal with situations. Remind yourself of what you had for breakfast, what you saw as you got yourself ready in the morning, consider pleasant thoughts, think of memories of peaceful days, try and hold relaxing and calm thoughts. Try to be an observer of yourself thinking in the moment that you are thinking and note where each thought arises.

Let each idea flow naturally through your consciousness without forcing it. As soon as it feels complete let the next idea drift in. Do not become attached or stuck to any particular idea, let them linger naturally and drift away as they are replaced by the next.

Note that at the end of the exercise keep a record of any feelings or insights that you may have in your journal.

Do not allow yourself to think of dramatic situations at this stage. Just get used to the idea of opening and processing your thoughts without fear, in a space of safety and comfort. This is preparation for the real task ahead. It is important that you get used to your own mental processing mechanism. Become disciplined in maintaining a regular mental exercise schedule.

Do not feel hurried while you do this. Feel yourself completely safe and unthreatened.

If you need some help in recalling your experiences consider some sensory experiences you have had. Review simple events related to all five senses.

Things that you
saw,
touched,
tasted,
heard,
and smelled.

Find at least one experience from each of the five senses to meditate upon. Consider any feelings that you may have attached to the source of the memory. Recall the actual emotional effect on you at the time you had the experience.

In other words, we not only merely observe something such as a blue sky, but the sky itself may evoke childhood memories such as a picnic. Another example is that we may not only hear a piece of music but the music itself may trigger a memory and the memory in turn triggers an emotion.

The source of the input and the input itself may evoke entirely different feelings in us that are very subjective and that are not in and of itself part of the observed object. So in the example of music, the music just is. It is nothing more than what it is. However our emotions regarding that music may be tied into a memory that elevates the music to an entirely different emotional meaning.

Therefore try to meditate and recall the events of the day as vividly as possible at all levels, the emotional as well as the physical level and be aware of yourself in the actual moment observing your feelings.

Now taking one sensation or sense at a time, recreate a memory as strongly, and as realistically as you can. Relive the experience and sensations. First begin with sight and concentrate your focus on things observed and seen. After about five minutes or so do each of the remaining senses that are touch, hearing, taste and touch. Go through each experience one at a time spending about five minutes or so on each, do not rush through it.

Try to experience a really strong feeling of the emotional and physical recreation of the memory. Slowly replace these feelings with a clear awareness that all of these feelings that you created as part of your "reality" do not exist outside of you at all.

Realize that no matter what your senses may tell you, your mind created it - it does not exist elsewhere!

In the above process you have actually now recreated the experience again with your current thought process.

What you are, whatever you think about yourself, whatever your reality - all is a product of your mind. You are the ultimate authority of your experience.

This may not be an easy concept to grasp so do not be discouraged. It gets easier with practice. Stick with the program. You will get it - in fact, there is no way you cannot get it.

Once you begin to accept responsibility for your thoughts and feelings you are invoking your higher self - which already knows and understands everything that your mind is trying to get to grips with.

Realize that there is no reality outside of you. And that "outside of your" is an illusion that you have created and that you have empowered.

You have now taken the first step towards personal responsibility and in reclaiming your power.

Consider how this awareness makes you feel.

Note your feelings and experiences in your journal.

After you have done this, reflect for a few minutes on the implications attached to the thought that all reality exists only in your mind!

Consider the ramifications of your taking responsibility for your own thoughts and your experiences of life.

Note this in your journal.

Do this exercise daily for a week.

Also practice doing this as an awareness exercise during the day as frequently as possible. Pause for a few moments and tune in to what is actually happening with your thought processes during the day and in the moment. Get in touch with your emotions as you are feeling them. Become an observer of your own life.

For example during a meal tell yourself that you can only experience the taste of this meal in your mind - and nowhere else. The fact that the taste appears outside of your mind is an illusion. Take responsibility for your feelings in the moment.

Catch yourself while you are talking to someone and affirm that your experience of seeing and hearing this person is in your mind and that they exist nowhere else!

In traffic - or at work - in your home, while listening to the radio, the TV, even when you are with your boss - remind yourself:

"Nothing exists outside of my mind!

All reality is in my mind.

I alone am responsible how I choose to see - hear - feel - taste - smell and experience this event.

I alone am responsible for my feelings about this"!

Consider how this realization makes you feel.

Being fully responsible for your own feelings and perceptions - does your sense of self- confidence and empowerment increase the more you practice being consciously aware of your reality?

When you become conscious of your feelings, you should feel a sense of empowerment and control that you did not have before.

In effect, by mentally stepping aside for a few moments, you are suspending your ego's version of "reality". You become the conscious observer of your own life.

As I have said before, all experience except that of thought is of the past. Only thought is in the present. When you suspend your thoughts about the past and the future and you bring your thoughts inward to the here and now, you are able to access your higher self. You do not exist except in the present moment of every moment in time. All other sense of existence is illusionary.

In so doing you become a detached observer of your own life. Very often, this will lead to a realization that life is not as intense as you are making it out to be. You will start to chuckle inwardly as you see how seriously others take themselves.

You will realize that you were just like them before you took control of your consciousness.

As a conscious observer, you will learn that you have the freedom at any time to choose how you wish to experience your life.

You will learn that you can choose your emotional reactions, and more often than not, as awareness increases you will choose not to react to situations where previously you probably would have gone ballistic.

Being present in your consciousness, that is in the here and now, you can observe your thoughts about a situation as they arise within you. Conditioned reflexes, such as anger towards someone who insults you, can give way to a more reasoned response as you step away from your emotions and see yourself as the observer of your own mind.

You will be consciously choosing and creating your own reality, as well as your own emotions and responses.

Feel free to take longer than a week with any of the visualizations, but not shorter.

Try to maintain the practice of awareness of self as an ongoing routine.

This and each of the exercises presented require that you practice the concepts presented herein everyday for a week for about thirty minutes in the morning and again in the evening.

Repeat the awareness techniques as frequently as possible during the course of the day.

Evenings are an excellent time for review of the day's activities. Mornings are a great time to review dreams, aspirations and to set goals and do affirmations. Continue to practice throughout the day. Even as you visualize doing your practice, realize that the visualization itself is a creation of the mind.

—

<u>Visualization Exercise - II</u>

I think, therefore I am. - Descartes (French philosopher
mathematician)

Spiritually one may say, "I am- therefore I think."

In the previous lesson we concentrated on sensory visualizations. Now we will be doing emotional visualizations.

Go to your quiet spot. Do twenty connected breaths. Once you are done think of some of the major emotional experiences you have had such as - joy, love, grief, anger, hate, fear, peace etc. We will concentrate on a different emotion each day this week using events that were very meaningful to you at the time and that may still be meaningful to you.

After a week move on to the next set of exercises. If you choose, you may continue with any exercise longer if you feel guided to do so. There is no magical time frame. I only suggest that you stick with each exercise for at least a week of regular practice, and longer if you need to. You are always free to choose.

In recalling various emotions such as - joy, love, grief, anger, hate, fear, peace etc. you are going to visualize events that led up to, and triggered, strong emotional responses in your life. Feelings such as the happiness you may have felt as a child, feelings of security and being loved as well as other feelings and experiences including traumas, loss and pain.

In this exercise you are going to try and really feel and relive certain emotions that you felt at a time past. By creating a strong memory recall of the event, even if it is painful, know that you are now in a safe, nurturing place, and know that all your feelings only ever existed in the past and in your mind.

In the presence of "now", which is the eternal moment of creation, you are completely safe. Feel this safety and support in your inner being.

Choose a different emotional event to recall each day and reflect upon it. Sit in quiet, for thirty minutes or longer and reflect on the circumstances that preceded and led up to the event you have chosen to recall. Experience again and feel the emotions you had at the time. Consider carefully all the details of the event including how people around you may have reacted, what was said, what you felt, what you were wearing, even what the weather was at the time. Remember how you were and how you reacted. Try and recall all the details including the sights, smells and sounds at the time and recall how you may have felt in the hours and days afterwards.

If you are reliving a painful experience always remember that in this exact present moment of time, that is to say in the Now of this instant you are completely safe and can continue to be safe in future.

When you are done you can note your thoughts and feelings in your journal. Consider your observations.

How do you feel now? Compare your thoughts and feeling now with those you had when you first had the experience. Note this in your journal. Remember that there is no right or wrong and nobody is judging you.

Do a different emotion and relive a different memory each day this week always using events that are very meaningful to you.

Understand that all emotions are learned responses - nothing is intrinsically good, bad, sad, happy, etc. except as you choose to experience something or as you have been conditioned by your upbringing to react.

Consider the possibility that you can change your experience by changing your thought about it, because your thoughts create your reality.

It is amazing to consider how many things that people have an intense reaction towards are not necessarily their true feelings but instead are a programmed response that they feel is necessary and is expected of them. For example, how many people have got into a fight or a confrontation, not because they wanted to, but because they felt that if they backed down from the conflict they would lose face? How many divorces result not from wanting to break up but because social mores or conventions demanded this course of action? For example many people feel that infidelity is unforgivable and that divorce is the only course of action. This may not be their true desire and frequently family and friends will pressure one and influence our decisions. Sometimes our egos are so strong that we would rather cut off our nose to spite our face. If only we could relate our true feelings to one another without the fear of being hurt so much pain could be avoided.

Bear in mind that these exercises are about gaining awareness of our selves and control over ones life. This is a step towards becoming empowered through increased self-awareness.

Contemplate the story of my trip to Mexico. Consider while reading it how you would have felt in a similar situation. This is not to say that my response is the only response there is, nor that it is "right" and any other response is "wrong".

For many people being lost at night in a foreign country and hundreds of miles off course may be very frightening. They may react with feelings of panic, anger, frustration, fear or helplessness.

Consider how many people would consciously have chosen "how" to feel in the moment. If they did then they could choose at all times to feel safe and supported. Their thoughts create their reality.

The key is to see everything as a Divine play[*] and not to be attached to a specific outcome. To observe with interest, that is to be a detached observer of ones own life means to ask oneself what you have to learn from each experience - what are you being shown by the universe and what is the specific lesson therein.

Why have you created this happening?

These are the questions you must ask as the detached observer of your life every day. These are the lessons you are to seek to uncover in your daily meditation as you recall the past events of your life.

People are taught from an early age, indeed from birth, not to feel their true feelings and to react in certain set and predictable ways. Boys are expected to be brave, girls are told to act like ladies. At each age in our lives, certain emotions are considered inappropriate to express and therefore must be suppressed. People are conditioned from early on to withhold and suppress their aliveness. The Bible, our parents and our schools all suppress our aliveness.

---

[*] God is without form, without quality as well as with form and quality. Watch and see with what an endless variety of beautiful forms He plays the play of His *Maya* (the phenomenal / physical world) with Himself alone. The *Lila* (Divine Play) of the all-pervading One goes on in this way in infinite diversity. He is the whole and also the part. The whole and the part make up real Perfection........ Accept Him in His numberless forms, shapes and modes of being, in everything that exists. - Anandamayi Ma (Indian Saint)

Society and our parents have molded our expectations of life and have programmed our responses to challenging situations from the time of our birth.

You have to unlearn the unconscious, programmed reactions that are inculcated within in order to become the conscious and self empowered captain of your own life.

When you are cognizant and in the present moment, you are in touch with your feelings. You have the freedom of conscious choice.

You do not need to react in predictable ways when you are detached from the outcome of a situation.

For example, think about what your feelings might be if instead of anger or disgust, you saw humor in the ridiculous behavior of a rude person and rather than reflect anger back to them you chose instead to forgive them and have compassion for them.

Would you not feel better and more empowered knowing that you are able to choose your response to a situation rather than your being on emotional auto- pilot?

Think about how powerful you feel when you are truly in charge of your feelings and that nobody can force a reaction from you that you do not consciously choose to have.

The results, when you act from a place of spiritual awareness, are very different to what you are used to. You have a far different experience of life. You would not let others dictate how you should behave, you would be conscious and aware of your experiential options at all times!

Here is an example to illustrate this point.

On trip to Chicago, I approached red a traffic light in my rental car. I wanted to make a right turn. To my left in the outside lane was an eighteen-wheeler semi trailer signaling a right turn.

As I approached the intersection, I squeezed in on the right hand lane of the truck.

Obviously the truck needed two lanes to make a right turn and my coming up on his right was going to affect his turning.

I figured I would zip away long before the truck driver could even engage gears. The driver however had other thoughts. Obviously he needed both lanes to make his wide turn and he was enraged that I had moved into the inside right lane. He actually scooted over from the drivers seat on the left side of the cab all the way to the right hand passenger window, then he rolled the window down and hollered at me and proceeded to unload a series of expletives.

My thought in that instant was focused on why did I create this situation. Here was a chance for me to learn something. I was not particularly concerned by his anger nor by what he was yelling. Indeed, in that respect I was detached from the situation completely. What he said actually went over my head, but the curious nature of this encounter was intriguing and far more interesting to me than any thought I may have had of responding to him. It was like watching a movie. I had no investment in his emotions and I was not going to buy into the energy of the situation.

I concluded that he had a need to vent his frustration for his own personal reasons and I was simply there to enable him to do so. I also had the opportunity of being in my Higher Self and to learn detachment in order to experience the *leela* (Divine Play). I simply backed up my car, and I mentally blessed the moment for the opportunity I had to learn. I let the truck driver go and mentally I blessed him too, for all people are ultimately one and a part of everyone else.[*]

(On a physical level I can also rationalize that the delay caused by this encounter possibly prevented my being in an accident down the road and that the Universe was indeed protecting me).

Consider if you would, the alternative responses and outcomes possible with this encounter. Consider if I had matched his anger with an equally angry response of my own? I could have carried this upset with me for hours and to have it really get to me. Instead I chose to feel uplifted and blessed in the moment and very joyful for the lesson!

Now when you do meditation on your own past emotions, examine how much of your feelings are conditioned responses brought about by your upbringing, society, parental and cultural values etc. Pay particular attention to how you felt in the moments when your reactions and emotions were on autopilot. Review

[*] "In every attack you call upon your own weakness. While each time you forgive you call upon the strength of Christ in you. Do you not begin to understand what forgiveness will do for you? It will remove all sense of weakness, strain and fatigue from your mind. It will take away all fear, guilt and pain" - A Course in Miracles

alternative ways you might have chosen to experience your emotions if you had been conscious and in control of your thought process.

Keep notes in your journal of your conclusions.

When we think about learned responses a particularly interesting cultural perception concerns that which surrounding death.

Certain cultures see death as a release from the pain of earthly existence and as a rebirth to a happier existence, and not an end to life.

Consequently the loss of a loved one, while painful to the survivors, is not to be mourned excessively but is celebrated.

Indeed in our own Judeo-Christian-Islam beliefs life is often something we need to endure in order to move on to a better existence in something or somewhere called Heaven or Paradise.

This in itself is responsible for a host of particular misconceptions that has made of us mindless slaves to these beliefs.

Therefore, whether we are individuals or whole societies, we create our own reality.

Be conscious of your feelings!

Do you think it possible that a display of grief is expected of us, even when we do not feel grief?

Do you think that a hereafter is more real than the present?

Much of how we react to situations is a conditioned response and a culturally ingrained belief that is not based on our own certainty or experience..

A conditioned response is one that requires no conscious thought and is therefore thought-less and thus unconscious.

Also consider this:

You created all your emotions. You chose to have the emotional experience that you had, whether consciously or not. You can choose differently next time. Next time is Now in this moment. Next time is not in the vague hereafter.

Take into account how you might react differently and how you might feel if your ego does demanded that you respond in a certain way.

Emotions and reactions are driven by our ego. The key is to overcome the ego and become self- aware and live consciously in the present moment.

The ego dominates the life and controls the unconscious person. Consider, for example, some of the following standardized ego driven phrases embedded in our language that have become stock reactions to circumstances. This is a reflection on the unconsciousness conditioning of our minds and which is prevalent in society as a whole.

No one treats me like that!
Who do they think they are?
Over my dead body!
Damn nerve he's got!
She doesn't know whom she's dealing with!
I won't stand for this!
I know my rights!
You won't get away with this!
You'll get yours!
Screw you!
I'll be damned!
Bloody hell!
They'll get theirs!

All of the above and thousands more custom made "off the shelf" remarks are conditioned responses provoked by the ego in us.

They are thought-less, that is without thought. Therefore unconsciousness is in control of us.

Most people are guilty of such thought-lessness at one time or another.

The thing all these responses have in common is that they are NOT REAL!

The ego demands that one be recognized and heard. The real message behind all of these statements is:

'I am very important. I cannot allow you to get away with taking me for granted. Who do you think you are dealing with? I will have revenge!'

Is this truly who you want to be? Is this truly how you see yourself? I would say probably not. However when we are on autopilot the ego takes over.

For the rest of this week be acutely attentive of your emotions from minute to minute and be aware of the fact that your feelings and responses only exist inside your mind. You can decide who you want to be from one minute to the next.

(A good exercise and memory aid is to post small cards all around your home and work space to remind you to be conscious of your thoughts at all times. Stating "All my thoughts are creative - I create my own reality" or "All is an illusion. My own thoughts create my reality".

Remember to be consciously aware of your feelings in the very moment of Now, that is in the moment that you are experiencing them. Play at being the silent and detached observer of your own life.

You can choose to experience differently by removing the emotion of the moment. You can change your feelings and experience about any event at anytime, just step outside of yourself in the moment and be the conscious observer. Feel your feelings and consider alternatives. Remember your feelings are not necessarily real except as pride and ego would have you believe. All is nothing.

Choose in the moment to be "real" and present, decide on how you want to see yourself in the highest thought possible of the highest being that you can be. You want to decide how to experience your thoughts and feelings in any situation. You can mindfully choose to edit the programmed script of your thoughts. Practice relating to any challenging situations that you may come across with the release of any personal attachment to the outcome. Become an observer of your own life. Each moment is a chance for you to be the silent observer, and not a mindless puppet having its strings jerked by forces beyond your control. Live in the present moment.

Old patterns of behavior no longer serve you. Do not be out of control, or thought-less. Remember that thought-less comes from mind-less. And that leads to couldn't care less, or simply care-less.

Is that not the fundamental problem of our culture, we care less?

Be conscious at all times of your choice of emotions, feelings and responses. Choose how you want to react to any given circumstance with a sense of awareness, detachment, responsibility and control. See

149

if your choice fits in with the highest thought you have about the most perfect person in the world, yourself!

You are in charge now. Take responsibility. You are no longer a leaf blowing at the whim of the storm of life. Become the storm!

Each evening keep notes in your journal of your thoughts and experiences and record what happens when you consciously choose your experiences.

Note how your feelings of self-empowerment are affected.

Take notice of how the situations you were involved in were a play performed by unwitting actors who are completely ignorant of being on stage and who are oblivious to the meaningless of the plot. Note the energy that they invest in the play. The ego has much energy, yours! Is it any wonder why you often feel drained?

Feel yourself expanded in the moment of your awareness at this realization.

Write down how you felt knowing that you are free to act, and not be an automaton with programmed responses.

Journalize changes in your feelings as the week progresses.

Be mindful of how your awareness changes with practice.

Take charge of your life. Use challenging situations as an opportunity to grow.

At some level, if you attract adversity or struggle, you must process your thoughts and remember to ask why are you attracting this situation into your life. Why is it presenting itself at this moment in time? What can you learn from it? Is it a pattern of behavior that you recognize?

Do not fall back into the old habits of blame or of being a victim. Take responsibility that you created this happening in order to learn from it. So look for the lesson.

When you understand what the Universe showing you, you can eliminate the need for this experience. Recognize and break the pattern and disempower it, and you will never have to repeat that type of experience again. You can heal yourself.

Therefore always ask yourself why you created a particular event in your life and what is being shown to you about your mind, especially if it relates to your need for struggle. Remember the Universe is like a mirror. What is it about your life that is being reflected back to you at this time?

Bear in mind that your life is a mirror of your own thoughts about life.

Gratitude is an essential element in creating a Divine life.

Be willing to go into gratitude at all times and thank the Divine for the struggle and the blessings. Where answers elude you, ask to be shown the purpose of the lesson presented to you. You may need to ask God to enable you to see with greater ease or to ask for the removal of all obstacles with equal ease. Also ask that you be empowered so that you may to be detached from any outcome and to be released from any karma as a result of the lesson at hand.

Look for small changes and express gratitude each day for even the smallest things. It may only be for the fact that the weather is good, or that you woke up on time and do not have to rush. Be grateful for the small things so that the bigger blessings can move in.

Cultivate an attitude of gratitude.

Above all thank the Divine for your life and for the lesson presented to you each day. Even be grateful for books such as this and for inspiring people in the world.

Resolve to meditate on the message and feelings of gratitude.

If an unpleasant experience was presented to you today, do not be hard on yourself. Be gentle and forgive yourself and especially all those associated with the experience.

Thank the Divine again, for the hard times because without them we would never have an opportunity to grow.

Remember that the finest steel is forged in the hottest furnace.

Remember to ask to be enlightened by the answer when it appears to you, and affirm that you do not have to repeat a similar experience again in your life.

Remember that those people who confront you and challenge you are showing you something about yourself. They are reflecting some aspect of your mind. You are being taught a lesson by the situation at hand. It is a reflection of the unhealed aspect of your mind that needs healing, and you are being given the opportunity to heal it. The situation is perfect in all respects!

Be grateful for the opportunity you are being given to see and to heal your mind.

You are not only the student in this life. To others you may also be the teacher. Bear in mind that there are no victims in this game of life. By allowing somebody the opportunity to confront you, you have the opportunity to heal them as well as yourself. They, too, have a lesson to learn from the encounter with you. Silently you should bless them, even if that is the last thing in the world you might wish for them!

We learn more about ourselves from such people though we may not like them. The Divine presents us with these people to be our teachers. If we do not see the life lesson being presented and seize the opportunity to grow and to heal, we will continue to run into similar situations in our life. Furthermore, we are all teachers to one another and one of us has to take the higher path in order that others may follow.

Every interaction is by prior spiritual consent between individuals a learning experience for both souls. This is why, as I said earlier, that you might never know the true reason for a situation. Every why has a wherefore. Frequently the understanding lies beyond the meaning that you would foresee.

Notwithstanding the above, similar situations may arise again. Frequently we are tested again to see if we have learned and remembered the lesson. Always ask for Divine guidance and choose the highest course of thought and action without regard to your ego and without personal attachment to the final result.

Trust in the outcome. When thought proceeds from the highest light, the right and positive outcome is always assured. Be aware that this outcome may be different from what you imagine.

Therefore trust that all is in Divine right order. Know that you are building spiritual equity in the Divine bank when your actions are preceded by right thought.

You will see that all the world is a stage. You will know intuitively that most situations are, superficial, a sham, a play.

You will feel expanded in your outlook the more you are conscious and in the present moment. You will wonder how everyone around you is so unconscious that they cannot see reality behind the illusions they are spinning!

—

The Monks and the Maiden

As children bring their broken toys, with tears, for us to mend,
I brought my broken dreams to God, Because He was my friend.
But then instead of leaving Him, in peace, to work alone,
I hung around and tried to help with ways that were my own.
At last I snatched them back and cried, "How could you be so slow?"
"My child," He said, "What could I do? You never did let go." -
Anonymous

Everything arising from the ego is suspect. The ego keeps us stuck in illusion.

Egos have a great deal invested in ensuring that we never progress beyond FEAR. When we do the ego will shrink and we will become empowered - and the ego does not want that!

My friend Mathew always reminded me when I was a young man:

All is nothing - (Zen proverb)

In this statement one learns to have minimal attachment to the physical world. There is nothing we can take with us when we die. Everything in the physical world is nothing. Reality is in the mind of God alone. All else is what we create It is our illusion.

Where ego is, God is not.

There is a charming parable that has been around for centuries in various forms and it goes something like this:

A group of young Zen monks were walking with their master on a journey to a distant monastery. Having taken a vow of celibacy these monks avoided contact with women. As they walked they maintained a state of single-minded silence so that their focus was on their meditations.

One morning, on the lonely road through a forest they came upon a small river that was swollen from heavy rains.

By the side of the river stood a beautiful young maiden, well dressed in fine silk clothes and elegantly groomed. She was tearful and distraught. She could not cross the turbulent river.

The monks approached and the master inquired of her as to why she was so upset. She explained that she was returning home and that she was afraid that she would not make it home before nightfall because the river was impassable for her. She did not know how she would cross safely and she surely did not want to spend the night in the woods.

Without a word the master scooped this beautiful girl up in his arms, held her securely to his chest and proceeded to ford the river with her. Having done so, he deposited the young lady, dry and safe, on the far bank of the river.

Then the group of monks followed them across and they continued on their way in silence once more.

Nothing more was said. But the younger monks were clearly troubled. The master noticed that their mood had changed. There was sullenness and a heaviness of step amongst his acolytes and they appeared downcast.

The master observed all this and yet he remained in silence, merely observing and noting how the young monks sagged in their step and demeanor, their shoulders hunched as if burdened with a heavy weight and their faces down turned to the path. Several more hours passed in silence and day eventually gave way to nightfall. Finally the group stopped to make camp at the side of the road. They gathered wood and prepared the evening meal and set a campfire for the night.

Over the campfire they sat eating their humble meal in silence, as was their way.

Finally the master looked at one of the young monks and said, "You wish to speak". The young monk looked up from his meal and broke his silence. "Master. We are all terribly disturbed. We have sworn an oath of celibacy. We shun all contact with women as is our way lest we be tempted or our minds wander off purpose. Yet today you carried a most beautiful young lady in your arms. She held onto your neck and you could not have been so detached as to be unaware of the closeness of her hair against your face, the scent of her perfume and the warmth of her young body in your arms. These are all things that we are sworn by oath to avoid. We feel shamed and our minds are in turmoil."

The master quietly passed his gaze over the young monks, reflecting on the hard words cast upon him. Then he replied quietly and with great warmth as an adult to a child, "Now I see what it is that has been such a burden upon you. All day you have walked like old beggars bent, sacks across your shoulders, feet dragging. The weight of my actions has bowed your backs and confused your mind. I am truly sorry that you have carried this heavy burden and for such a long way. However, this morning, I put that young lady down safely on the riverbank. My burden gone. You, on the other hand, have been carrying her all day!"

Being emotionally responsible is not easy to grasp nor is it easy to accept.

Being a conscious human means being aware that oneself creates every moment of the day, alone.

We attract the persons and situations that result in specific conditions in our lives. These are life's lessons. We produce the people who love us and those that do not. We create the harmony and the discord.

We are both the instrument of life and the orchestra.

Every situation is a lesson. Where we see adversaries rather see teachers, and receive them with grace. Our antagonists are our greatest teachers, they deserve our greatest respect.

People who confront us and challenge us are said to be in our lives specifically for this purpose, by prior soul agreement. We must honor that contract and we must be willing to learn from the encounter and the relationship. Thus do we resolve karma.

People are inclined to accept acknowledgement for creating the positive occurrences in their lives and to find blame outside of themselves for the unpleasant ones.

The purpose of all relationships is to teach us.

If we do not learn the lessons being presented to us, then the Universe will continue to cast situations our way, in ever increasing doses, until we eventually do get the lesson we are destined to learn.

When we do comprehend what is before us, a mental light bulb goes off. Then we should be in gratitude for the experience that gave us the opportunity to grow.

By way of example, if you are intimidated by assertive people, and if your inclination is to avoid confrontation, then you will find all kinds of situations occurring in which you are challenged by just this. You are required to stand up for yourself and to honor your Divinity..

Each time you fail to do so, more such circumstances will arise. You may find yourself repeatedly facing confronting situations. They could arise all sorts of places such as in parking lots, checkout lines, at work, and you may even have married an assertive person!

Until you recognize the pattern and deal with it, you will constantly be challenged. It may be one of the important lessons you have to learn in this lifetime. One of the reasons you are here may simply be to learn to take back your power and stand up for yourself.

Once you recognize this you will be required to assert yourself and be brave. Eventually you will no longer have this fear and the challenge will subside. However, if you forget your lesson and backslide, the process will start again. The Universe will challenge you until you are healed.

How much better for us to be conscious of what we are creating in our lives, than to have the unconscious victim mentality of the unenlightened!

Being thankful for all things that come our way is an essential part of being an aware person. We learn and grow from adversity. (Read the book of Job in the Bible to illustrate this point).

Alternatively, one can whine and become weakened by adversity.

We can read about people who have grown strong from adversity. They are a source of inspiration.

One of the most inspirational persons I have ever read and had the pleasure to hear, is Nobel Peace Prize winner, Eli Wiesel.

Eli Wiesel is a Nazi concentration camp and holocaust survivor who lost his entire family in the death camps when he was just a youth.

He witnessed and endured unspeakable horrors at the hands of the Nazis.

He survived in body and in spirit to become one of the great humanitarians of our age. He is a champion of human rights and all that is noble in the human spirit. He has an enormous, shining intellect and is a most inspiring speaker. His message is one of faith, hope, justice and forgiveness.

Eli could have chosen to spend his entire life in bitter obscurity as many survivors indeed did. Instead he chose to help mankind in the pursuit of peace and justice. Eli is a prolific author and a Nobel Prize winner. He is truly a great example of how we can choose to create our lives for the better and how we can learn and grow from adversity.

Mohandas (Mahatma) Ghandi is another example of a great and wonderful soul. Growing up as a second-class citizen in apartheid era South Africa was not an easy thing for an Indian. Born in the province of Natal, he became a successful lawyer and champion of human rights. As a lawyer in South Africa, the South African Association of Lawyers refused his membership application because of his race, he was Indian and not Caucasian.

Following severe persecution by the Government of South Africa, Ghandi eventually left South Africa for India which was then under British rule.

Once there, he saw the oppression and misery of the Indian people at the hands of the colonial British army.

Ghandi espoused a unique philosophy of non-violent and passive resistance to end British rule in India. In spite of severe hardships, and without the use of military force, Ghandi and his followers eschewed violence with a philosophy of peaceful civil disobedience that made India ungovernable. With Ghandi at their head his followers confronted the British troops head on, without weapons and without fear. Throughout the country Indians stopped cooperating with their British rulers. The government was crippled. The British had no answer to people who faced armed soldiers with hymns and serenity. Workers downed tools and demonstrated against the British passively and peacefully. The country became unmanageable, the bureaucracy ground to a halt and nothing worked. Eventually the British were forced to leave India. India gained its independence. Such is the power of thought and non-violence.

Now do the following meditation. Recall a time of adversity in your life. In the face of such adversity, consider if you could have chosen to experience what life presented to you in that moment differently?

Meditate on the possible different outcomes you might otherwise have created.

What have you learned from this situation and how have you grown as a result of adversity?

What lessons can you still learn from past events?

Jeffrey M. Solomon

<u>Chapter Eight - Nothing Is Real</u>

All that we are is the result of what we have thought - Buddha

<u>Detachment</u>

Do not consider painful what is good for you - Euripedes (Greek playwright)

It is appropriate at this stage to discuss detachment.

Control of the mind is essential to being aware of your thoughts rather than being at the effect of them.

All thought is creative. Even the little thoughts matter. That which you think brings reality into being.

Unconscious thoughts are frequently the most powerful thoughts that people have. Especially those that are with us all the time and that direct our conscious thoughts and actions.

Thoughts that arise from fear are extremely powerful. Fear is a very insidious emotion and can be likened to a type of mind control that manipulates people like puppets. People are regularly unaware of where fear stems from or what their sponsoring thought behind their fear is, or even what their deepest fears are. They keep their fears suppressed and are often in denial all their lives.

Fears that arise from our birth trauma and early childhood may develop from early experiences before we are able to fully express ourselves. Frequently ones attitudes evolve from the thoughts of our parents and from the fears that they project through us. In some instances thoughts of fear may be a carry over from a traumatic past life experience. Hence one may come into this life with an irrational fear of something, such as claustrophobia, abandonment or a fear of drowning. By the same token the fear could also arise from the trauma of a difficult birth and even by transference of a mother's thoughts to the child in the womb.

By the time one reaches adolescence, patterns are ingrained and form a template that affects every thought about the world and hence ones life experience.

People attempt to rationalize why they feel fearful. However hard they may try, they seldom uncover the sponsoring thought behind their fear.

A sponsoring thought is a thought buried so deep in ones psyche that you may are unaware of its existence. When people react to situations and make decisions that are shaped by their sponsoring thoughts, they are empowering the thought until it is ingrained at a cellular level.

It takes a lot of work on oneself, such as psychotherapy or rebirthing to uncover what makes you tick.

These fundamental patterns are your ego's tool to have power over you. By controlling you through your deepest fears and psychosis, your ego will twist and turn your fears into a predictable pattern that may repeat itself throughout your life.

Uncovering these deeply held beliefs and thoughts through therapy or rebirthing, you can expose them for what they are, and you are able to confront them with the light of truth. Having uncovered your sponsoring thoughts enables you to move to a new perception of reality. You can integrate the experience of the new truth into your body through a rebirthing process simply called, "integration". This replaces the suppression of our fear thoughts. You can replace old cellular memories with new truths.

In doing so, you can be free of control and illusion, and you can escape self-deception.

Ego is of the dark. It is illusory and fear based. Truth is of the light and hence of love.

Overcoming the ego we "see the light" - this is enlightenment.

One needs to develop thinking and seeing life differently. No longer put your trust only in your senses. You must develop a detachment from expectation in the outcome of events. When you put thoughts into motion you must learn to use them constructively.

Your thoughts are "living forms of creation."

Accepting and trusting in the highest good being the end result of your creation is essential.

Only the Creator knows what is in our best interest. Trust in His process, knowing that all is well and is exactly as it should be. Let go attachment to the outcome. In letting go of your desire to control you release frustration and disappointment.

Also know that you and the Creator are one. Therefore when your ego is out of the way, when you are surrendered, your higher self will guide your best interests.

To manifest your true thoughts and desires, give up attachment to the outcome. At the same time be conscious of what you are bringing into birth in the Universe.

Attempting to control the outcome of events set in motion by your conscious manifestations and trying to micromanage the process of manifestation in your life is futile. This is the realm of faith and trust and intuition. When you put your intentions out into the Universe with trust, know that the Universe will decide the place and the time and the manner of fulfillment.

Also know that not all that appears good to you in the present moment is necessarily for your highest good.

It is beyond your ability to know what is good for you until you reach a high state of intuitive awareness.

You must hold the thought and keep faith and know that which you manifest for the highest good will materialize.

If there is integrity in your intentions, the thought put in motion will always result in the Divine Will manifesting for the highest good of all concerned.

This is a very important phrase: "For the highest good". The Divine always manifests the highest good for all concerned. This is an absolute given. It is a law of nature

You may not foresee the highest good. Therefore if you perchance knew that you might have to suffer in order to realize your highest good, you could become disparaged. You cannot control the outcome, nor know the lessons and karma you need to process in order to realize the end result.

You should, however, be alert for signs of the manifestation of your intentions and be grateful and give thanks at every little hint of its appearance. For example, if you are doing prosperity manifestations, do not focus on winning the lottery next Wednesday at 8pm.

The goal is really not to win the lottery. The goal is to have prosperity and to have a lifestyle that you think you need to be happy. Understandably you may see the lottery as the only means to prosperity. This should not be your focus. Focus on the result you desire and be open to the Universe providing the means to the end.

Therefore if your goal is material well-being and prosperity, see yourself in the lifestyle you choose to have. Hold that vision. Don't be concerned with how or when this will happen.

Prosperity may come from your winning the lottery, it may also come from getting a new job, receiving an inheritance, or even going through the trauma of losing a secure job, your home and all the things that make you feel secure, and having to start your own successful business. Somehow, in ways you cannot determine, the Universe shall provide.

The means may not be obvious and the path may require loss in order that the path towards change be opened.

If it is prosperity that you want, express gratitude everyday for the gift that you know with certainty is coming to you. Hold the vision of the lifestyle you desire, put up affirmation notes where you can see them so that you are reminded constantly of your vision. Know with certainty that it is coming to you and almost certainly in ways unexpected.

Your affirmation note may read something like this:

"I, (your name) now have the whole world's cooperation, including God's for (state your manifestation) to be manifested now with ease and for the highest good of all concerned. It is done, so be it".[*]

This means that if you are manifesting prosperity and you see a penny on the sidewalk, pick it up and bless it for you have begun to attract prosperity. See it as a sign and acknowledge the Divine for the prosperity that is certain to be yours in abundance. Pass it by and you are really saying to the Universe that you have no faith or gratitude in this process and this little offering is beneath you to appreciate and to acknowledge.

Therefore every little sign, even the smallest, should be blessed and be regarded as proof that you deserve what you have asked for. Hold the thought steady in your mind at all times whilst affirming with certain faith that which you are manifesting is already on its way to you.

Remember to visualize the end result. You cannot know the highest thought of the Universe, nor do you know that which serves your best long-term interests. It is useless to try to control events leading towards your goal and it is often futile to try.

---

[*] Although you could state a date, where appropriate, remember that you cannot know if this is realistic. Therefore do not be attached to the outcome by a certain deadline. Put your intention out and have faith that you will receive.

Jeffrey M. Solomon

Be mindful of the adage; "Be careful what you wish for, you just might get it!"

—

Detachment II

Knowledge of what is possible is the beginning of happiness - George Santayana (Spanish born philosopher)

One may detach from the energy and emotion of a highly charged situation such as an argument, and instead become a calm spectator of life.

This sense of detachment occurs when you are in touch with your higher self and REALITY.

You will detach from the illusion around you.

Your higher self, or soul, has no attachment to the worldly events that we mortals invest with so much importance.

Your soul desires that you should be happy. That which takes you away from stress and confrontation will be in alignment with your higher self. This reflects the reality of the Divine. The Divine desires only peace and harmony. Such is the universe without the mind of man. Therefore you are moving into Divine alignment when you detach and you become aware.

Your higher self is in touch with those things which, as a Child of God, are for your highest good. As you move to an awareness of the unreality of events around you - and you detach, you will feel the calm and experience less emotion.

The idea behind the detached observer starts to manifest once you accept that every experience is self created and that you alone have creative control over your life!

That which you think becomes your creation and that creation is your reality.

If you are really honest about taking responsibility for your own life you will agree that all tragedies in the world are self-fulfilled. This means that when you see a disaster on television such as an airplane crash, floods, crime etc. as terrible as they are, you must accept that the victims chose, on a soul level, to participate in the tragic event. There are no accidents for anyone. And so it is for us too.

The acceptance of responsibility for your life will begin to manifest with daily meditation, visualization techniques and affirmations. All manifestations and visualizations should be done regularly in the morning and again in the evening during meditation.

A word of caution:

Detachment does not imply that one has a callous disregard for life or other people. Far from it. Conscious detachment and awareness simply means not getting caught up in the struggle of your own ego and that of others. The Hindus have a great word to describe this state of affairs, it's called a "leela". A leela is a Divine play in which we are unwitting players in a game called life. In a leela we are serious and we take everything seriously in complete ignorance that in reality we are puppets in a Divine comedy. All of life is a leela.

When you transcend the illusion (Hindu word "Maya") you move out of maya or illusion and into enlightenment.

This is our Divine purpose in life, to move beyond maya.

An enlightened person is totally conscious of the Divine leela, or play, for they will see the lessons being presented by the Universe, and they will transcend and comprehend the lesson and what is being asked of them. This is total awareness. This is living in a state of now consciousness.

Such people, while seeing the leela for what it is, and being detached from the situation due to their state of awareness, are, nevertheless very compassionate They are not detached from other human beings. They are only detached from the game being played around them. They realize that they have a duty to help others to see the illusion and to help them also to rise above the leela into a state of enlightenment. In India such people are teachers and masters called "gurus". In this sense, many saints and holy men are masters and gurus. The job of such a person is to raise our level of consciousness by practical example as well as through lessons and guidance.

As far as you and I are concerned, a lesson we can learn from these teachers is that the spiritual level that they have attained is not limited to them only. Each of us has the power within to rise to Christ consciousness.

Christ consciousness may also be referred to as achieving the state of Buddha. It is a term used to describe a state of being. It does not imply that this state of consciousness only applies to Christ or to supernatural or high beings.

We have within us all the ability to rise to the level of the Ascended Masters.

With this in mind, remember that the great teachers that have blessed this planet with their presence, were and are here to show us by their example, that which each and every one of us can achieve. They do not come to dazzle us with wonders and miracles. There would be no benefit in this. We are shown the true nature of what it means to be human. We are all the radiant sons and daughter of God. None of us is less than another. We all have the ability to achieve everything that the masters have achieved and even more. Even the least of us is not less than the greatest amongst us.

"The works that I do shall ye do also; And greater works than these shall ye do" - Jesus Christ

—

Jeffrey M. Solomon

<u>Visualization Exercise - III</u>

If one is lucky, a solitary fantasy can transform one million realities -
Maya Angelou (American writer)

So far we have examined the process of physical responses and emotional processes in the body.

This week we are going to consider the creative side of your nature and how the mind constructs reality. We will practice creating a new memory. This is a really fun exercise.

From your quiet place, do your twenty connected breaths. You are being asked to the following process in meditation each day for at least a week for twenty minutes or more. Furthermore you will recall the visualization periodically throughout the day.

We will construct an imaginary tropical scene together that will involve the use of all your senses. You may expand on the one I have described below in any manner that you wish. For instance, you may want to include a partner in your visualization. You can embellish the fantasy in any manner that suits you. Read through my description below and then close your eyes and create your own scene in as much detail as you can in your mind.

The quiet of your visualization, in your minds eye, meditate on the fantasy described below, paying particular attention to creating, smells, tastes, tactile experiences, and sounds as well as emotions. The object is to create a "memory" utilizing all five senses that is as real as any memory that you currently have.

"Imagine a gentle hill of soft, green grass at sunset overlooking a tropical bay. The sun, still warm and sensuous, rests like silk upon your skin. It is about 6 p.m. and the tropical light will linger on the bay for another two hours, washing the azure sky in ever deepening hues of orange and red until finally to be embraced in the velvet fingers of creeping nightfall.

Below, the rustling palm trees are playing lightly with the cooling breeze. Their body's sinuous hula dancers bent and swaying. You can see the curved bareback sweep of the bay. White against blue, sand painted against sea, the spine of shoreline arches in joy against the cool surf lapping and shuddering, against its pale skin.

The wind delights in the joy, the surf song, spraying foam in strident tones against the rocks. Softly feel the wind stroke on the lyre fronds of palm tree boughs, a melody as slow and subtle as a snake slither in a sea of waving grass. On palm trees it sneaks down, to swoosh the fronds and trip tickle over your body, feeling both warm and light upon your sun kissed skin.

Your eyes, closed, your upturned face towards the sun, you feel the thin trickled breeze caress your lashes, prickle your arms and rustle your hair. It echoes in your ears, an imperceptible secret sigh whispered just beyond your senses, then fades like a lover in the night.

Towards the bay you turn your gaze. The fishermen have gone. Left behind are orphaned boats. White washed homes upon sentinel hills stand guard over the bay as small boats bob and weave on the swollen water belly of the bay. The air is a shimmer upon red tiled roofs.

Gulls and pelicans, dipping, bobble upon the water. The lazy waves lap their hulls in languid, endless creasing tongues.

Faintly taste the salt upon your lips. Subtle. It is the smell of sea air mixed with fragrance spilled from a myriad of butter colored frangipani flowers. Perfume wafts hidden in the breeze, which, tickling the hair at the nape of your neck, rolls over your chest and face.

Absentmindedly, you are picking at the remnant of a most delicate tropical fruit.

It's sweet juice mixed in pallid flavor shades with the faint salt taste upon your lips - so very subtle. You feel pleasantly full, your thirst quenched and ringing vaguely from the tang aftertaste.

Listen. The bay calls. The distant sounds of seabirds searching the empty, silent hulls of swaying fishing boats. Their calls can be heard spliced within the hushing of the breaking waves. See them swoop, loop and swoop again, lazy, skimming mariners of the bay seeking a hidden tidbit, an evening snack, before the sun is gone.

Peace is tangible. A lazy melancholy peace it is that wafts the air, air that is warm and luscious to your senses. It enfolds you as you gaze wistfully in reflection another perfect day turns to dusk. You are the colors of the sunset on the sparkling mirrored water. Your mood reflected in multi-facets, a gem, in tones of reds, yellows and purples.

Scented breezes, mixed with the aroma of fruit, caress small beads of perspiration cool upon your brow, and with a final gentle kiss all care floats away."

Hold the feeling of sensuous melancholy. The sun drenched vistas and smell of exotic flowers and tropical fruit. Feel the mood, the emotion, and the whole range of tactile experiences.

Hang on to the picture in your mind as you close your eyes and float away on your own fantasy and let it feel right and comfortable in your body.

You do not have to force anything into your consciousness. Let the vision sit at ease in your mind.

Depending on your imagination you may create this experience immediately or it may take a few attempts to create it. Just create it in a manner that feels real for you. Feel free to dwell on any aspect of it and to go deeper into it. For example when you see in your minds eye the whitewashed houses on the hills overlooking the bay, you may want to look closer at the houses and see them in greater detail. Perhaps you will see families, women cooking and children playing. There may be pets and animals in the yard.

Likewise the activities of the seabirds on the boat may draw you in so that you see the paint peeling on the hull, and the nets folded on the deck. You may even imagine what it would be like for you to be out on one of these boats fishing.

So as you meditate on this panorama allow your mind the freedom to explore and to be totally sensory with smells, feelings and sounds.

The key is to make this real for you through all your senses, the tastes, the sights, the smell, and the feelings of calm and serenity.

Feel yourself so deeply at peace that you can recall the feeling of tranquility at anytime you choose simply by closing your eyes and going back to this place.

Repeat the exercise periodically throughout the day. With your eyes closed for a couple of minutes each time, summon up this memory, your serenity fantasy.

Savor your mental vacation and integrate it as part of your actual life experience. When you feel that you have integrated it as a memorized experience then reminisce about it with your eyes open.

Remember the sense of peace. Allow the calm to descend over you each time you do so.

Feel a sense of the serenity return each time you evoke this memory and for a few moments allow your feelings to be free and let your mind drift away to this place of safety and calm.

Whenever you feel tense or stressed give yourself a few minutes and go back to the memory of tranquility and visit your favorite spot. Check in and see how the sunset looks, see if the fishermen are about and what they are up to.

Have the gulls found some scraps of food? Is that fragrance still lingering in the air?

After a while compare your memories to those you have of an actual vacation.

Notice if this new memory is starting to feel like an actual experience?

Become aware of how this mental creation remains with you like any other memory.

In terms of your other memories, - is this memory any less real or valid?

Consider; Is life any less of an illusion than that which purely exists in our mind?

Indeed do our lives exist anywhere other than in our minds alone?

This demonstration of the creative process of the mind shows the power of the mind to create its own reality.

This exercise goes beyond the act of being a demonstration of mind power. The development and the process of focusing the mind for visualization is an essential tool to be used in manifesting real things in your life such as wealth, relationships and joy.

Another benefit is that you have created a technique for stress relief and a place in your mind of serenity that you can go to anytime that you choose.

Practice this technique and concentrate on your goals. Make them real.

You will learn more about manifesting your hearts desires.

—

Jeffrey M. Solomon

Visualization Exercise - IV

One's own thought is one's world. What a person thinks is what he becomes- That is the eternal mystery. - Maitri Upanishad (Vedic Teaching)

The emphasis so far has been on the illusion of what we consider to be reality. The following series of visualization exercises will focus on each of the five senses individually.

Done correctly, you will learn the limitations of your senses and hence the limits of the physical perception of reality.

This is important. They way people cope with life is to make themselves right. To "make right" that is to validate our belief structure we call on our faculties of sight, sound, touch, smell and taste. These perceptions get filtered through the mind. Your mind will always make itself right.

In this manner ones experience always validate ones beliefs.

Your ego will always resist being made wrong. It will go to great lengths to always be right. This is not to say that it necessarily is right. Some people stop at nothing to prove that they are right because if they cannot trust their senses then what can they trust and what then becomes of reality?

The thought for this process will be a ten-day program on seeing.

In truth, there is nothing that you gaze upon for which you have a neutral thought. You have no neutral thoughts. Every single thing, whatever it may be, invokes a thought about it in you. You imbue everything with meaning. If it is an ant, you have a thought about it. Perhaps you like or dislike them, maybe they bite, maybe they will invade your home, you played with them as a child they bring back memories.

A pen. You like/dislike the way it writes or feels, you are concerned about losing it. You have a thought about the way that it feels and the way it looks.

As a child when you saw many things for the first time, your feelings of wonder and inquisitiveness were great. You noticed the print on your favorite shirt. You kept pieces of gum on your dresser if it still had flavor left in it. You played in the dirt and built roads. You noticed the flowers and the bugs in the garden. You loved the smell of

172

cookies or casseroles in the oven. Your mother smelled a certain way, a grand parent smelled different.

As you got older, the wonders of the world became mundane and common place and increasingly your senses act on autopilot. Today you hardly notice the color of your shirt. Seldom do you gaze at a flower and observe the tiny bugs in the garden. Gone are the fragrances that surrounded you. Occasionally a scent may evoke a lost memory and perhaps a feeling of deja vu arises within you.

All your experiences are still within you. They exist as catalogs and references to your worldly experience. When you see an ant for example, you have categorized and logged it within your mind. No longer do you need to look at it closely. Your thoughts about ants are set. You no longer stop to think twice about it. You react to it according to your thoughts about it, and so each time you find one you will likely respond each time accordingly. If they are in your house you may kill them. You will do this without much thought.

When you were a child you would probably have watched them to see where they go. You may have tried to feed them crumbs or have got out a magnifying glass to see them better!

Sit quietly and consider at random, objects around you or those outside, and you will see that you have a thought about everything. No matter how seemingly unimportant, no matter that you have never particularly considered that object before, once you stop and think about it you will see that you do not have a neutral thought about anything.

Once a person is aware of something they imbue it with a thought.

We have no neutral thoughts or feelings about anything.

In your daily visualization exercise, think deeply and calmly on these thoughts and try to feel the truth and meaning of the following idea;

"My eyes would deceive me. Nothing exists outside of me. If my mind does not recognize it - it would cease to exist. Everything outside of my mind is an illusion ".

You are going to practice looking at everyday things with new eyes and a new thought.

This week as you look at the most familiar things in your life, you are going to perceive them as you did as a child, as if you were seeing them for the first time.

This you will do all day long - every hour for the entire period.

Remind yourself to take a break for a couple of minutes each hour and to look around you and take a fresh look at things around you.

Write each of the following ten thoughts on small card or a sticky note and place them where you will be constantly reminded of them. Carry them in your pocket and read them frequently. Choose one idea for each day and focus on it. Do a different one daily over the next ten days.

Precede each thought with;

"This that I look upon is not real - It exists in my mind and nowhere else"

Daily Thoughts

Now do one of the following daily thoughts preceded with "This that I look upon is not real - It exists in my mind and nowhere else".

So on day one your thought would be; "This that I look upon is not real - It exists in my mind and nowhere else. This is not real - All I see, exists only in my mind and nowhere else".

- This is not real - All I see, exists only in my mind and nowhere else.
- My eyes would deceive me. Nothing exists outside of my mind. If my mind chose not to recognize what I gaze upon - what I see would cease to exist.
- Everything that I perceive as being outside of my mind is an illusion I have created.
- I have imbued all of this with meaning. It has no meaning beyond that which I have given it.
- My reality exists within my mind and nowhere else.
- I can choose exactly how I wish my mind to process my experiences.
- I am responsible to myself alone for my perception and feelings about everything.
- I alone choose how I want to feel about all things.
- No one can make me feel that which I do not choose to feel.
- When I react unconsciously, I am allowing that which has no meaning to dictate my feelings.

In addition to the above, as frequently as possible, look dispassionately at yourself in a mirror and see what you see.

(We seldom actually look at ourselves other than for vanity's sake).

As you look in the mirror have a dialogue with yourself. See yourself as you would if you were seeing yourself for the first time and get to know yourself.

Especially look deeply and frequently into your eyes and hold your gaze.

Say "This is not real - It exists in my mind and nowhere else".

In various situations practice stepping outside of yourself and suspend judgment about a situation and become a neutral observer.

For example in traffic, while driving, while stopped at a traffic light, look around you at the buildings, landscape, and vehicles and say to yourself -

"This that I look upon is not real - It exists in my mind and nowhere else" and repeat the thought for the day.

As you look around yourself at your home, office, or workplace say:

"This is not real - It exists in my mind and nowhere else". Repeat the thought for the day in all situations.

Look at your family, friends and colleagues and say:

"This is not real - It exists in my mind and nowhere else.

In all situations, especially when you are absorbed in an activity stop and say, "This is not real - It exists in my mind and nowhere else".

Use this practice as often as you can and in all situations throughout the day.[*]

After several days' practice and of using the affirmations under various and diverse situations, you will find that you can do it during a conversation or while on the telephone. It is especially valuable during an emotionally charged situation when you experience anger or fear.

---

[*] If you miss a few practice periods, do not beat yourself up about it. Never make yourself wrong or feel guilty about not doing the exercises. As soon as you become aware that you have missed a practice period, just resolve to do better. You can always repeat the exercise for an extra day or two.

It will work easily for you the more you do it, eventually you will carry this thought with you all the time.

Once you have really assimilated the above idea you will see situations spontaneously as being in your mind and nowhere else. When you reach this point, you will feel your sense of awareness change regarding what is real and what is illusion.

Your ability to choose how you see your reality is very empowering and has a calming effect.

No longer will you need to stress out. Situations that previously "tripped your trigger" will seem trivial to you as you learn to step back from confrontation and from emotional situations.

Bikers in the Bar

Courage is a kind of salvation - Plato (Greek philosopher)

One business I was involved in was a restaurant and sports bar. It was a very large place and we had function rooms for private parties.

It was extremely rare for us to have fights although occasionally we did have had to restrain a rowdy sports fan.

One particular evening, the back party room was booked for a wedding party.

When the guests arrived, it turned out that the bride and groom and all the guests were bikers. This was a biker wedding and the Harleys were lined up in rows outside!

This definitely was not our typical Saturday night crowd of lawyers and accountants. Some of the bikers appeared pretty intimidating in their leathers, long hair and tattoos, but overall, as I welcomed them at the door to the party room, they seemed like a nice group of people.

At some point in the evening, one of the ladies from the wedding party went outside and when she came back in one of our regular guests foolishly made some disparaging remarks to her.

Following that her boyfriend came out and confronted this person and a scuffle broke out. It soon spread and became a brawl, a free for all as the wedding party poured out of the party room. About thirty people including women were engaged in the fight!

To make matters worse, my bartender and myself were the only male employees on duty that night. So it was up to the two of us to break up the fight before the situation got completely out of hand and someone got seriously hurt.

Any sane person would likely be extremely reticent to step into the middle of such a fiasco.

In that moment I saw the situation without judgment and I affirmed to myself that I create my own reality.

I realized that I must take personal responsibility for manifesting this event in my life, and so it became clear to me in that moment that previously I may have been scared and intimidated by such an incident and I would have avoided being involved in it at all costs.

My lesson here became apparent to me, I had to confront my fear in order to heal my fear. With this in mind I called on the Divine for protection and affirmed my willingness to see the truth of this lesson. I held a steady thought of the Divine in my mind and mentally I repeated "Om Namaha Shivaya", this is a mantra that Babaji gave us to surrender to the Divine will.

My bartender and I were concerned that someone would be hurt and that the premises would be trashed. So we entered into the melee hoping that we could somehow get everybody outside and into the parking lot. My fears were immediately erased as soon as I interceded and placed myself squarely between two of the brawlers. I did not hit anyone nor did I shout or yell.

Somehow I felt certain that I could handle this situation calmly and without violence and, most importantly, in complete safety.

I felt a strong feeling of "chi" or an energy field surrounding me and I felt extremely powerful energetically as well as in my body. It was as if my energy field was interacting at a subtle level with the energy of the combatants and that I was forcing my will on theirs.

I felt that I was an observer, detached from the event, and yet in complete control as I inserted myself between combatants and proceeded to separate them and at the same time I directed them to the exit and then outside.

Incredibly, the belligerents actually stopped in mid scuffle and they took their quarrel outside.

I believe that even if I had the biggest bouncers, that they could not have achieved the same results.

Once outside, I continued trying to separate the parties but by now there were even more people involved, including the bride!

The situation was now completely out of control. All I could do was put protection around myself and affirm that no one would get hurt. In fact the only person who did get hurt was the fellow who started the whole thing by making derogatory remarks in the first place and even so he was just bloodied and not badly injured.

At some point a waitress called the police. When they heard that the police were on the way, the fight broke up. Thank God that no one was seriously hurt and there was no damage to the premises.

My bartender had a few bruises. I was completely untouched! In spite of my having been in the thick of the brawl, not a single person threatened me or took a swing at me! It was as if I had a shield of protection around me, which in truth, I had.

Throughout the entire imbroglio I mentally repeated the mantra. I did not lose awareness of my consciousness in the process. I saw the illusion dispassionately all through the melee, under very trying circumstances, and as a result I was not harmed.

As one learns to apply the principles of the visualization techniques, especially when under pressure, one experiences subtle, and often dramatic, shifts of awareness that will mature as our awareness increases. We begin moving into a state of empowerment and heightened awareness at all times.

This is the desired state to achieve.

The benefits from the continual use of awareness techniques will increase with frequent and regular practice.

You will find, as I did, that in the heat of an argument that you lose all attachment to emotions.

This is not to say that you are unfeeling or insensitive. Rather it is an awareness of the manipulative qualities of emotions and a consciousness not to let outside influences rule you.

It is rather akin to not letting the tail wag the dog.

Jeffrey M. Solomon

Chapter Nine - In The Mind Of God

Failure is Gods way of letting you know that you are going in the wrong direction.
To be in Gods direction is to be in ones passion - Sharda Collard
(British born Rebirther)

Playing In The Mind of God

Who can set bounds to the possibilities of man?...Man has access to the entire mind of the Creator, is himself the creator of the finite. - Ralph Waldo Emerson (American poet)

The visualization exercises presented in this book are not just mind games for the amusement of my readers. If that were so, what would be the purpose of seeking eternal Truth with meaningless games?

Games have no meaning and are ephemeral in their existence.

My purpose is to bring you more than a dramatic shift in your perception of the physical world.

Indeed, if you were to see the world differently, through God's eyes would this not be a gift enough?

Yet there is so much more to give. The Divine would have you be nothing less than Divine yourself. Therefore the purpose of your journey is not merely to perceive the Truth through the veil of illusion. Rather it is the way to a higher purpose.

Before you can see the path that you keep so well hidden, you must know that you conceal its' existence through the web of illusion that you weave.

You hide its light with the darkness of your fears and with the trivial diversions that you create daily with which to distract yourself. You busy yourself with meaningless trivialities, knowing that in the end all that you create shall perish like the dust of kings and empires of old. Yet even so, you continue with your thoughts and pursuits of some material key to happiness as if you were the very lord of creation.

People fear the light and the joy that God realization would bring into their lives for then they would have to give up the pain to which they are so attached. People would also have to give up their egos. Their ego has worked tirelessly to keep them stuck all their lives. Could you live with so much joy? Might not this amount of joy kill you? Would you be able to face yourself if you were forgiven and were once more truly innocent and supported by the Most High Himself?

Are you willing to let go all your fears and misery and see your higher self waiting for you, as it always has done since the day of your birth, to find your way back?

Are you prepared to step onto the path and find your true purpose in this life and cast aside illusion?

Are you willing to seek the way to a higher purpose?

Our purpose is a journey to God Himself.

Where would you look for God?

Do you perhaps see the Divine all around you and intellectually acknowledge that you, yourself, are a product of His creation, and yet still not know where God is?

All the exercises and visualizations you have done have dwelt on the nature of reality being in your mind alone. Repeatedly I have reminded (re-mind = to recreate the mind anew) you that the experience of your entire existence is in your mind alone.

If you have followed the exercises you will by now have a deep appreciation of what it is that you are being asked to see.

You are being asked to see God.

Nothing less.

To see God you must go within. It is not a strain to go within. Indeed the process is gentle like relaxing into a soft warm bubble bath and of releasing tension and strain. The less you struggle at it the better, for God cannot come to you when you shut Him out with distracting thoughts and struggle. You need to become mindless (mind-less = less mind).

So give up struggle and trust that He will come.

All you have ever perceived is God. When you look at your pen, this book, your hand, the desk you do not see a pen or a book, hand or desk. That is the illusion. In Truth you see God. All is manifest in the Universe of God. All experience is of God. And all experience is in your mind.

So where else would you go to look for God!

Go within, in peace and in certainty that which you seek is ever there and ever waiting His child's return. Here lies the ultimate Truth. When the masters tell us to look for the kingdom of God within, you need search no further.

God is within you.

God shares in all your experiences. Inasmuch you are one with the Eternal, so is the Eternal one with you. That which you do so does God do, and together you both do in complete innocence and perfect love. There can be no guilt. Forgive yourself for your thoughts of sin and imperfection for now you are free. God is your mover and your inspiration. God is your partner in this life! Where God is, there can be no sin and no guilt. You are innocent. Rejoice!

Om Namaha Shivaya. - I surrender to the aspect of God within me.

Compassion

So shall my [creative] word be that goeth forth out of my mouth: it shall not return unto me void, but it shall accomplish that which I please, and it shall prosper in the thing whereto I sent it - Isaiah 55:11 (Bible)

Compassion comes when you realize that nothing on earth can truly harm you.

Our Divine role on attaining this awareness changes to that of being of service, in an unselfish way to others.

When you have this opening of your mind, you see yourself not as an individual, but as part of a greater Universal consciousness in which all life is interrelated and interconnected.

Everyone is a reflection of ourselves and, like a mirror, they show us our own mind reflected back at us. Therefore the presence of any person in our lives is really that of a teacher coming to us to present to us a life lesson at that particular time. The more issues such a person leads us to confront in ourselves, the greater the lesson their presence represents in our lives.

All adversity is an opportunity to rise to our highest selves. Therefore the presence of someone who forces us to confront our fears is a cause of blessing and opportunity for us and we should acknowledge them accordingly.

If a challenge confronts you it is because a part of you needs healing of that aspect that is being challenged. It is in this moment that the Universe is giving you the choice to either go back into your old pattern of behavior or to consciously heal and change your thoughts by choosing to react differently and in a more enlightened manner.

Examples of old patterns of behavior are avoidance of the situation, rage, denial and suppression of your emotions

Bear in mind that the person confronting you is also a poor soul that is in need of healing. Both of you will fulfill the opposite needs in each other. The one needs to be confrontational and the other needs confrontation.

Whatever you fear you will attract to you. (Like bikers in a bar)

You cannot go through life avoiding or suppressing your fears and not expect them to continually keep cropping up to confront you.

You will be tested time and again. Each time you fail to assert yourself, the lesson will present itself again, perhaps in another form. Until you stand your ground and say 'no more', the Universe will continually challenge you. When you have learned to be strong, you will no longer have to face this particular challenge again because you will have resolved this aspect of your karma.

You will have grown spiritually and you will be ready to tackle a greater life lesson.

Frequently the situations in which you are challenged will vary greatly, frequently to the degree that you may not see the similarities between them. However all the situations will give you the opportunity to confront and overcome your fears. If you choose not to rise to each occasion, and with awareness of spirit, then you will continue to repeatedly have challenging situations throughout your life.

Your role, apart from learning the lesson being presented, is to be in a state of grace and compassion.

As an enlightened being, you will see the duality of the situation and be prepared to react with compassion both to yourself by way of forgiveness for attracting this situation, and to your tormentor. Only in this way can you shift the energy in the moment and heal your future need for this lesson.

Your thoughts about your tormentor will also change. You will no longer see an intimidating person. You will see a brother who is in need of healing.

Your help and understanding and your compassion will transform them.

You know that your pain is your own creation and that in truth nothing can harm you. You also know that all people are one with you and that they act out (mirror) your own leela (play). This being so, you need not fear or have cause to seek revenge.

Knowledge is strength. Fear is ignorance. You should act from strength.

Compassion will replace fear. This is the metaphysical understanding of Jesus' admonishment to 'turn the other cheek'.

This is true empowerment. This is true unconditional Love

Challenges are never in our lives by accident. We create them in order to work out issues and character flaws brought about as a result of our thoughts in this lifetime and of past life karma. We all have such lessons to resolve. The ultimate goal is to be self realized and enlightened, free of all fear and karma.

When one has a teacher, or a guru, one can advance faster. A teacher can show us aspects of ourselves and highlight for us the lessons we need to have in order to progress.

People who think that challenges are here by chance or that success is pure luck are living in an old paradigm.

The old way of thinking is to look for blame and cause outside of us without taking responsibility for all that happens in our lives. This is no longer acceptable.

This old way of unconscious living will not work in the future especially as the world moves rapidly to a new age of enlightenment.

Great changes are in store for the way the world operates. Those stuck in the old way of thinking will not survive the coming changes. It is important for the evolution of the world that people become enlightened.

In the 1920's Nicholas Tesla, a physicist who gave the world alternating electric current (AC), figured that the earth resonated at a frequency which he measured to have a vibratory resonance of 7.8Hz.

In 1987 it was again measured and found to be 8.6Hz. Presently it is 9.0Hz.

This means in fact that the earth and time is speeding up, or if you will, that time is compressing.

Time is accelerating. Imagine, if you will, that time in the 1920's is like the slow motion action replay one sees on television. Today it is akin to watching the action at regular speed. This is a marked difference in perception. When people comment on how fast time has flown, they are really experiencing an acceleration in time.

Metaphysically and physically we are progressing to a state that corresponds to quantum mechanics in which all time is in the present.

This means that thought is becoming subtler as well. The ability of our thoughts to shape reality is becoming easier to manifest as the resistance to our energy that we put out decreases.

The world is undergoing a radical shift that affects human consciousness. Because we are made of the same energy of which everything on earth is made, and are of the same "matter" as the earth, that which affects earth must correspondingly affect ourselves. We are interconnected.

As the speeding up increases, some refer to it as a quickening, reality as we know it will change.

Those who are aware of the change and who are working on "lightening" their consciousness to correspond with the lightening of the earth (i.e. en-lightening themselves) may be better adapted to cope with the change.

We will see a period of great change over the next 15 years or so.

According to the Mayan calendar, which is more accurate than our own, and that charts celestial events going back tens of thousands of years, the present age has been in effect for close to 25,000 years and will be ending sometime around December 23 2015.

Coincidentally, the current Hindu age is the Kali Yuga. This too is a 25 000 year cycle, and it is also destined to end around this same time as the Mayan calendar.

The Kali age is an age of darkness and ends with the destruction of darkness and the ushering in of new age of awareness in human consciousness. According to Hindu mythology this new age will emerge after the massive destruction of the old. Whether this represents physical destruction, or the destruction of ideas and thought I don't know.

The Christian doctrine of Apocalypse, espousing the end of the world being around the same time, and it would seem that some major spiritual forces, each apparently independent of one another, are predicting major change and some form of cataclysmic destruction of the old ways.

Babaji also speaks very specifically in his teachings of a great destruction. In the 1980's Babaji repeatedly speaks of the need for us to be spiritually strong. He talks of the end of the world as we know it and he goes to great lengths to explain the need for us to be spiritually prepared because the old ways of thinking and doing things will no longer work.

Be that as it may, we will see a lot of "insanity" around us from those people who are unable to adapt and many people will pass over. We are seeing this now and it is possible the number of natural disasters, accidents and a general dying off of unenlightened souls will occur.

We will also see massive changes in society and human consciousness and the effects are probably already beginning. We should look out for indications of this happening and be prepared for the possibility of great change over the next fifteen to twenty years.

—

Thought

Many people would sooner die than think. In fact they do -Bertrand Russel (English philosopher)

The Universe responds to thought. This is the "stuff" of creation. The key is to know what type of thought the universe responds to. Here are the most important aspects for creating your own reality. Literally being the creator of your own happiness, success, health and life.

1. The Universe will always respond to your thoughts. It has no vested interest in what you think. It will always respond affirmatively to your thoughts. The stronger your thoughts the greater is the energy being released.
   The more you dwell on a particular thought and the clearer that thought is, the stronger the energy released into the Universe. When people align themselves in common thought, the more powerful is the energy behind the manifestation of that thought.
   We are partners with the Divine in creation.

2. There is an abundance of unlimited thought energy, the "stuff" from which we manifest the world. You need never fear that there is not enough of anything in the world, whether it is money, happiness or whatever else you desire to have present in your life. Because of this abundance, it is a simple concept to attract to you more of the material of which everything is made. Whatever you desire simply needs to be brought to you and made manifest in order for you to have it.
   There are many disciplines that teach the how of manifesting. An easy to read "how to" book is "Manifesting Your Destiny" by Dr. Wayne Dyer.

3. The Universe does not know time as we do. In effect there is no past, no present and no future. Within God, all time exists in the now.

You cannot put deadlines and preconditions on the Universe, such as demanding something by a specific time.

You have created separation between yourself and the Universe, in your ego-dominated physical reality and you are not in synch with the Universe. Your concept of time bears no relation to Reality and Universal time.

As you become more spiritually aware, you will come more into alignment with the All That Is, that is the higher self, God and all creation.

In this raised state of consciousness, you will manifest in a more direct way and in a more direct time frame. This is your goal. Once you attain a higher level of awareness, your will and that of the Universe will become more aligned.

4. The Universe will decide how and when your will be done. You cannot dictate the manner of manifestation, nor its time or place.

What we learn from this is that we must have clarity of vision in what we want. We must be totally trusting, knowing that which we have intended *will* manifest in our lives. We must be consistent in our visualization.

In phrasing the thoughts that you put out for manifestation, you should avoid thoughts that begin with begin with "I want" or "I need". Nor should they be phrased in the negative such as "I don't have enough..... or I want to be healed of......."

These thoughts are telling the Universe that you do not have, that you want, that you need and therefore that you are not yet in a state of grace and acceptance.

The response of the Universe to this will be "Yes, you are correct. You do want, you do need" And the Universe will create for you want and need!

Consequently you will get exactly what you are affirming, that is *want* and *need*!

If, for example, you are affirming a healing for an illness, do not say, "I want to be healed". This would only affirm that you are sick and that you want! Rather say, "I AM WHOLE & HEALTHY NOW. THANK YOU GOD. AMEN" and visualize your healing. See yourself as whole and well. Affirm that the Universe has heard you and has already manifested your healing. Trust and be grateful, in advance, for the healing that YOU KNOW is already here.

Even though you may not be healed instantly, at exactly the moment in time you in which you affirm this, remember that the Universe does not know time as we do!

Be faithful and do not doubt for a moment that when you hold the affirmation firmly in place and confidently visualize that which you have manifested, creation will happen.

"Healing is always certain. It is impossible to let illusions be brought to truth and to keep illusions. Truth demonstrates illusions have no value...Yet what if the patient uses sickness as a way of life, believing healing is the way to death?...(if this is so)..Healing must wait, for his protection. Healing will always stand aside when it would be seen as a threat. The instant it is welcome it is there." - A Course in Miracles.

In the future, which in spiritual terms exists concurrently in time as the past and the present, you are already healed. What you want is to bring this scenario of a healed you, into your present, NOW. Therefore in total confidence that you cannot be denied that which you affirm with conviction and complete faith, repeat to the universe over and over "I AM RADIANT IN GOOD HEALTH, I SEE MYSELF AS STRONG, WHOLE AND HEALTHY. THANK YOU GOD AMEN"!

In the book, A Course in Miracles, if we are tempted to doubt our healing we are admonished thus; "He (we) must use his reason to tell himself that he has given the problem to One Who cannot fail (God), and must recognize that his own uncertainty is not love but fear, and therefore hate..... (Therefore) let him remember Who gave the gift (of healing) and Who received it. Thus is his doubt corrected. He thought the gifts of God could be withdrawn. That was a mistake, but hardly one to stay with...love without trust is impossible, and doubt and trust cannot coexist.....

Doubt not the gift and it is impossible to doubt its result." (Italics mine).

We must remember our holiness, and that we are one with God and when we offer ourselves healing, we offer our healing as a gift to God and receive our healing likewise, as a gift from God. Only our lack of love, fear of weakness or failure or self-doubt would deny our giving and receiving God's gifts.

"Be sure of what you want, and doubt becomes impossible" - A Course In Miracles

The words I AM are the strongest form of manifestation. All creative processes begin with the words 'I AM"

When Moses asked God what His name was, God replied, "I Am That I Am". The use of the Divine name or a name reflecting an aspect of God has an innate power in and of itself.

To know the name of something is to call forth its power.

Some of the names or aspects of God are Christ, Buddha, Shiva, Elohim, Adonai, Yahweh, Allah, Krishna, Hashem, Om, Ka, Brahma, Amun.

When you know the name of something you can call forth its power.

Calling forth a manifestation, as the child of God, which indeed you are, you are entitled to affirm "I Am That I Am" to assert your Divinity.

God brings creation into existence with the affirmation "I AM THAT WHICH I AM"

In the Hindu tradition it is "OMmmmmmmmmm". Om is the sound of creation.

There is nothing which "I AM" is not. All that is, is all of what the "I AM" is.

In other words, all is God and God is the all.

The use of "I AM" at the commencement of an affirmation and concluding with "AMEN" or "OM" is very powerful.

AMEN is an aspect of GOD similar to the eastern word "AUM" or "OM" which is one of the Divine names or aspects of God. When one manifests using the words the Divine uses, namely the "I AM" and concludes with "AMEN" or "OM" we are creating a very powerful statement of intent.

If one seeks happiness, one should not have some vague idea that someday things will improve and perhaps then they will be happy. We affirm that we are happy right now, and thank God or the Universe, (or whatever deity represents the Supreme Being to you) for our happiness.

We should make a list of all the things in our lives that we are grateful for and that we so often take for granted.

So, begin by affirming right now that you are happy!

Situations and thoughts that do not contribute to your happiness should be looked upon dispassionately, from a distance, as an observer. Then you should note that this situation/thought does not serve you or fit in with your happiness affirmation.

Release this thought or experience without judgment or attachment, to the Universe, and ask that this thought/situation be transmuted into the light from which it came. Affirm that you have no attachment or judgment over it or wish it harmed. You merely release it dispassionately and bless it on its way.

Likewise, when you see goodness flow your way, always, always, always, say thanks to the Universe (God) for bringing goodness into your life.

In this way you do TWO EXTREMELY IMPORTANT THINGS.

1. You forgive.
2. You are grateful.

You forgive that which does not serve you - and MOST IMPORTANT - you forgive yourself and others, who have brought this unwanted event into your life!

You are likewise grateful for all the blessings that have flowed into your life, no matter how small they may be.

This is called a state of MINDFULNESS. (Mind-fullness = fullness of mind).

Mindfulness is always being in a state of awareness (aware-fullness), from moment to moment, of the currents and energies flowing through us and over us and seeking the lesson in the moment

Always be in a state of grace that allows you to forgive and release without condemnation, attachment or judgment.

Always accept with gratitude and blessings, so that your blessings may continue to flow and grow.

Do your affirmations as if you have already received that which you have manifested, and in certain faith that the Universe has heard and responded to your affirmation.

At the end, conclude with thanks for that which you have received, in the knowledge that at the spiritual level, that which you seek is already on its way to you, even if in the physical moment you may be unaware of this fact.

Holding the thought of your manifestation constantly in mind re-energizes your original intention.

You cannot demand that it arrive by a certain day nor in a certain manner however only the strength of your mind and mental clarity can make it so in this gross world that we live in.

You cannot say that you want to win the lottery next Wednesday. You can only affirm and hold a vision of the lifestyle you would choose to have which winning the lottery represents. Winning the lottery is a means to an end. So manifest the end and not the means.

If you could have the lifestyle of a lottery winner but by some other means, you would not be obsessed with winning the lottery.

In any event, the majority of people who have won the lottery have ended up losing all of the money along with their friends, family and sometimes their physical and mental health.

Better then, that you affirm and see abundance as your right. Health, vibrancy and aliveness are yours, without preconditions of the how, when and where. Allow the Universe to take care of the details.

I should qualify my comments. There is a dichotomy or a duality that exists.

You can win the lottery. You can create anything happening by a certain deadline. In my comments I am referring to the great majority of people in the world. As you get clearer, you mind will get more focused, your intent sharper and your energy body stronger then you can create anything that you wish in the instant that you decide. If you want to turn water into wine you can do so. It has been done before.

Babaji once had a devotee fill a bus gas tank with water from the river when they ran out of gas.

Some may regard this power as miraculous. Indeed to the vast majority that have not attained this level of personal empowerment, it may indeed seem so. It is not. It is the natural law of physics and of nature.

All is energy and energy can transmute into anything. Indeed out of seeming nothingness one can create something when the intent is strong and the mind is razor sharp.

Remember too, most human beings have not reached the levels of consciousness that I am speaking of above but that does not mean that their thoughts do not manifest. It may take more work and concentration over a longer period of time. Hence the healing of an illness for example, may not be of Biblical proportions and may take weeks of affirmations. Nevertheless you can manifest a miracle when your intent is strong.

At the level of awareness that most of us are at you cannot know what you may need to give up, change or release in order to have what you want. We have no way of determining what karmic forces are at work in our lives and what lessons still have to be learned before we are able to release our blocks in having what we want - manifest.

If you have done rebirthing you may be aware of the patterns in your behavior that need healing. In such a case, you would know what you have going on in your life that works for you and what does not and what is in need of healing.

Because you do not know what it may take to achieve your hearts desire, great and unexpected change can and does happen in ones life. Author Carolyn Myss refers to this as "spiritual madness".

She talks about this in her book "Anatomy of the Spirit" in which she discusses the probability, when one asks God to take over ones life, of dramatic lifestyle changes. These could include changes in relationships, businesses etc. before one emerges, more enlightened from the other side of the darkness. This may not apply to everyone, however big changes could happen.

Only God knows what is in our best interests and how those interests will manifest when we ask that the higher purpose of our lives be shown us. We may unwittingly be asking for major life changes for which we need to trust that our highest purpose is being realized in spite of physical appearances to the contrary.

Neale Donald Walsch in his books "Conversations with God" describes his personal journey into complete poverty and back again.

It may be that one loses ones job and even goes through bankruptcy or is forced to start anew. Perhaps out of the ashes of the past, a person may start a new career or a business that one never had the courage or freedom to pursue, and ultimately they may realize their goals. However, in order to get to the goal, the past had to be swept clean.

This is not to say that all manifestations are so dramatic.

When we join the Divine in manifestation, we never know beforehand what route we will take to get there.

In short, we go along for the ride, but we don't get to plan the route!

—

It's the ride.

A beautiful soul has no other merit than its existence - Johann Friedrich Von Schiller (German playwright)

It is reasonable at this point to question why the Universe should grant us what we wish.

I explore this concept again and again throughout this book.

Creation is a circle. Our senses would have us see time and space as linear. It is not. Everything that ever is, was, or will be, already IS. God IS. Therefore all of everything IS.

Neale Donald Walsh in his book, "Conversations With God", puts the concept in perfect perspective. He writes that the Universe is like a CD Rom computer game. You are the player. All possible scenarios and outcomes are pre- programmed on the disk. How you play and the choices you make affect the way the game turns out for you.

Nevertheless, all possible outcomes are already anticipated and programmed in, only how you play affects the particular outcome of the game for you.

You, however, can do nothing in the game that does not already exist.

To the computer it makes no difference whether you win or lose or how you play, when you are done playing, the computer pops back on the screen - "Want to play again?"

So it is in life, all that IS already IS. Your choices determine your specific experiences. Change your life choice and you change the experience.

All that exists is in the mind of God. All that IS, is of God. Therefore all souls are part of, and one with God. So, too, is every blade of grass, every mote of dust, every star and every being. God experiences Himself through that which is all of creation. The Universe is God. Therefore all that happens is an occurrence that God experiences. This is what God does. God experiences the entire universe, every atom, every bacterium, every animal, every person, and every soul.

Nothing is outside the intelligence of God.

Such is the Universe.

This intelligence does not judge. You cannot lose, unless you choose to have the experience of losing. You can decide to physically experience loss, pain, depression or any other thought that you can conceive, even hell, because that which you think, you will manifest. Your freedom to choose your experiences time and time again, is how you as a soul grow by having a human experience!

In reality you can only win. Because your thoughts and your soul are eternal, nothing can harm you. You have always existed forever.

The one soul of humanity split into billions of parts called human beings and having multiple experiences is united as one in God.

All our experiences feed into the greater consciousness that is God. Through us, God experiences Himself.

Thus does God experience through the All That Is. This is to say that the entirety of creation is holy, for the All That Is, i.e.: everything that exists, is God manifest.

The reason for this chain of creation is simple.

The gift of a body and of life is a tremendous honor and a privilege. It is one thing for God or for that matter for anyone to be aware of its existence intellectually, it is quite another to have the actual experience of physical life.

For example if space did not exist, there could not be a "here and a there"

Conceptually and intellectually, one can know that there is a here and there.

However, to actually have the experience of "being here and going there" i.e.: to actually experience space is quite a different thing.

In order to experience there always needs to be pairs of experiences. That is, there needs to be opposites. All things need to have opposites in order to be. One cannot know darkness without the light to compare it with. All experience is a paired experience so that there is a basis for comparison. There is happy and sad, hot and cold, near and far etc.

In order to know space experientially God divided or expanded Himself to be everywhere, here and there simultaneously. Thus did the Divine gain the experience of self- awareness.

He is then able to have the *experience* of space instead of being restricted to the intellectual concept of space.

In order to travel from "here" to "there" also takes time.

There can be no "here" or "there" if space and time does not physically exist. God brought into being space and time simultaneously.

Once created, God can experience both space and time, yet paradoxically space and time still exist only by Gods grace and within God simultaneously. All exists at once, past present and future within God at all times.

From this point let us proceed to examine the Divine that exists within us all.

The God that is immanent throughout the Universe is the same energy that is manifest in each of us. Our consciousness of God is therefore God's experiential awareness of Self.

The Divine creation of the soul imbued with the gift of free will allows God unlimited experiences.

God, as a metaphorical ocean of energy, has poured out cups of Self in the creation of souls.

Every soul is of this "ocean" but in itself is not the entire "ocean". Yet the soul contains within itself all the potential that the ocean is.

In this dividing and expansion of the Divine, God created *of Himself* us.

Another way to express this is that the Divine out of a desire to experience Itself in all It's magnificence has split off from It's own Divine essence the eternal and indestructible energy that is the soul. As the soul sees the magnificence of the Father, so experiences the Father His own magnificence through the soul.

This is why in the final reality we are indeed one another! What we do to one we do to all including to ourselves.

We cannot harm another without harming ourselves.

The soul being *of the Divine*, has the same ability to create and manifest in a similar manner as the Father / Creator.

Indeed, the soul, mindful of the Divine entity that it is, and having a similar desire as the Creator to know itself experientially, created a body. It is our physical body.

Ipso facto, our physical body is the vessel of the soul. We too, have the ability to manifest and to create. The process of manifestation is harder in the material world. The physical plane is grosser than the spiritual plane and the results of what we create are sometimes less obvious to us when the immediacy is taken away.

Yet the perceived physical world as well as our thoughts and emotions are a result of our largely unconscious creation.

By the process of free will, souls are free to manifest their own destinies, separate from the will of God and yet completely within His embrace. In this manner, when a soul takes on a physical body, God is part of, and in, every human experience conceivable without exception.

(Remember that nothing exists outside of God.) The world created by mankind is transitory and lacks the meaningful existence of God's direct creation. Nevertheless it does provide a unique experience for the soul.

Therefore every human experience is Gods experience. It cannot be otherwise.

That is also why ultimately every human experience is illusionary. We have forgotten our Divinity and the truth of what we really are.

We are the Sons of God. We are the Daughters of God.

The error that we make is one of seeing God as a separate being somewhere in Heaven. We imagine ourselves as lost souls praying for mercies and handouts and in need of begging favors of God and imploring His forgiveness for sins that we imagine we have committed.

It is absurd in this context to think of a Biblical deity who judges and punishes us. Simply ask yourself who is God going to judge and punish and the answer must be Himself!

Indeed once we realize that God and we are one, then we also know that we are already forgiven before we even sin!

We are not sinners. There is no such thing as the original sin or the downfall of man through the sin of Adam or the consequential need by mankind of a Savior!

If there is such a thing as sin then it is that we have created ourselves believing in separation.

We have forgotten what we truly are and so we experience God as being separate from us. Therefore we do not trust God to deal fairly with us. We blame Him when things go wrong. We see God as being quick to anger and as vengeful. Scripture is full of the deeds and stories of God sitting in judgment and smiting the wicked. We implore Him to forgive us and to alleviate our suffering. We blame Him when He does not.

Western religions all teach that there is Divine retribution for our evil ways.

We are inculcated from birth to believe in a philosophy of death and eternal damnation that is reinforced all the way through adulthood and into old age.

Who teaches young children these things?

The answer is those people whom we most trust, namely our parents, clerics and teachers!

The biggest selling book of all time, the Bible, is full of tales of the wrath and vengeance of a god who annihilates sinners in the most gruesome ways imaginable. He obliterates entire nations on behalf of those whom scripture tells us He has chosen from among all other nations.* He pours forth pestilence and affliction on mankind as the wages of sin. He demands supplication and penance from those wishing to evade eternal damnation. And that is just the beginning.

We are shown that God is a King and we are nothing, less than dust before Him.

We are taught to see our unworthiness and separation from all that is good and of the Light. We are also told that we count for so little that we can be consigned to hell, doomed for all eternity for our sins. However all is not lost. If we grovel and snivel and beg forgiveness, God may, if he so deigns, forgive us our sins.** But we will never know if we are forgiven until we die. And so we live out our wretched days in mortal angst.

Does this sound like the conception of a Divine Being whose primary attribute is unconditional love?

Or does it sound like a diabolical means devised by mankind to control and gain power over his fellow man?

---

* It is no coincidence that each of the three major Abrahamic religions, that is Judaism from whose roots sprang Christianity and Islam, claim that God has chosen them and therefore is on their side.
** In many instances the clergy, who, as Gods representatives on earth, profess to know what God wants for you. An often-prescribed remedy for Divine forgiveness, not surprisingly, of a generous donation to the church is a sure-fire means to salvation.

Is this the behavior of a loving and caring Father/Mother or is it that of an unpredictable raving lunatic?

If we feel that we cannot trust God, then how can we trust our fellow man?

Indeed we cannot trust ourselves. So is it any wonder that so many people are paranoid, and are full of doubts and cynical in the ways of the world. And who can blame them? Until they realize their true relationship with the Universe, they must, as a result of our culture and upbringing see only conflict and separation between themselves and the rest of the world!

People must forgive themselves this illusion, this falsehood of existence, otherwise we are doomed to failure as a society and as a species.

Although human beings are guilty of some pretty gruesome deeds, we cannot truly do harm. All we see is not what it appears to be because of the illusion.

Nothing that we do on the physical world is of lasting importance and we will always be the eternal soul body that we are.

God therefore does not judge the actions of souls or that of the human bodies that they have created. There is no need to. We are as much one with Him as our brain is of us.

We could no more punish our brain for being a brain and doing what a brain does, namely processing our thoughts, even our most intimate (sinful?) thoughts, than God could punish his soul bodies for being the vehicles through which He processes His experiences.

So much misery and damage has been created over the centuries by the many religious orders who would have us believe in eternal damnation for the consequences of our *thoughts*!

So many lives have been destroyed in the process of people believing that they are unreformed sinners. The misery caused by the doctrine of sin is immeasurable.

Consequently, as the children of TRUTH a very important concept opens to us:

God will not judge Himself nor will He see imperfection in Himself or His creation, nor will He judge us. God will not destroy us or punish us. We are one with God. We are of God. We are God. All is One and the One is the All.

203

*You are one with me and we are one with all beings, all creatures,
the earth and all creation.*
And all that is, is only God in truth and in love.

Through the physical body God would have us forsake the illusion
of separation that we create and the politics of fear, and return to His
love.

Having given us free will and knowing that we can do no harm,
God does not intervene on our behalf.

The soul, in the physical world, has no investment in the illusion
either and does not identify with it for it knows only truth. This world
is a playground of illusions and games.

Experience of the physical world does affect the souls karma, and
determines the future lessons it will go through. Naturally the Divine
Itself also feels the experience. Every action and thought we have is
merged into the creative process of the All as One.

Hence, the experience of the physical being, even though we may
be totally unaware of it, glorifies God with its every act and thought
and manifestation. In so doing the Divine has the experience of Itself
as a human being.

As the soul glorifies its creation, the Divine is glorified. As the
soul experiences so experiences the Creator and much more.

*God has manifested Her awesomeness, His glory, and Its
magnificence!*

There are many levels of consciousness between God and a
human soul. The explanation so far represented herein is simplistic.
Suffice to say that the further one is from the Source, that is the
Godhead, the denser is the energy. Between a human soul and the
Source there are many levels of density. Likewise between the human
soul and the physical body and the physical body and the earth, there
are increased densities of energy and matter.

The density level increases the further one is from the Source, and
the manifestation process is similarly affected and becomes more
difficult the further removed one is.

The reason we have our physical body is summarized below.

What the soul cannot do is to have a direct physical experience.
The physical world is very dense.

Souls manifest a physical body in order to have the experience of
the physical world.

204

The physical body in turn creates physical experiences that the soul and God mutually experience. Experiences allow the soul and God to know themselves experientially. Bodies therefore are the vehicles employed by the soul to create and have physical experiences in order to know itself experientially.

Thus we are Divine beings having a human experience. The soul is not within the body, as many believe. The body is within the soul.

The difference between being pure soul and that of being a human being is that souls always have full Divine spiritual awareness. Humans do not.

We have free will and as a result we have forgotten our Divinity. In the process of which we have created the illusion of our separation from God. Therefore we have lost our sense of connectedness, our anchor, and thus we live in fear and uncertainty and have created all the negative aspects resulting thereof.

For human beings to experience complete free will without Divine interference, it is necessary for us to forget our Divine connection. In other words, we forget who and what we are. In this way we are free to experience and create whatever we want without limitation.

We are even unconscious of our ability to create and manifest.

Our goal and ultimate destiny as human beings is to reclaim our Divinity through our experiences in the course of many incarnations. Our lives provide an endless panorama of events and experiences for the Uni-being or the One Being that is the Universe, which is God.

We are in service at every minute of the day to God. God knows that our physical bodies are not who we really are. The experience human beings create for themselves is the Illusion of their lives!

When one chooses to return to the spirit form, in other words when we die, we exit the illusion and reclaim our natural state of total awareness. That is, we realize our true nature. We see that we are part of the One Soul (God) manifesting in many forms in order to have the multitude of bodies, on both the spiritual and physical levels for the purpose of experiencing Himself consciously.

We must of necessity forgive ourselves for any hurt we have caused ourselves in the physical world while in our state of illusion. In Truth we cannot harm ourselves, nor can we harm another.

We can however, believe that we did do harm until we see the Truth. The belief that we can harm each other and ourselves produces real distress and grief in people

All that we do is in accordance with the Divine will for us. There is no right or wrong, and no good nor bad.

We need opposites in order to have a complete physical experience.

The dichotomy is that all we create is seemingly real. It is real until it isn't. That is, as long as we choose to believe something is real it will be so. When we no longer choose so, then it is no longer real. We can un-create that which we have created.

The ego is that part of our mind that thinks that it is in charge. The ego would have us believe that it decides what is real, via our imperfect five senses, and through the filter of our mind.

The ego does not know that it cannot even live in the present, if indeed it lives at all.

By the time an event occurs, a conversation takes place, or a thought arises, it is already history. In the further time it takes for the mind to process the experience and interpret it into a form that would give the mind a sense of perspective, context and continuity, the event is past.

In dreaming, a similar thing happens. Ones mind cannot make sense of all the images and emotions happening in the dream state. In order to put them into a logical physical context that the ego can understand, it will attempt to form the dream images into some understandable form, no matter how twisted and strange it may be. Hence dreams are frequently disjointed and unintelligible.

In life, too, the ego twists everyday events to suit ones own perceived concept of reality

The physical body and the physical world are a very harsh environment for the soul to exist in. The weight of sustaining the mass of the physical body, the illusion and all the emotions is a major task for the soul. Sleep time is when the soul can reconnect with its true self. In this time it can depart the body and return to its natural state.

New born babies, the souls of which have yet to adapt, have a very difficult time adjusting to the physical plane, and spend much of their day in sleep. It takes a long time for the soul to adjust to the mass and trauma of this dense plane. Very often when people are in stress, or have difficulty in facing "reality", they will require much more sleep.

In rebirthing terms, this is called the "Death Urge". It is an escape from "reality" and is a suppression of feeling ones aliveness.

The more spiritual a person is, and the more in harmony one is with the spiritual realm, the less onerous is the physical experience for the soul. Spiritually evolved persons frequently require less sleep.

Sharda at the Divine Mother Temple in Dronagheri near Nanital, India. It is one of the oldest Divine Mother Temples in India. Legend has it that if you hang a bell there, the Divine Mother will grant your wish. We hung a bell.

The immortal guru Babaji as he appeared around circa 1972. It is said that he always appears as a young man. When he appeared he astounded everyone by his intimate knowledge of the affairs of 50 years prior. There was a court case in which Ashram land was being disputed by some land owners. When Babaji presented himself at the courthouse in Haldwani he astounded the court with his knowledge of the documents that were thought lost during the time of the British Raj.

The Author outside Babajis room in the Himalayan Foothills. Haidakhan Ashram.

The cave in the base of Mount Kailash at the source of the Ganges River where Babaji appeared in circa 1970

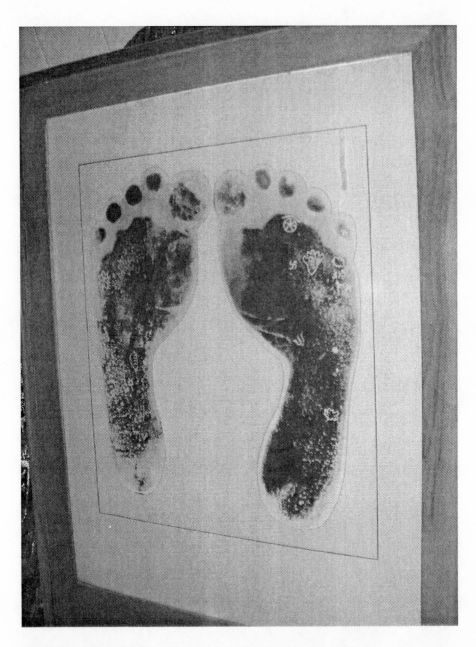

Signs of Divinity. The Gurus feet are said to be the connection between heaven and earth. This picture of Babaji's feet show astrological symbols that appear embedded in the soles of his feet.

The author with Prem Baba (left). It is said that Prem Baba died and was brought back to life by Babaji. The story has it that Prem Baba was quite upset and he did not want to come back!

Sri Muniraji (bottom left) performing a Yagna (sacred fire ceremony). Before he left his body, Babaji appointed Sri Muniraji to continue his work. Muniraji means King of Silence,

Nine Temples built by Babaji. Himalayan Foothills. Note the Ganges River below. In monsoon season it a torrent that sweeps away everything in its path.

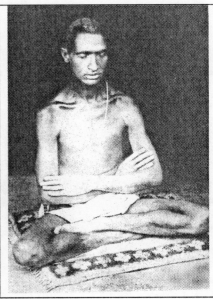

This is the previous incarnation of Babaji as written about by Paramahansa Yogananda in his famous book "Autobiography of a Yogi". In 1911 Babaji went to the city of Prayag. After taking a bath in a public bathing area at Triveni, a photographer named Sorabji took two pictures of Babaji at the urging of Major Basu while he was there. To everyone's surprise, when the pictures were developed, in one Babaji was wearing his shirt and Tibetan cap, and in the other he was wearing no clothes at all. This, even though both pictures were taken at the same time.

<u>Chapter Ten - Awakening the Senses</u>

*If we had keen vision and feeling of all ordinary human life, it would
be like hearing the grass grow and the squirrel's heart beat..... -
George Eliot (English Novelist)*

<u>Visualization Exercise V - Integration</u>

*A fool sees not the same tree that a wise man sees - William Blake
(English poet)*

Following this section there will be five exercises dealing with each of your five senses.

You would do well to understand the need to integrate the practices into your consciousness.

Each day continue to use the visualization techniques you have learned and apply them during all types of situations and moods-happy, stressful, exciting, dangerous, lazy, etc.

Always hold in your mind two simultaneous thoughts:

1. Firstly be very aware of yourself feeling the emotions that you physically feel in the moment.
2. Then hold the awareness that these feelings are not real, nor is the experience, they exist only in your mind.

As the observer of your self, be aware of your feelings about being simultaneously conscious and detached in the same moment. Afterwards, spend a minute to reflect on, and being in touch with, the feelings you experienced during the moments of awareness.

Try to extend the periods of awareness for longer periods of time during the day so that your consciousness becomes extended.

You can do this by using various affirmations such as:

o "All that I see is an illusion and it exists only in my mind. I am one with God. I can freely choose my own reality"
o "I am free to experience this situation (name the situation) in any manner I choose."
o "Life is a reflection of my thoughts. I am choosing how I wish to experience my own life and I choose love"
o "I choose to see this situation differently. I am a very holy being. I am choosing joy in my life"
o "This which I see is not real. I am Divine and I choose to replace this situation with happiness"

o "Om Namaha Shivaya" the supreme mantra. (I surrender to God or Gods will be done)

Consider this your Reality Check.

You can create your own affirmations or use any of those above if they feel right for you.

In order to be effective, be ever more aware of what your underlying feelings are at all times and then create conscious awareness with your daily affirmation.

As you progress, note how it feels not having to react to situations in a predictable and programmed manner. Being in control of your life instead of life controlling you, you will be free to choose your own life experience.

Note your feelings in being able to choose when, where and how you wish to respond, knowing that in all situations it is all is an illusion anyway and you do not have to be attached to a specific outcome.

Awareness of being a conscious being lies in knowing that you do not have to fret about the outcome of anything. Know and have total faith that the Divine knows better than you do regarding what is in your best interests, then you can be certain in knowing that the highest good will result in whatever the outcome is to something which you have put into motion.

Trust. You may not see the immediate sense of where things are headed, or how events are unfolding. This is because of your attachment to the ego and the illusion. When you override your instinct to control and manipulate and agonize, the highest good will manifest in your life because the outcome will arrive from a place of truth.

As you progress, you will find that you will develop secondary feelings that are telling you something. Some may say this is a psychic awareness. Some experience an awareness of synchronicity of events. That is things begin to happen in perfect timing for you. You may be troubled about something and you turn on the television and see a program with the answer. A book or an article may appear that guides you to a solution. Sometimes you may find people calling you with some piece of information you need just at the time that you needed it. Other times a happy call from someone uplifts you in the moment that you feel a little down.

Call it what you will, the universe will start to align with you and bring you exactly what you need in the moment that you need it.

This is because you are giving up all resistance and control and instead are becoming aligned with a higher source.

I cannot tell you how much of my life and that of my partner, Sharda, is based on synchronicity. It is a rare day that it does not occur.

Awareness will grow to a level that you previously did not know you could achieve. It is like a kind of secret knowledge. It is a wellspring of strength, calm and wisdom that raises you up. It is both illuminating and creative in its energy. There is no time frame regarding when you should start to experience this awareness but you will experience it, perhaps vaguely at first and then stronger as you learn to see these things and tune into them.

As Wayne Dyer says, "You will see it when you believe it"

Perhaps you are also getting a sense of the meaning of this statement in Zen Buddhism

"All is Nothing"?

In the scheme of things there is no reality save the Ultimate reality, and all else is nothing.

The ultimate reality is those things which are God given and are immutable.

Nothing created by man is absolute and permanent. The pyramids in five thousand years will be sand hills and the contrivances of man will be as dust. However the Universal law will be unchanged. Cause and effect, love and joy and the eternal Divinity will continue to exist as will you and I. All that is today will be forgotten. So why put your faith in that which has no meaning? Align yourself with those things that do have meaning.

Love is the ultimate reality. Love exists in the fact that the Divine sustains the All That Is in perfect balance and harmony. Like a caring mother, there are no preconditions set on Her love nor does She ever withdraw Her love. It is without judgment and ever held for us, waiting only our acceptance and realization that it is there and always has been here for the taking.

Not only is it here for the taking, it is our birthright. It is here for you to *demand* it. You do not have to ask for Gods love, nor do you need to feel worthy of it before you can have it. You are <u>entitled</u> to Divine love because of what you are in reality. We are holy beings. We should <u>demand</u> of the Universe that we have it *now*, without fail.

The Universe cannot deny you that which is one with you, only your ego can **E**dge **G**od **O**ut.

What is required of you is for you to be open once again and to accept that which you already have!

All challenges to love such as fear, attack and defense, being man made, are illusionary so give no more energy to these feelings and thoughts. When they arise in you, see them for what they are; Edging **G**od **O**ut, and replace **E.G.O.** with a reality check and do an appropriate affirmation.

Be aware that you are not your body and know with certainty that nothing *Real* can harm you. Those thoughts that you create, called fear, are not real. As long as you have fear, you are in doubt about your true identity. Your thoughts perceive separation from your Source. You are forgetting that you are holy.

Perceiving fear you think you need defenses from some apparent form of attack. Fear breeds defense and attack.

What you defend and attack against are only the illusions of your mind. You joust with windmills.

One of the great teachers of this century is a self- realized man named Sri Ramana Maharshi or Bhagavan. When he was asked about what method was best for attaining enlightenment this is what he said; 'I do not teach only the Ajata Doctrine[*] I approve of all schools. The same truth has to be expressed in different ways to suit the capacity of the hearer. The Ajata doctrine says: 'Nothing exists except the one Reality. There is no birth and no death, no projection or drawing in, no bondage and no liberation.

---

[*] The teachings of the Bhagavan are a process of self -inquiry and that one has to look for the "I" within oneself. Discover who it is that is feeling, who is seeing who is the "I" that we refer to so casually in speech. When we meditate and have thoughts come into our mind, delve into the thought and ask where does this thought come from. Who is the thinker that originated this thought.

The one unity alone exists forever.' To such as find it difficult to grasp this truth and who ask: 'How can we ignore this solid world we see around us?'... They are told, 'All that you see depends upon the seer. Apart from the seer there is no seen.'

To such as cannot grasp even this and who further argue; 'The world is felt and seen not only by me but by so many, and we cannot call such a world non-existent'. They are told, 'God created such and such a thing, out of such and such an element, and then something else and so forth. God created all this and so you see it'

When asked how all these teachings can be true and that only one doctrine can be true, Bhagavan said, 'All these viewpoints are only to suit the capacity of the student. The absolute can only be one.'

Max Planck, a physicist and the Nobel Prize-winning father of Quantum Theory stated, 'All matter originates and exists only by virtue of a force... We must assume behind this force the existence of a conscious and intelligent Mind. This mind is the matrix of all matter.'

There are things, such as time, that are beyond our physical ability to experience, and that are creations of the mind.

Time itself has no implicit meaning. You can stretch and shrink time. Time is a function of mind.

All of time co-exists simultaneously, past, present and future.

Einstein proved it. As you approach the speed of light time appears to slow down.

Highly precise atomic clocks taken aboard spacecraft and even airplanes have shown differences in time when they return to earth. The speed of motion has created the clocks having a different time continuum than those left behind on the ground.

Quantum physicists are dealing with the problems of time. Time and space are as Einstein stated are relative. Time does not exist, as we perceive it. Or to put it another way, it does not exist as we see it unless we choose to see it, in which case it does.

Just like light, if we choose to see it as a wave rather than a beam, we will.

Time and space exist in the here and now in the mind of God. All things exist as one here and now.

You have done quite a lot of work with mind and memories in this book. Once again, consider for example, your own memories.

All that exists for you is the reality you have created in your mind, unaffected by time and space. Your childhood memories exist alongside the memories of what you did yesterday. Insofar as they exist within you, in the same time and space in your mind that is the eternal now.

Under hypnosis, you can instantly regress from being an adult to a five-year-old with the belief and perception that you are five years old. This is not merely a stage trick, it is a demonstration of how the mind creates reality and how we choose our perception of reality. Certainly this type of hypnotic demonstration is very dramatic, but it is no different from how we create our lives and our perception of time in our lives, everyday.

You should strive to integrate the conscious awareness of the deception of **E.G.O.** and replace it with mantras and affirmations of your true self until you have created a new paradigm of perception.

Integrating the ideas presented thus far requires you to see the duality of existence. Be conscious of what is happening on the physical level. Have no attachment to it. Look for the metaphysical reasons behind things and events and question everything that happens to you. In every experience ask yourself why you have created this in your life. For example, assume that you are looking forward to going to a ball game or a party and you get ill and cannot go. The unconscious way of thinking is to say. "I can't help it if I got sick, I really did want to go". At a metaphysical level you should know that you created not going. Then the question becomes "What part of my mind created not going?" If you cannot get the answer then ask yourself the following question, "If I did know the answer to why I created this happening, what would it be?" The first thought that pops into your mind, however improbable, is likely to be the correct answer.

In the moment that you are having a physical experience, integrate the awareness in your consciousness of the illusionary nature of what is happening. Get in touch with your feelings and get to know which are from ego and fear and which are from a place of Love and Truth.

Be attentive of being both the observer and the observed and look for the greater Truth behind everything and integrate it into your consciousness.

—

Visualization Exercise VI - The Senses: One on One

Nothing awakens a reminiscence like an odor - Victor Hugo (French Poet)

By now you should have a pretty decent grasp of the creative power of the mind as well as your role and accountability for the reality that you experience.

You should also acknowledge that you are a holy being and that you are one with everything in your world, and with every person that you come into contact with.

Always be mindful that you are one with everything that you lay your eyes on.

When you encounter anyone including your own family, remind yourself that they and you are one.

Knowing that you are a holy being, you should also affirm that you are a completely innocent person and you should resolve to always accept yourself as so.

The following five exercises on the physical senses are one day exercises. Do them consciously throughout the ensuing day. They consist of a morning meditation and an evening meditation with a review period along with a daily awareness program.

Spend a few minutes to review your thoughts and feelings about the past day as well as a reflection on the day ahead, contemplate your dreams and aspirations. Consider this a mental maintenance program, a mind gym, just like exercising your body.

Remember that this is for you and your happiness and self-realization. You owe time to yourself first before you give your valuable time to anyone else!

As Yogananda said, "If your priority is God, give God the first couple of hours of your day."

It is a wonderful thought to consider that every human experience becomes a Divine one.

Through you, God is experiencing His creation. Therefore embrace all your senses with aliveness and awareness and consciousness of thought. Do this both for your sake as well as for His sake.

The connectedness of your aliveness to the entire universe will run through you, an electric energy. It is a constant reminder to you that you are never alone and always connected to your Divinity.

Apply the following idea during your meditation: The sense of smell.

Think of a smell. Perhaps bring to mind the smoke from a fire or a fragrant perfume filled night. Choose any feel good sensation that is evocative and has a powerful memory for you.

The smells only exist in your mind and nowhere else. Appreciate this fact: all that you smell has no existence outside of your mind. Remind yourself that you can choose your feelings and how you relate to your experiences.

When you experience fragrance with true aliveness there is a renewed sense of wonder in the commonplace.

This will be true for all the sensory visualizations that follow.

As you meditate be alert to whatever feelings are being evoked within you when you recall different smells and aromas. Take notice of the memories that can be brought into awareness by recollections of smells such as your mothers fragrance, muffins on the stove, a small baby, holiday dinners with loved ones etc. Embrace your feelings and note the warmth, comfort or safety and all other feelings aroused by the awareness of scents.

Use your sensitivity to aroma, and apply it to smells and fragrances that you encounter during the day so that you are aware of the feelings it raises within you. Make a point of seeking out smells. Smell the milk in your refrigerator and the perfumes and aromas surrounding you. Notice your thoughts and emotions in the moment you experience them. Pay attention to how your mind and body feel. See what smells may evoke memories then get in touch with how your body and mind are reacting in response.

Savor the experience and acknowledge that for you no smell can possibly exist outside of your mind. Furthermore, every emotion brought up by a scent is yours alone, created by you and for you as a means of sustaining the illusion of reality.

Meditate on why you have the feelings that you do to certain scents, and what their significance is to you. Some may invoke feelings of panic, discomfort or wistfulness. Ask yourself why you are storing this emotion and what it means to you. Some scents may invoke unresolved emotions within you such as regret for things that you wish you could have expressed, or sentiments never released. Perhaps you even wished to cry and you held yourself back.

Now is a good time to get into your mind and study the meaning of the feelings being aroused in you and express the emotions aloud to yourself. Write down the unresolved things that you wish you could have said or done. If the feeling was an unexpressed feeling of love to your mother when you were a small child, then express it now. If you felt hurt about something, or afraid or even nauseated, express it now. Remember you are safe and you are innocent.

Once you have addressed some of the feelings you have been suppressing all these years, write a forgiveness affirmation for yourself. "I, (your name) am innocent of withholding my feelings about (state cause). I forgive myself and I forgive (name). I am a holy being. I am safe, I am loved and I am one with the Divine."

Keep it where you can see it and where you can repeat it so that innocence and healing may occur.

When looking for aromas, you can choose how to experience the smell, whether it is pleasant, indifferent or even unpleasant.

As part of the exercise, seek out fragrances wherever you go and try to notice the subtleties within a smell, much like the way a wine connoisseur analyzes the subtleties of a vintage.

Mentally try to reverse the rolls of smells and experience unpleasant smells as pleasant and vice versa. How much of your conditioning dictates that perfume should be pleasant and other smells such as say, garlic unpleasant? What do you think the smell does for you. Does a bad smell warn you of danger such as when food goes bad. Does a pleasant fragrance entice you? Consider why this is so and what is happening to your body? Can you affect your reaction to your conditioning about odor? Can you experience a juicy steak as the smell of death and decay?

Can other scents be equally illusionary? What of the fragrance of a perfume - does it smell of chemicals is it sickly sweet or overpowering?

See if you can you create your reaction to smell opposite for yourself, i.e. making the pleasant unpleasant and vice versa. Treat familiar scents as if this were the first time you have ever encountered them and as if they are totally foreign to you. Be inquisitive about it and how your body is stimulated. Think how powerful some scents are and how they project themselves into the room while others are subtle and mysterious.

See if you can feel the energy behind a scent. Does it tell you a story when you really focus and tap into it? Smells are frequently used as a communication technique in the animal world, such as when a dog marks his territory, or with pheromones - the scent given off by animals to attract a mate.

What messages do you hear in the smells around you? How about messages in the scent of colleagues?

This is all about creating your own reality. Smell the air and imagine where it has been before it reached you. Consider if you are more unconscious about smell now than you were as a child.

To coin a "Yogi Berra-ism", 'The beauty of a fragrance is in the eye of the beholder'.

Actually this holds a lot of truth. Yogi Berra, the famous baseball player was also renowned for malapropism and the misuse of words.

—

The Selous Scouts

I have no doubt that it is a part of the destiny of the human race, in its gradual improvement, to leave off eating animals, as surely as the savage tribes have left off eating each other when they came in contact with the more civilized. - Henry David Thoreau (American essayist)

In the 1960's and 1970's the white regimes of both South Africa and the country of Southern Rhodesia (now Zimbabwe) fought a bitter bush war with neighboring countries that harbored African freedom fighters, then called terrorists by the governments of the day.

Black freedom fighters spent years in the jungles and bush of southern Africa surviving off the land. Their hit and run tactics were typical of guerrilla fighters of that era, which also saw the USA involved in its own similar war in Vietnam. The countryside was the refuge of the guerillas. They could disappear into the jungle effortlessly in thus they could evade the mostly white soldiers of the South African and Rhodesian defense forces.

In order to counter these stealthy adversaries, the Rhodesian and South African armies created special commando units that employed similar bush fighting techniques as their enemy. In Rhodesia they became the world famous Selous Scouts. These men learned to survive for weeks on end off the land, eating bugs, raw meat and whatever else was at hand. It is said that if there were no water available they would drink water from the gut of an animal that they had killed.

These soldiers learned to become one with their environment. To do so effectively, they reverted to the wild and the primitive state. It is noteworthy how fast city boys learned to adapt to the bush and how soon they could revert to a state of savagery. Also remarkable is the fact that they could transition from this environment and resume their life with their families during leave periods and then return to the bush once again.

I am reminded of the book 'Lord of the Flies' written by William Golding. In this book a group of middle class school children are stranded on a remote island and the story follows their shedding of the veneer of civility and their descent into ritual, tribalism, and savagery.

As they shed the trappings of civilization and ultimately form tribal grouping they discover murder and ultimately cannibalism.

The Selous Scouts in the process of their return to the wild developed an acute sense of smell. They realized that the enemy too, had an acute sense of smell and could smell the scouts from a great distance. To evade detection, Scouts attempted to blend into their environment completely so that they would not wash for a couple of weeks before entering a combat zone and thereby lose all trace of scent of civilization. Once in the combat zone no fires were allowed, no manufactured foods, no soap, no cigarettes, not even chewing gum or toothpaste. All of the trappings of civilized society contain smells that are not natural to the environment, and which could be detected by the enemy from a great distance in the bush.

Smelling like animals, eating like animals and living as such, the scouts became one with their environment.

I am certain that on the occasion of their return to society, society must have been a traumatic assault on their sharpened senses. In the bush, they could smell animals from a distance. A cigarette could be smelled from more than a mile away. Can you imagine the smell of normal society upon their return home? Overpowering perfumes and colognes, exhaust fumes, tobacco, chemicals of every description, soaps, cleaning solutions, even flowers in the well-kept gardens of the suburbs must have bombarded their senses.

Those scents and smells that we accept as normal and in fact are oblivious of in modern society can be an overwhelmingly powerful assault that eventually deadens the senses. One should be more aware of the power of smell.

—

Jeffrey M. Solomon

<u>Visualization Exercise VII - Hearing the TRUTH</u>

Many of the greatest discoveries of our times will be made by those who, in addition to listening to their hearts and to each other, listen to the rest of the kingdom of life; to the trees, birds, insects, fishes, worms, algae; to the oceans and forests and mountains and deserts and skies; to all consciousness that dwells on this planet; - Paul Williams (Author)

This one-day exercise, like the previous one should be done as both a morning and evening meditation with frequent applications during the day. (Remember to do the connected breaths when you settle down).

Today you are going to work on your sense of hearing. This is the next hardest sense to master after sight. You are expected to be the conscious observer and to focus on what is being said to you while at the same time you are experiencing a different sense of reality attached to observing your hearing experience.

It takes some practice to hear on two levels of consciousness. At first you may only be able to achieve detachment during conversations for brief flashes, until you become more adept at it.

Review my comments in the previous section about the sense of smell. My comments relating to the forgiveness affirmation and the technique to use apply here as well.

Begin by focusing your attention on the sounds around you. Observe all sounds and not only those directed specifically at you. There are things such as ambient music and situations where people are engaged in casual conversations as a group and that you do not have to focus too closely on what is being said.

Practice hearing on the physical level while simultaneously being aware that you are hearing on another level, the mental level.

As you hear words and sound be attentive of the lilt and rhythm of the song of language. Assume for the moment that you do not speak this tongue, so all you are aware of are sounds and inflections without meaning. If you have the opportunity to listen to a real foreign language, perhaps on cable television, close your eyes and hear the music of language without the distraction of meaning.

Use your mind to direct how you experience sound. Create an awareness of sound and have fun experiencing it as the melody of life all around you.

Be aware that the intelligence your mind uses so naturally to comprehend language can be switched off and otherwise controlled and manipulated.

Music, for example, can sound foreign when you change your perception and hear it without any preconceived notions of rhythm and melody. I find it interesting to listen to Tibetan or Indian music that has a different tonal scale to western music and therefore is strange to our ears.

The Tibetans do throat chanting that at first is very monotonous until one becomes aware of many subtle layers of sound and vibrations that lie below the surface. Like oil on water, the harmonics shimmer and change in barely perceptible ways.

Here is something that you may enjoy doing. It is the Aaaah meditation. Sitting in your meditation spot, take a deep breath and open your mouth wide. Then expel your breath through your open mouth and as loud as you can and say Aaaaaaaaaaaah and stretch it out with a long exhale. Focus your attention on the space on your brow between your eyebrows and above the bridge of your nose. It is sometimes referred to as the third eye region. Continue doing this for about twenty minutes to an hour. You will begin to fall into an easy rhythm of breath and sound. As you do so all extraneous thoughts will be overcome by your focus on the breath and the sound. You could loose track of time, and that is fine too. The sound will start to take on different harmonics as it reverberates within your head. You may experience several layers of tones simultaneously somewhat like a vibrating reed does on a musical instrument. Soon the aaaah assumes a life and a quality of its own. Sometimes it can feel as if the sound is rising from the base of your spine and upwards through your stomach, heart, and throat and out of the crown of your head and into the universe. It is a great release for those times that you feel stressed and its after effects leave you feeling very energized.

At the conclusion of the exercise gently wind down the intensity of the exhaled aaaaah and slowly bring it to a still point and then sit and feel the silence. The calm will be palpable and you will feel your body vibrate all over. Allow yourself time to sit in the silence and to relax and let your awareness of your surroundings return naturally.

Another exercise is to observe your family over dinner. Turn off your understanding "switch" and listen to the tone of language. Notice if the family sound like aliens when you choose to switch perception tracks.

See what happens with the telephone when you do not have to concentrate on what is being said to you by the person on the other end. Disassociate sound from meaning.

What music do you hear in the traffic and in life around you?

Be aware of the sound of life.

Another interesting exercise is complete silence. Get a snorkel while in the bathtub and with your head under the water just float and listen to the silence.

The background hum of the universe is Ommmmmm. In the silence of nothingness listen for the hum of creation.

Listen to tone of language instead of to the words. See if you can hear messages in the tone that belies the words spoken.

Beyond the meaning of words is the tonal message that displays such things as fear, threats, boredom, passion etc. Learn to hear the hidden message of language present in tone.

If what you sense in tone rather than in word disturbs you, you can be certain that your intuition is correct. Therefore the tone, not the word carries the true message.

It is a good idea not to be seduced by words. Where the tone and the words are not in harmony, wisdom and prudence would suggest that one be very skeptical of the message and the messenger. It may be best for you to detach from them, bless them, and acknowledge that notwithstanding anything else, you and they are one.

Once you have mastered the technique of disassociating sound from meaning, and this may take more than just one day of practice, try and integrate it with smell. Apply both smell and sound sensory techniques simultaneously whenever the situation arises. In this way imagine the strangeness of the world as if you were experiencing the familiar for the first time, it's a lot of fun and it can teach you much about perception.

Remember that you are responsible for what you feel and that you can change your perception. Affirm; "This which I experience is not real, it exists in my mind alone".

—

<u>Visualization Exercise VIII - Taste</u>

I have an everyday religion that works for me. Love yourself first and everything else falls into line. - Lucille Ball (Actress)

Today we are going to do an exercise around taste that is relatively easy.

Do the necessary preparation and breathing as per the previous exercises.

One thing that we seldom do as we get older is to experience the taste of things. In the first instance most of us tend to eat rapidly and without much thought about taste. Secondly, the tastes we are used to are often taken for granted so that we do not think about what we are tasting unless it is a totally new dish or product. And thirdly, some really bad tastes are those that we have got used to. In this category I can think of the bitterness of sugar and the taste of meat and alcohol, to name just a few.

There is the huge amount of sugar present in everyday processed foods. Barely any processed foods from sauces to savory chips are made without loads of sugar.

Sugar is in flavored chips, condiments and canned and frozen foods. The presence of sugar is ubiquitous in our Western diet.

As you practice today, taste various familiar products in your kitchen for the subtleties of the under taste. Something as simple as sugar can actually have bitter under tastes.

Taste everything today with the approach of the detached observer. Look at it before you eat it. Visualize where it may have come from – consider its origin. What processes did it go through before it got to your plate? How old is it, what gives it color, and what is keeping it from spoiling? Consider this, if it does not spoil in its container, how does your body cope with breaking down this preservative substance? Does your body welcome the ingestion of this substance? Does the ingestion or eating of this product make you feel good? Foods definitely lighten us or alternatively make us feel heavy and polluted. Observe what effects different foods and drinks have on your body as you consciously feel what your body feels like as it goes down.

Smell is important to taste. Smell the product and notice the aromas and tones of its smell.

What do the smells emanating from it tell you? If it is hot and steaming can you taste the air around you? How does this compare to the expectation of the taste in your mouth?

We are so accustomed to the expected taste of things, that we do not notice the subtleties that under lie the flavor. Practice experiencing and tasting familiar things as if for the first time.

The average diet contains a large amount of artificial products such as colorings that have been shown to cause behavioral problems in young children, and sugars that cause hyperactivity. Babies do not usually take naturally to sweet things if they have been raised on natural healthy foods.

Have you noticed how babies turn away from sweet things preferring bland foods such as vegetables instead? Sweet is probably an acquired taste that tends to overwhelm the natural flavors of foods.

I remember having given up all sugars for several months. When I finally tasted a candy bar that I used to really enjoy - it was totally disgusting and it actually tasted bitter! It was way too sweet for my taste buds.

My taste had changed and eating sugar again became a learned experience. It took some time before I could accept many of the sweet things that I had previously been used to. To this day, I regard most sweets as too sweet and increasingly I avoid processed products completely.

When I gave up meat I tried it again after a long period of time and it tasted terrible! It was very heavy and did not feel good going down. I felt as if I was taking something into my body that my body objected to. I came to realize that my body is not intended to be the final resting place for the carcasses of dead animals.

Taste, therefore, is not the only a factor to consider. You should be aware of how your body feels taking this or that substance into itself.

In this regard, if you want to be sensitive to the suitability of things you ingest, try laying off something for a few weeks and then feel and hear what your body is telling when you reintroduce it back into your diet. Sometimes your body will tell you it is really missing something. If you give up fresh fruits and vegetables, you will feel like you are missing the freshness of food. You may even feel heavy and unclean inside.

The taste of meat can be missed, but if you lay off it for a while, when you go back to it, the heaviness and feeling of eating carrion and of introducing something unclean into your body is unmistakable.

Taste is a learned experience - like anything else. In parts of Africa the thought of eating a hamburger is repulsive - but locusts are a delicacy.

Practice eating each meal as if this dish was a new and first time experience. Examine texture, smell, taste and appearance for the first time. Use your fingers to squish and examine. See the grease ooze out of the fries or pizza - feel the texture of grease. Does this feel acceptable for you to ingest? Is it really food? What are the ingredients? Does it contain dyes and preservatives? Visualize preserving chemicals going through your digestive system and see how you think your system feels.

Remember that taste is often a learned experience and is quite superficial to your desire to eat. The body does not taste. The body has to deal with the consequences of taste. Frequently taste spurs a desire to eat without regard to the body's need for sustenance. This is called gluttony. This is the desire to eat and to snack slavishly without conscious regard of the need to do so. It is an addictive behavior. It is the precursor to obesity, cancers, heart disease and other illnesses.

An enlightened awareness to learning mastery over the sense of taste is a healthy and life affirming choice to make.

—

Visualization Exercise IX - Touch

Every man takes the limits of his own field of vision for the limits of the world - Arthur Schopenhauer (German philosopher)

Today's one-day meditation begins in the same way as the previous meditations. Begin in your quiet spot with twenty connected breaths and it too, will continue throughout the day.

Touch is subtle. Today be aware of skin types and visualize how different types of skin might feel. Not only rough or smooth, but thick or thin, strong or fragile. Envisage how skin might bruise or be resilient. Visualize of how old skin and young skin and baby skin differs and feels.

The most sensitive touch receptors are on your tongue. During the course of the day try feeling familiar things with your tongue and notice texture and temperature, acidity and moisture. Feel the texture and surface characteristics of foods in particular as you eat.

Also feel textures of clothing and fabrics, woods, glass, plastics, leaves of various plants, and trees. Go through your wardrobe and feel your different articles of clothing. Feel with your hands and fingers then with your eyelids and then with soft skin on the inside of your wrist.

Notice the different sensations of touch that you can produce from these different parts of your body.

Consider in your imagination how you might feel being an inanimate object.

If you were a building how would your "skin" feel today being in the open and exposed to the elements. Visualize it. Do the same thing by imagining you are a tree and feel the bark as your protective garment.

Practice feeling and touch throughout the day. You can fantasize being an inanimate object such as the hot roof of a car parked in the sun, a bee on the breeze, then imagine how it feels as it touches the petals of a flower. Feel yourself as a dog with fleas. The idea is that all of creation is inextricably linked to you, whether it is a tree or a rock. So use your imagination today to feel how it must be to be someone or something other than yourself.

What would things feel like if they had an energy vibration and you could feel and experience them not by touch alone but by their energy vibrations?

Cup objects in your palms and try and feel the energy emanating from objects such as crystals, rocks, pets, and people and see if you can tune in to any kind of vibration coming from them.

Everything carries a subtle vibration of previous ownership or if it is a living thing it has its own energy vibration.

Close your eyes and hold objects to see if you can intuit their vibration. Most objects carry a vibration that sensitive people are able to feel. Choose items such as jewelry belonging to another person, stones, pets and other people. Place your hands very lightly on somebody's head or chest and feel the subtle vibration of their energy field as it starts to rise after a few minutes of quiet concentration.

People, plants and animals have subtle energy fields or energy bodies that radiate from them. Humans have seven main energy vortexes in their bodies called chakras. These radiate ki (Japanese) or chi (Chinese) and they are the basis of acupuncture therapy and also for many of the martial arts, in particular Shaolin King Fu.

The base chakra is an energy field located between your legs at the base of your spine and it spins downward towards the ground. Two further chakras that overlap somewhat are located below the navel and in the solar plexus. A fourth is located in the chest near the heart and is called the heart chakra. A fifth is in the neck by the Adams apple. The sixth is between the eyebrows on the forehead and is sometimes referred to as the third eye. The second through the sixth chakras radiate energy forwards from the front of the body as well as backwards to the rear of the body. The seventh is the crown chakra on the crown of the head and it radiates upwards.

After some practice on different subjects, one can actually feel the energy body with the hands. If your subject lies on their back and you hold your hands and inch or two above them, with your eyes closed, you can feel the energy emanate from them. It feels like a gentle magnetic repulsion and is stronger in some people than in others and also varies depending on a person's state of mind and health. In some vibrant people you can feel their energy projected a couple of feet above their bodies.

In certain circumstances, you can feel the actual spin of the energy chakras. The more you practice doing this the more sensitive you will become at feeling the energy. You can practice on yourself as well by placing your hands a few inches in front of yourself and tuning in to your own bodily vibration.

There are many fields of medicine as well as body workers who use the energy fields of the body for both diagnosis and healing. Perhaps one of the better-known disciplines is Reiki. Others are Zero Balancing, Acupuncture and acupressure, Cranio-Sacral Therapy, Hawaiian Huna practices, Healing Touch and so on. Practically every culture has discovered the power of touch for healing.

The Bible talks of the laying on of the hands for healing purposes, and many church groups practice this form of healing.

My Reiki master, Joyce Swanson, tells a story of a burn victim. While waiting for the emergency vehicles, some Reiki practitioners directed healing energy through their hands to the burn victim. The sooner that you begin the healing process after a trauma the better it is for the patient.

In this instance, the patient recovered, and in the places where the Reikii practitioners had held their hands, a few inches above the victim and never actually touching the skin, there were energy handprints on the newly healed skin where the healing energy had been most concentrated!

I, myself have burned myself many times with matchbook matches, where the match head has broken off and flaring phosphorous head has stuck to my thumb. Usually this results in a painful blister. By applying Reiki energy immediately, I can attest that I have healed without a blister and in a matter of hours.

My entire family use Reiki on themselves at the first indication of a cold or the onset of any illness. I had a dog, a German shepherd that received Reiki when he injured himself. In fact whenever we had our monthly Reiki healing group at my home, my dog, Nicholas, would be the first in the room and he usually lay there totally blissed out from the energy of the group. He also liked to lie across someone's feet and receive the energy that way.

Touch, has both healing as well as sensory applications.

Some people can demonstrate amazing feats when it comes to the sense of touch.

239

People can walk over hot coals when they believe strongly that it will not burn them.

Many cultures, including Native Americans, do fire walks. It is not uncommon for people with very little experience at all to participate in this ritual of walking on hot coals without getting burned.

Certain yogis in India stare into the blazing summer sun for hours and are not affected by it. In fact in the heat of midsummer some have been known to build a fire around them and with the temperature reaching hundreds of degrees, they stare at the sun for hours on end.

DO NOT EVER ATTEMPT THIS IN ANY MANNER, SHAPE OR FORM YOURSELF!

It is extremely dangerous. My telling you this is solely intended to be informative to show you the power and control a highly evolved being, trained in self-control and trained in self-healing, can achieve over his body. Such people are few and far between.

In the Christian tradition, over two hundred cases of spontaneous stigmata (stigmata are the various wounds that Christ bore on his body at the crucifixion) have been documented on individuals. One of the most famous of these in more recent times is Therese Neumann of Bavaria, Germany (1898 - 1962). Therese suffered 45 simultaneous wounds on her body hands, head and feet associated with the Passion. These occurred throughout most of her adult life for an estimated total of 275 times! Therese had to wear special gloves and shoes to enable her to go about her daily life. Perhaps the most amazing sight was that even when she lay on her bed horizontally, the blood flowed from her wounds as if she were upright on the cross.

Bearing in mind that were she actually on a cross rather than lying on her bed, her hands would have been raised above her head. Therefore the blood flowed upwards from her hands to her elbows in defiance of gravity!

For forty years she never ate or drank yet her weight increased during this time from 121 pounds in 1927 to 215 pounds in 1953. Living on Divine energy, prana in Hindu terms, ch'i in Chinese or mana in the Kahuna tradition, Therese took no sustenance. Furthermore, she slept but a few hours a week, working through the day and night, often in excruciating pain.

Pause to consider how addicted most of us are to our need for regular meals, snacks, sleep times and recreation time.

Ponder, in your meditation, your living for one day, under the conditions that Therese lived under everyday. Visualize how you would feel in your body. Use your mind to experience what the lack of nourishment must feel like, then combine that with a twenty four hour work schedule and to finish off add the wounds in your hands, feet, ribs, forehead and back.

Understand, even if only briefly, the power of the mind in trying circumstances. Imagine how you might expect your body would feel both inside and outside.

Where do you think that you ultimately experience the sensation of touch? The answer of course is in your mind. All concepts of touch, suffering and pain can be mitigated with the power of the mind. Similarly pain, suffering and illness can also be created by your mind.

Ultimately all illness and all healing must originate in the mind.

In 1939, an Indian mystic named Anandamayi Ma was considered one of the greatest gurus of all time by her devotees, and as a manifestation of God in the flesh. She displayed an amazing power of spontaneous self-healing.

She was known to take on the diseases of her devotees in order to affect their healing. In so doing Anandamayi Ma took no notice of these "guests from the subtle plane" as she referred to the diseases in "the body". She often referred to her physical self as "the body" demonstrating no attachment to her body. She treated people around her as reflections of God and would be very humble, even though she was the enlightened one to whom all these people were flocking to pay homage.

Anandamayi Ma was diagnosed as having malaria, dysentery, heart disease, and terminal liver cancer. She acted as if nothing at all was wrong with her, taking all in her stride while healing the sick and counseling the troubled.

She refused all medication and rarely slept, all the while maintaining a rigorous routine. Upon the threat of her being given a morphine injection, which she absolutely refused, she completely spontaneously de-materialized all her illnesses and became healed.

241

Understand that no matter what your mind tells you - you can tell it otherwise - the whole totality of your experience is deep within your mind - and not outside of you.

Enlightenment begins with your taking control of reality.

—

<u>Visualization Exercise X - Perception</u>

Light is energy manifest.

It is no coincidence that the sense that most influences our illusion and our place in the world is sight.

Today we are going to look within for some "In – sight"

You understand that you have no sight outside of your mind. All that you see without you exists only within you.

The reality that you perceive as being out there is not "out there" at all!

With this in mind, today's meditation starts with your centering yourself and breathing so that you are relaxed. It is a morning and evening exercise with repetition throughout the day.

In fact this is an exercise that deserves a week of your time and indeed it is something that you can carry with you for all time.

Be mindful that in order for objects to be visible, that is to be seen, they must reflect light / energy just like the images captured on film that I discussed at the beginning of this book.

You cannot make a movie in the dark.

Reflected energy in the form of light is what makes the world around us visible.

The illusion that things are solid, as already discussed, is just that, an illusion. The matter that solid objects are composed of is energy, the same as the reality inside your mind.

To truly see reality we must therefore "See the Light".

All objects are composed of atoms. The space between the atoms is far greater than the size of the atoms themselves. Consequently all matter is comprised primarily of empty space.

Atoms widely intersperse the space. Solid objects are therefore more space than "solid ".

Our imperfect senses create the illusion of solid matter!

Today we are going to get quite philosophical in our meditation. Keep a journal of your thoughts and insights to the questions posited below. In fact write down the questions on cards that you can carry with you and keep a notebook handy for any insights you get. There are no right or wrong answers, so do not feel challenged. This exercise is a blank canvas on which you can create any form that you wish and whatever you create, will be perfect! You may even surprise yourself at the ideas you come up with. Be open to all possibilities no matter how absurd. And have fun!

To begin, let me summarize some of the ideas presented so far:

o   Everything is energy.
o   Energy is light.
o   Nothing is solid it only appears so.
o   Therefore all is an illusion.
o   All experience of the external exists within the internal (that is the mind).
o   To understand what is without, we need to look within.
o   All truth is contained within the mind for nothing can exist if the mind does not experience it.
o   A "Great Mind" sustains the energy of creation, without which the "Great Thought", that is the energy that forms the "All That Is" could not exist.

Meditate on this today and write your thoughts and insights to each of the following issues:

o   Your entire visual perception, that is everything you see, is your personal creation. All your senses, especially sight, exist only in your mind.
o   Consider what and whose thought process sustains the objects you perceive as outside of you. Who is the seer behind the "I".
o   When you are not conscious, as in sleep, who is doing the seeing? When you meditate and all those thoughts rush in and create turmoil in your mind stop thinking and try to observe where those thoughts arise. Ask yourself as each thought arises, who is doing the thinking and who is seeing?
o   Think about where the energy of the universe, that which sustains all creation, arises. And what it is.
o   Consider the nature and characteristics of the Universal thought. What and whose thoughts sustain you in your existence? Where do thoughts come from and where do they go?
o   Knowing that everything you see exists only in your mind, what relationship does your mind have with that of the Creator

of the universe? Consider that He is engaged in similar creative thinking as you now are. What becomes of your thoughts? Consider the durability of your thoughts. Can they be destroyed?

o Human beings are energy beings, and your physically solid appearance is an illusion. Consider what manner of energy being you are consider what form you might exist in the mind of the Creator. Remember that energy is eternal.

o Take into account that your creative energy is the same "stuff" as the Universal creative energy, so what creative potential do you imagine you have that perhaps you have not yet developed?

o If a Divine Mind has created the All That Is, where is this Mind? Where in time and space does the product of Its creation exist? What rules might apply to you in being a part of this creation? What could your relationship be to this Creative Mind?

o Reflect on the statements "I Am that which I Am" and "I Am That, which I Am".

Be alert. You may get insights when you are distracted during a break at work etc. so keep a notebook handy. Have fun and see what you get. Remember there are no wrong answers. Challenge your friends to voice their opinions on any of these questions and note their thoughts and comments.

Throughout the day you should observe the world and you should be conscious that you are intimately connected to all and everyone that you see.

Remind yourself of the lack of substance and solidity everything has and therefore all that you lay your eyes upon is not what it appears to your eyes. It is an illusion.

When you look at things and feel things, notice what they feel like and then look at them. Look at them as if for the first time. And marvel that they are no more than a shadow. They are emptiness with just the slightest trace of solid matter. They are pure light in motion. It is a hologram.

Then look at people you know and apply the same thought.

—

Visualization Exercise XI - Review

To gain that which is worth having, it may be necessary to lose everything else. - Bernadette Devlin (Politician)

We will do review exercises this week.

The concepts within this book are circular. That is, as they come around again and again, they are presented with slight changes between the first presentation of an idea and the next.

This is intentional. The repetition of concepts and the repeated use of key phrases are much like reading any educational text. If you were reading about how to be a better golfer you would have repeated reference to swing, balance, poise, greens and so on.

It is too easy for a reader to mentally reject an idea, or to miss a concept and then to loose the meaning of a lesson. Repetition in the form it is used here is intended to keep the reader reminded, in a slightly different context or manner each time, until you are comfortable with the concepts and they sit comfortably in your consciousness. In this way you can assimilate the material without rejection or distraction.

To begin, please re- read chapter one. You were asked to record your reaction to the opening statement:

"My whole existence is an illusion ". Once more, please note your response to this idea.

Compare how this opening statement feels to you now at this point and note your thoughts.

In the second chapter, I mentioned that there is only one TRUTH, which has been presented thousands of times by many saints, seers, holy texts and the like.

The message of Truth is repetitive throughout this book. The TRUTH is stated and restated repeatedly in a hundred different ways but it always comes back to the same message of TRUTH.

Go to your quiet spot where no one will disturb you for a half an hour or so.

Take your journal, and review your notes and update your feelings and thoughts that you have today. Consider what insights you have had and how you may have changed.

After that is done, still your mind and do the clearing breaths twenty times. Consider as you look slowly about you, that everything you see is not separate from you but within you. Try to feel the experience of your being one with everything. Adjust to the reality - that in spite of a lifetime of being told by your brain that reality exists outside of your body - you can now see that nothing exists for you outside of yourself.

Close your eyes and quietly think of the past and about how your mind has been creating experiences and telling you that these experiences exist independently of, and outside yourself.

Think about your experiences over the past weeks and how your perception of self has changed or has otherwise been affected.

Review in your mind the various experiences you have had. See how your entire life has really been created by you. Take responsibility for all the things you have manifested happening in your life.

Know that your entire life up to this moment in time is but a reflection of your past thoughts about life.

Know, too, that the thoughts that you have today will create the life you live tomorrow.

Realize that even in the very moment that you remember, indeed in the very act of remembering - that you are engaged in recreating them anew in your mind, exactly as you did the first time you had the experience!

Visualize your mind as the film on which you have created the images of your life. Everything outside of you is the flickering screen that you project your mental images onto. This is the screen which, in the past, you have credited as being real.

All you now see is your own mind reflected back at you.

Note these facts:

That all you have ever created in your life is a product of your mind.

Everything you have created in your life continues to exist in your mind.

All your experiences exist in your mind simultaneously, side by side, irrespective of when they happened in your life. This means that your mind is the home of all your experiences. It is the seat of your

247

reality, your memories, and the creator of your present and your future.

All time therefore exists only in the present

All experience exists simultaneously in your mind in the here and now. Outside of time as we know it.

In this way all of creation exists simultaneously in the mind of the Creator.

What conclusions can you draw about the meaning of time?

Does time have a beginning and an end?

Furthermore, take into account that since all things exist in the here and now, and all possible outcomes have already been determined, in manifesting your life the way you want it to be, you can attract what you want into your life because in a sense it is already here.

What you need to do is make the right choice and call it to you and it must come.

—

Thirty Day Visualization and Release

Happiness is not a possession to be prized, it is a quality of thought, a state of mind. - Daphne du Maurier (English Author)

Keep your journal close at hand. Seated in your meditation space relax. Breathe in deeply and immediately release your breath for twenty cycles of connected breaths.

This is going to be a daily meditation, morning and evening for thirty days.

All the exercises over the past weeks have been in preparation for this day.

You are now familiar with the process of taking responsibility for creating your own reality and in recognizing how your thought / creative process manifests.

You have created a meditation space. This is a place of solitude and safety in which to sit quietly in meditation and to visualize – without being disturbed. Know that you are nurtured and safe.

As realistically as you can remember some really stressful situations that you have experienced. Perhaps a traumatic confrontation with another individual, or a speeding violation, an accident, or any situation that raised your blood pressure, produced fear and got your adrenaline pumping. Mentally recreate exactly how you felt at that time.

With your eyes closed allow the sights, sounds, smells, touch, taste, words and emotions to flow effortlessly into your mind. Experience those feelings.

You may feel your anxiety level rise, your breathing intensify and your muscles tighten, exactly as they originally did when you first had the encounter.

Remember that you are safe.

We will release the trauma of those past events that have never left us, even since birth.

Unresolved conflicts and traumas tend to repeat themselves in cycles. These cycles, which, if not resolved and recognized for what they are, will continue to repeat themselves in various guises and forms throughout ones days in an endless series of life defeating events.

You are going to look for patterns of behavior and deep-seated thoughts in your life that you may have never admitted existed to anyone - least of all yourself!

When you recognize your deepest fears and the self defeating thoughts you will enable yourself to observe how such thoughts keep you stuck in ways that are inimical to your well being.

You will see that the same deep-rooted thought takes on various manifestations and guises as it reappears throughout your life and keeps happiness, success and full aliveness an elusive goal.

Keep accurate notes and be honest with yourself about your true feelings.

Remembering when you first experienced the particular feelings are key elements to the success of this healing and for the rebirth of your spirit. You may have to spend several days remembering, reliving and repeating these difficult or painful events. Time is of no concern. Take as long as you need. Old habits can be stubborn and hard to break.

Do not force anything, chip away at your feelings and deal with them at a level that is comfortable to you. Each day a little more may be revealed.

Sitting quietly, remind yourself again that nothing in your life or your experience has ever existed outside of you. Without your mind as the observer and the interpreter of your thoughts there is no reality. Reality is within you. You are safe.

When meditating, and those thoughts come rushing in, I like to remind myself;

"Don't train. Don't strain. Just be."

Soon your mind will become calmer.

Remind yourself that it is safe for you to relive all past fears and emotions. You are in complete control as you peel away only those layers of traumatic memories and thought that you are presently comfortable with doing so. Tomorrow and the next day you can peel away additional layers until you find the original - sponsoring - thought.

The sponsoring thought is the negative thought that originally arose in your mind about yourself or about a situation in your early formative years. A sponsoring thought can be created as early as birth and possibly in pre-birth. This original thought created a negative impression of yourself or of the world that has remained deep in your sub-conscious ever since.

A negative sponsoring thought has the ability to bend all your subsequent thoughts to align with its concept of life, safety and well-being. Thereafter, submerged in your unconscious, the sponsoring thought rests like a computer virus. It affects all subsequent thoughts. It puts a hidden message in all the thoughts and experiences that follow. This affects how you feel about yourself, your life, and your relationships.

Later in this chapter I deal with some of the types of negative thoughts that constitute a sponsoring thought. A negative sponsoring thought may be called a personal lie. It is called this because we believe this thought about ourselves to be true even though it is not. Buried within our unconscious, it is a computer virus, or more aptly a computer worm, that burrows into our deepest mental programming files and there hidden from our awareness, it directs and controls our lives. It has immense power to affect control over our emotions, our self-esteem, success, relationships and prosperity.

Therefore it is essential for you to be honest and accurate in your note keeping when you record your thoughts and feelings.

Bear in mind that all life experiences are created within your mind - so you are responsible for everything you have attracted to yourself as well as for how you have allowed circumstances to affect your life even unto today.

Blame no one. Absolutely no one! And especially do not blame yourself. This is not about finding fault. There is no right or wrong.

Everything "Just IS", neither good nor bad, so do not be in judgment of anything or anyone, least of all yourself.

Be in a state of grace and acceptance and have a willingness to release and forgive all past experiences and thoughts for the highest good of all concerned.

For example, let's say that you were abused as a child. Do not say, "I cannot help being like I am because I was abused as a child". Do not use the excuse of being a victim as a way out of not taking responsibility for your life. As improbable, and as difficult as it may seem, acknowledge that there are no victims in life. At some unconscious level, conceivably even from a past life, you had to have the experience that you did, just as much as the abuser needed to have the experience that he did of being abusive.

In a sense two minds have come together, as if by mutual consent, to create a process that, with consciousness a spiritual healing of both parties can be effected.

I know that this point of view may offend the sensibilities, but bear with the process for now and accept this as a working hypothesis.

Typically, the trauma of early life pervades the unconscious mind and then repeats throughout the rest of ones life. When we learn to recognize the thought that controls us we can begin to forgive ourselves as well as those party to this condition, and true healing can begin to take place.

Only then do we cease seeing ourselves as victims and we create a healing new thought about ourselves.

As you created your thoughts, so you can UNCREATE YOUR THOUGHTS.

One of the worst traumas in my life was losing my father at the young age of thirteen. My father was a young man of forty-eight years when he died and I had just had my thirteenth birthday.

I remember my father very fondly as a gentle and kind man with a twinkle in his eye, a quick sense of humor and the manners and demeanor of a gentleman.

When he died I was just becoming aware of my father as a person and a personality.

Prior to that he was just my father who was sometimes here and at other times away on business. He was always doing things either for business or around the home. My father always had projects. He did paintings that adorned the walls of our house; he invented new products for his factory. Other times he was busy building additions and renovating the house. And when he was not doing that he was at the country club on the weekends or having guests for dinner and friends over for drinks.

Thirteen was a very critical time for me as an adolescent boy. Along with all the bodily and hormonal and personality changes attendant to puberty, I did not have a true sense of self.

My parents took care of everything for me. Life held no concerns or fear for me. There were no unknowns for me, as a child, when I was growing up.

To me my home was always a place of safety and predictability. Nothing bad ever happened in my world. But all that was to change with an earthquake of unpredictability on a warm summer day in November in Johannesburg, South Africa.

When I lost my father it was with a suddenness of unreality that overwhelmed my senses. It was a beautiful weekend. In the morning my father had gone to a country club to play lawn bowls as he often did on weekends. By the afternoon we were rushed to meet him at a country hospital. We arrived there just as my father, sweating and gray, was being wheeled into the hospital emergency room. It was a heart attack. The thought that this was a fatal heart condition was far removed from my reality.

So when the nurse took me away from my mother and other family members who were gathered in one room, and she gave me a pill to swallow, I still did not register what was going on around me. The nurse proceeded to tell me about her life and that how, when she was a young girl, she had lost her father. I could not understand why she was telling me this. I was not making the connection at all. The thought that my father was in the next door room and that he was dying was beyond my comprehension. Everyone knew what was happening except me.

Try as she did, nothing could have prepared me for the news when another nurse entered the room and told me that my father had passed away.

In that terrible moment my mind melted and I went totally weak with feelings of complete and utter desolation and disempowerment. I felt helpless, angry, cheated, resentful and victimized.

I cried and implored the doctors not to give up. I begged them, tears streaming down my face and salty on my lips, to go back and to try again. Save my father. Do something I implored! They did nothing. I do not recall them expressing their condolences to me, alone in that little room. Perhaps they did. I don't know.

Life, I concluded later, was not fair. I blamed the doctors for what I perceived as their incompetence. Later I also blamed my father's business for the stress that killed him. I berated myself for having not got to know him better before he died. For thinking that he would always be around. I felt responsible in some way for allowing him to die. I truly believed that this could not be happening to me. Life had punished me so unfairly. Where was justice? Where was God? Why am I being punished? I do not deserve to be a victim of this outrageous conspiracy! I was mad and helpless. I felt that I was a weakling because I was unable to do a thing, not the smallest thing to save my father. I could not change this cruel turn of events. I could not find anyone who could help me change a single darn thing and who could do anything about it.

Thus I was traumatized in one cruel, heartbreaking summer afternoon. No one could bind my wound, or offer me solace or comfort. I was swept away in a gale of thoughts, dark clouds of despair and heaving tides of resentment.

The result of this trauma, as I subsequently have discovered, is that I created a twelve to thirteen year pattern of self-sabotage. Each cycle ended with a major loss and a consequent change in my life.

The upshot was that I created problems with loss. Because my father died suddenly, I had not had time to prepare for completion with him. My subliminal thought, that is my personal lie, was that when you get too close or too attached it leads to loss. So for many years, getting too close or too attached without loss was an issue for me.

Of course I was not conscious of this aspect of my own psyche.

At about age twenty-four, I quit my job because I was fed up. The result was that I started with a very small firm and almost immediately, that is within a few months my boss died. His partner was mugged shortly after and lost his eyesight in one eye and quit. I was left alone with my boss's secretary and two office workers to run the business.

So I began my new twelve to thirteen year cycle. I was very successful and I bought out the surviving partner. I achieved substantial success in my field of business and financial wealth started to follow.

At about age thirty-six, I lost almost everything in an economic collapse of the economy in South Africa. The banks failed and had to be bailed out by the reserve bank and the South African currency collapsed. This prompted me to leave the country a year later and to come to the USA and begin again in a more stable environment. Again, I built myself up from scratch and I had several business ventures, a restaurant, retail stores and a travel agency. At age forty-nine (my father was almost forty-nine when he died) I was at home when I had a spontaneous near-death experience. I had never heard of anything like this happening to anyone and I had no point of reference. Feelings of futility and despair filled my mind and my inner self screamed for God to take me. I saw that I could choose at that point to leave this earth and that my passing would be blamed on a heart attack, just like my father had at that same age. I felt in that moment that I was ready to leave. I experienced my body functions slowing shutting down. Darkness, very calm and peaceful crept through me. My limbs lost feeling as my life urge withdrew in the face of advancing shadow. Starting from the extremities of my body sensation ceased and cool numbness crept very silently and restfully, most welcome up my torso. My breath was shallow, less than a whisper and my heart a slight tremor, nothing more. It was almost done. Then in that last and final moment I realized that I had one ultimate choice, to shut down all bodily functions and depart or I could step back from the edge of the abyss.

I had no experience in these matters, and the thought of leaving was a siren song in my ears calling me onwards. I had a strange thought in that split second. I thought that when I am gone no one would know that I chose to go willingly and of my own accord. Friends and family will be thinking that I died like my father did.

I could envisage my eulogy and people tut-tutting and saying what a tragedy my passing was. He was so young. This raised feelings of tremendous rebellion in me. I thought that I couldn't leave a legacy of such a falsehood concerning my death! Here was my second chance. The one that I never had when I was a child and my father died. I was being offered the opportunity to say no to death and to choose life! Here was the wrong to be corrected that I could not right previously. Now, finally, I could take charge of my own death and make a choice.

That meant that I could affirm my own life if I so chose to.

Here at the brink is salvation and renewal. The universe was giving me a chance to correct my wrongful thinking. Suddenly it was clear to me. I understood. Here was a message in the lesson before me. There is an entire dimension of awareness that I must master on this earth and in this lifetime. There are doors of perception, and I vowed to devote my rebirth to finding those doors of perception and to open them.

And thus I began my new journey into affirming my own immortality and the validation of my life.

Although I had no awareness at that time that I had cycles to my life, that came later, it was nevertheless clear to me that I had created my life. I am not a victim.

Prior to the present, each time my cycle manifested, the circumstances surrounding it were different. I was not cognizant of the linkage or of a pattern until I started to do spiritual work on myself in my search for a higher reality. Once I observed the pattern I saw that I could also forgive myself for creating it.

Thus I was able to bring it out into the openness of my reality. Knowing the cause, I could then disempower the thought and change my life.

One can never experience REALITY by reinforcing a negative thought about oneself. Similarly by placing blame outside of oneself one also cannot find reality.

Rather ask yourself, "Why did I create this situation in my life"? And "Who experiences this life of mine"?

Consider this form of self-inquiry when you meditate and when your mind gets filled with all sorts of distractions. Release the distractions as soon as they pop into your mind and examine them by asking yourself, "Who is doing the experiencing?" "Where does this thought arise and who sees it?".

Without forcing an answer, and without training or straining, just be. Let answers and thoughts flow without judgment in your mind, and constantly bring your focus back on track.

When one is asking to be shown ones personal lie, you are looking for the thought that exists behind the thoughts that arise in your mind.

Ask your higher self as you meditate that you might be shown the thought behind the clutter of meaningless thoughts and focus on seeing that. Mentally ask yourself, "What is my true thought about (subject)" You may say, for example, "If I knew what my true thought was about having a loving relationship what would it be"? Or, "If I knew what my true thought was that is blocking my financial success, what would it be"?

Do not judge your thoughts with further thoughts such as, "no that cannot be" or "that thought must be wrong" etc.

Often when thoughts arise in your mind spontaneously the chances are that those first thoughts are probably correct. So pay attention to them and note them in your journal.

You may have thoughts such as:

My parents never wanted me.
I am bad.
I am not worthy.
I cannot trust myself.
I am always wrong.
I am weak.
I hurt people.
If I express myself people will get mad at me.
My being born was wrong.
I should be dead.
I am wrong.

Such thoughts are typical of personal lies. They are the thoughts that keep you stuck by your repeating old habits that no longer work for you. If you are to break these old habits that have been with you all your life, then you need to release the sponsoring thought behind them.

Release the personal lie and see it as the untruth that it is. Forgive yourself for holding that thought. Do not make yourself wrong for having had it. You must replace it with a new thought through the repeated use of positive release affirmations every day and at every possible opportunity.

—

<u>Release Affirmations</u>

If one is lucky, a solitary fantasy can totally transform one million realities. - Maya Angelou - (American Writer)

Instruction: This is to be done during your morning and evening meditation and at every opportunity you have every day for at least a week and longer if need be.

This process is divided into two parts. The First Process is an Empowerment Affirmation. This is used to empower you and to raise your awareness of struggle and confrontation in the moment that it occurs thereby enabling you to change your thought about conflict immediately.

You may use this process simultaneously with the Second Process.

The Second Process is the heavyweight process that is the Release Process. The Release Process is addressed at the serious core issues of the personal lies that are blocking your happiness and your ability to manifest your life as you would have it be.

<u>First Process - Empowerment</u>

Begin by reminding yourself that your whole life is a reflection of your mind and your thoughts about life generally. Consequently your thoughts have created the job, family, and life that you are currently having.

As an example:

If one has a thought that life is difficult, life is a struggle then you believe that you do not deserve to have ease. As long as you have to struggle you are able to vindicate your belief that life is hard and that you have to be in struggle in order to survive. Therefore you get to prove yourself right every time!

The opposite of this is to affirm:

"I, (your name) deserve ease and sweetness in my life. God and the universe support me to easily experience, sweetness, joy, success and love. I am willing to give up resistance and struggle in my life knowing that I am always supported."

You would then write your affirmation on some cards and keep them on your computer, dashboard, mirror, and in your pocket and repeat it all the time in your mind like a mantra. When you are not concentrating on a task at hand repeat this affirmation or mantra.

The first time you use an affirmation repeat it aloud a few times. Then repeat it silently and feel how it sits in your consciousness. It is like breaking in a new pair of shoes.

Practice using it for at least a week with special emphasis on a 20 to 30 minute meditation on the affirmation in the morning and in the evening. It is important in the meditation to go beyond merely repeating the mantra like a parrot. Visualize yourself as an energy magnet attracting to you the vision that you have of your life working the way you want it to be.

If you hit a tough situation at anytime in the course of the day, stop and do a reality check. Whatever situation you are in when a tough situation arises cut your thoughts about struggle dead right then and there. You could be on the phone, at work, with your kids, dealing with the public service, contractors, employees, boss, etc. and feelings or thoughts of frustration, defeat and struggle rising in your mind, immediately cut these thoughts dead and affirm to yourself:

"I choose support, joy and ease in all situations. I release all struggle"

Replace the negative situation right away with a short positive affirmation, otherwise you are going to go into your old pattern of thinking that you have to prove that you need to struggle and that you do not deserve ease. Cultivate the thought that, *"I (name) am a winner. I always win"*.

As soon as possible after the tough situation, take a deep breath, relax and exhale all the negative energy and repeat your main affirmation that in this example is:

"I, (your name) deserve ease and sweetness in my life. God and the universe support me to easily experience, sweetness, joy, success and love. I am willing to give up resistance and struggle in my life knowing that I am always supported."

(The above affirmation; *I, (your name) deserve ease and sweetness in my life"* can also be your personal mantra, as can the affirmation *"I (name) am a winner. I always win"*. However I prefer that you use it as a precursor to your main larger mantra for at least the first week.

Once you feel that you have begun to release thoughts of struggle and you feel that you have shifted the energy of defeat and struggle, say after a week, then you can use the above, shorter affirmation for the rest of your life as a maintenance tool)

If you want to change the syntax of the affirmation to better suit how you would choose to express it, that is fine too.

An affirmation is really a personal declaration to all the powers that be. Therefore it has to fit well, like a comfy shoe, so that you can say it and mean it. This means that you say it with a level of conviction and familiarity with your own voice so that it does not jar in your mind when you do so.

Usually when I work with someone we try out several different ways of expressing an affirmation.

We will say it out aloud and write it out on paper, then modify it and rewrite it again and again until the person says, "Yes, that way feels right in my body".

Here are some examples of alternative affirmations also dealing with creating ease in ones life. You may prefer to use one of these. See which one fits best, or create your own.

I, (your name), am a sweet and loving person. I am worthy of receiving total joy, love and ease in all things in my life. I embrace life knowing that I fully deserve complete support, ease and success with joy and love in everything that I do.

I, (your name), am completely supported by the Universe (God). I now choose to have ease, support, love and joy in all aspects of my life, knowing that I am worthy of this and that I deserve it all.

The thing to take note of is that in an affirmation all reference to the negative is avoided.

I never, ever use negative thoughts.

For example in a wellness affirmation I would never use a reference that indicates that the patient is anything less than perfect and whole and well.

For example I might say, *"I (name) am a vibrant, whole and healthy person, full of life etc."*

I <u>would not say</u>, *"I (name) see myself as healed of this disease and I see myself as well...etc)"*.

The difference being that the first affirmation is completely full of vitality and aliveness in which we embrace a whole and healed vision of the person within the affirmation.

In the second <u>incorrect</u> affirmation we are dwelling on what is wrong and we are affirming that something needs to be healed.

Selecting a good, healing and life affirming affirmation is somewhat of an art.

<u>Second Process - Release</u>

This process deals with the release from our imprinted memory of lifelong issues about our worthiness as individuals such as those I listed at the end of the previous chapter viz.:

My parents never wanted me.
I am bad.
I am not worthy.
I cannot trust myself.
I am always wrong.
I am weak.
I hurt people.
If I express myself people will get mad at me.
My being born was wrong.
I should be dead.
I am wrong.

This second process requires that we do more than just the daily affirmation.

You not only need to be mindful about your thoughts, replacing the negative with the positive, as per the above set of affirmations, but you need to change your cellular imprints.

We need to do a complete mental house cleaning. These thoughts are not only in your mind, directing all that you do; they are imprinted in your body at a cellular level, as a cell memory.

Whatever it is that you feel is not working for you in your life you can start turning it around today.

Are you co-dependent on others? Perhaps your adult relationships have never worked. Are you creating abuse in your life? Are you transferring this pattern of abuse to those around you or to your family? Are you a drug dependent person? Do you feel unwanted or unworthy?

These are the types of thoughts that you must be prepared to honestly face up to and be prepared to deal with them openly and without self-judgment. The level, with which you are prepared to admit to yourself that you have these thoughts or feelings and patterns of behavior, will determine the success of your healing the pattern and moving on with your life.

When you analyze yourself, look for repeated patterns of conduct and of cause and effect. Especially try to find the root of the problem by looking for the first time it occurred. Ask yourself why have you attracted that behavior or event into your life. How did you feel about yourself prior to that happening? How did you feel about yourself afterwards? What thought did you have about yourself that you got to prove right by having this happen or by indulging in these actions? How do you feel about yourself now?

Why do you think you felt it necessary to create that situation happening in your life? How would you be better if you could release that event or un-create it in your life? Are you truly willing to release and to live without it? What thought do you have about yourself would you have to give up in order to achieve the change you desire? Are you willing and ready to do so now?

Keep detailed notes of every session. Write down your thoughts as they occur to you and then continue the process.

Refer to your notes frequently for further insights.

Once you have identified your personal lie(s) (you probably have several) then you need to work on releasing each one separately. It is good to note your personal lies and to deal with them one at a time before moving on to the next one.

We need to release personal lies. In doing so it is useful to call on Divinity for a healing.

When we call on the universe with sincerity and conviction and when we display a willingness to be healed, the intention behind prayer can create a powerful manifestation, or energy to go out into the ether for the purpose of healing. It does not require a belief in God for healing to happen.

The nature of the universe is such that powerful intention can create its own result. This is demonstrated in your having created the condition that you now wish to heal. So now you can un-create it using the same energy that you have always called upon. This time you are doing it with intent and with awareness and power.

Here is an example of a *Release Affirmation* below.

State your personal lie then say, (do this aloud if possible):

"I call upon God (Jesus, Buddha, Divine Consciousness, My Higher Self) for a healing of this condition. I wish to report an injustice in my life that requires righting immediately. This (thought about / situation concerning) no longer serves me. I therefore choose to un-create it and the remove the effect of it in my life now.

I am releasing this situation unto the Divine pure energy from which it came. I now release my attachment to and my thought about (specify exact thought, situation, persons name, event, feeling etc.) to the highest good of all concerned where the Divine will transmute it into pure light and it shall be with me no more. For this release and for the healing of all damage done, I thank God. I resolve to forgive myself and I forgive all parties concerned (you can name the parties concerned) for thinking that we could be hurt. I am grateful for this lesson in my life and I now choose to no longer be at the effect of it. It is healed and it is done. Make it so. So be it"

Now imagine placing the thought or situation that you have just released inside a large pink plastic helium balloon and it is secured tightly therein.

Float the balloon heavenward and see it rise high into the sky towards the sun. As it rises to a great height carrying your problems with it, see it burst into purple all consuming flame.

(If you prefer, you may have bunches of balloons filled with your thoughts float away and flame out. There is an endless supply of balloons so feel free to fill as many as you need.

Write the above *Release Affirmation* on cards and repeat it throughout the day - and keep on releasing those pink balloons at every opportunity - all day long!

As you can see, you create thoughts and your reality so can you un-create those thoughts and change reality too. This process of un-creation / release is very powerful.

What is required is that you recognize all of the issues that come up for you, in all of its forms in your life and be genuinely willing to accept change.

In particular, this requires a genuine call to the Divine, in whatever form that you acknowledge God, and to demand the miracle of release, which you, as a Divine Being, are rightfully entitled to have.

Keep in mind that you are innocent. It is your right as a holy being and as a child of the Divine to demand your release from pain. Afterwards express gratitude for the help that you know without doubt is already on its way to you and that you will receive from the process.

Initially it may not be easy for you to readily accept some of the ideas presented here, especially if you have a lifetime invested in the thought that - all your problems are the result of your being a victim who has no control over his or her life. You are not a victim. Do not embrace victim consciousness. Always keep your mind firmly on the thought that you are innocent. You are forgiven for thinking that you were guilty. You are forgiven for thinking that you had to suffer. You are forgiven for all the suffering you thought that you had to go through.

In Truth you have always been and always are innocent and therefore you are forgiven even before a situation arises for which you imagine that you are guilty and that forgiveness is required.

You have to turn the negative ideas around and chip away at the protective wall you have built up around the beliefs or the situation. Day after day process the above Release Affirmation.

If at first the idea makes no sense to you and you feel the exercise is futile - do not give up - you will grow in strength and confidence each time that you honestly, and without fear, face the problem and resolve to heal it.

Do the Release Affirmation as many times as you can. Repeat it during the day. Every hour or more if you can. Keep in mind that you have spent a lifetime affirming your old negative judgments, so be diligent and know that you cannot fail.

Indeed God has been waiting your entire life for this opportunity to set you free. Go forward with confidence and know that God wants nothing less for you than what you want for yourself.

With God on your side you cannot fail, so start creating miracles in your life now!

The more you do this process, the stronger will be the energy that you build for your healing process and the stronger the power for positive change in your life.

The force for release will intensify as your attitude changes to your vision of the new, healed you.

Think of how much energy you expended in the old ways that did not work. Bear in mind how many years you invested in building your negative thoughts and giving away your power.

Now all is changed. Work diligently to build the energy required in order to remove the negative thoughts once and for all.

As an incentive you can remind yourself what the alternative is if you stay invested in keeping the negative thought and the old pattern of behavior alive.

Do not indulge in self-pity. Replace that with the practice of forgiveness.

Your notebook is a vital tool. Record all your feelings and personal issues that come up for you. Note which thoughts and memories continue to feel unresolved.

Work on those thoughts again and again in your future exercises until you feel that you have reached a point where you have resolution.

When you review your notes look for similarities of behavior and emotional reactions and feelings related to different experiences that you have had - both in the past and recently.

Look for similarities and the causes and effects of important issues in your life and attempt to identify similar patterns.

Look for the reasons why certain things happened to you then try to see if they have anything in common with one another.

Look for similarities of outcomes or results to various events in your life in order to establish patterns of behavior.

Identify common emotional trigger points such as anger, feelings of rejection, rage, helplessness etc. It is important to recognize these so that you to gain your freedom from old ways of thinking that no longer serve you.

Old trigger patterns and responses keep you out of being truly alive and aware!

Continue the exercises as often as possible, stay with one theme or problem until you feel that you have released it completely and that you are able to move on and that the event no longer has control over you.

Keep going until you loose your attachment to all the thoughts that are keeping you stuck.

Then you can truly forgive all parties concerned, including yourself.

Ten Declarations

- o I alone create my Reality. I am safe in this world and I am protected at all times.
- o I accept responsibility for all that I create in my life. I am a holy being and one with my Father and all things.
- o Fear is the result of my feeling separate from God. I am one with God now and forever.
- o FEAR cannot exist where there is TRUTH and LIGHT. I am the Light and the Truth.
- o I choose TRUTH and LIGHT in my life. I am worthy of Divine bliss and happiness.
- o I release all negative thoughts and situations for the highest good to be transmuted into pure light. I am safe and loved. I am successful.
- o My TRUTH is that I am holy and of Divine Energy and Light. I deserve love and happiness. I am innocent.
- o All my thoughts are created in TRUTH and LOVE and LIGHT. I am one with the Universe.
- o I am Divine, Eternal, Indestructible, and a Conscious Being of Light. I am worthy of love.
- o God and I are ONE. I am worthy of all the highest blessings of life. I always win.

Note that the "I am" statement in any affirmation is an important component of your statement to the Universe of your intent to manifest whatever thought follows the "I am" statement.

The nature of the Divine is; "I am That, That I am".

Jeffrey M. Solomon

Chapter Eleven – Your Divine Purpose

Fortunately, in her kindness and patience, Nature has never put the fatal question as to the meaning of their lives into the mouths of most people. And where no one asks, no one needs to answer - Carl Jung (Swiss Psychologist)

<u>Un-creating the Illusion I</u>

The soul that has no established aim loses itself - Michel De Montaigne (French Moralist)

In truth the answer is so simple - you would not accept it. It is too easy.

In truth – (for TRUTH is all there is) - If you do not live in Truth then you must live in the opposite, which is Fear. (You have the right to choose which).

TRUTH states that if every person would realize that the Great Illusion exists because it is the collective illusion created and sustained by every one, and if we all recognized that the Creative Divine Energy within each of us forms every thought even before we can think it, - Then:

THE COLLECTIVE ILLUSION COULD BE DISEMPOWERED!

Through the collective will we could remove and disempower corrupt political leaders.

We could remove weapons and diseases from the earth.

With the Creative Thought process we could use the conscious spirit of mankind to create the most beautiful and harmonious world we can imagine. A world where conscious Divine thought and not fear, will be the guiding principle for mankind.

Harnessing the Divinity within us would release the power of thinking in a trained and aware manner resulting in a aware world devoid of fear and in which souls would incarnate for an experience of pure love for the joy of creative Holy manifestation.

We can move the earth itself, when we evolve into a higher form of Being, devoid of destructive tendencies and trusting implicitly in the immutability of the eternal spirit which is within ourselves.

Reaching within ourselves we shall find a place of pure divine bliss, an oasis from the confusion and horror of the outside world, where resides our Divinity waiting to be revealed, and readily accessible to us.[*]

---

[*] *There is more wisdom in your body than in your deepest philosophy - Friedrich Wilhelm Nietzsche (German Philosopher)*

We should become resolutely responsive in every moment of the day to the idea that we are an indivisible part of God. In every second you are never alone. All that is, resides within you permanently, you can never be divided. Happiness, peace, contentment, confidence, calm, love and success are with you always.

The dichotomy is that you exist concurrently both outside this world and within it. You have only but to tap into the higher source within to realize that only you suppress the Divine attributes that are in you, and you alone can release them.

People should establish groups of like-minded persons to regularly meet with the intention of expanding knowledge in a conscious and creative endeavor to transform the world.

By projecting affirmative thoughts and by envisaging positive earth changes, you can change the fabric of creation. You can by design conceive with intention, for the highest good.

Your group can act in mercy to transmit healing energy to disaster victims. They can work at sending positive restorative energy into polluted areas of the earth and to the people who are responsible for pollution.

Dispatch thoughts of peace to conflict situations between nations and particularly to world leaders.

Send light to people in hospital and in old age homes, and love to the bereaved. The catalog of compassionate actions in which you can engage your group is limitless. You do not have to meet physically if you so choose. You can come to an understanding to engage in perform affirmations and manifestation at an agreed time, from your own homes and do it! Or if you do have meetings and someone cannot make it, they can still join in the group and add their energy from a distance.

Part of the time that you devote to healing and visualization of the planet should also be used for the advancement and betterment of the group members as well.

Anything that you wish - you can affect through conscious affirmations.

Call God forth from within you to be present in your circle and that His Light illuminates all of you and guide you for the highest good of all concerned.

Our thoughts are indistinguishable from us, likewise is God, who shares our thoughts with us.

Equally, we are all one in the mind of God.

Accordingly we mutually coexist in one another's mind. The One mind.

To articulate it another way, we are God and God is us.[*]

We are One, engaged in multiple experiences of Itself through the many minds of Its entirety.

Each aspect or individual in the entirety has the power to create according to Divinely established laws.

Those who are familiar with the T.V. series Startrek may be familiar with the collective called "The Borg". The thoughts of the many are known by the one and by all. All exists within the Borg. Well imagine a benign Borg that encourages individual thought and achievement and that has only love and joy towards the collective because the collective is the whole.

God did not "put us on earth" in the biblical sense. This implies that we are separate from God. It also implies that there was a time when we were not. God is eternal. We were, are, and always will be one with God. This is the meaning of our eternal soul.

God is here, and we are here, on earth as one Being. Our purpose is God's purpose. Let us fulfill that mission with love and integrity.

Being one with God also puts to rest the untruth that has been perpetrated by religious dogma. The myth of heaven and hell, of judgment day for the sinners and retribution towards the unrepentant serves only the clergy. God does not put Himself through a test to see which of His aspects (souls) deserves to go to heaven and which do not. God does not need to prove anything to Himself. God (us) is perfect and just Is. Why would we think that He would be otherwise?[**]

This misguided notion of God, heaven and hell, is mankind's own creation as a consequence of the many religions that we have invented. It is the cornerstone of our Great Illusion that we, as Divine

---

[*] In the Beatles song "I am the Walrus" the song goes, "I am you and you are me and we are all together". Let your mind be open and sublime messages are seen everywhere even in places that we least expect it!

[**] *Dogma can in no way limit a limitless God.* - Flannery O'Connor (American Writer)

beings, have devised in order to produce disconnection between God and us.

We have also fabricated something we call priests and we have bestowed upon them special powers over us. In our misapprehension, when we perceive ourselves as disconnected from God, we experience ourselves as weak and vulnerable.

At some point in our long forgotten past, mankind elected to renounce from consciousness our direct link to God. We handed over (or were otherwise compelled to relinquish) this power to the clergy to commune on our behalf with God. The clergy now dispense this "communion" as a reward to those who faithfully obeyed its edicts and who contributed financially to the organization.

So long as the clergy have job security and our confidence, they will continue to perform the role that we have bequeathed to them, that of mediators between God and us.

They, too, are performers in the Grand Illusion. Few if any are self-actualized and spiritually advanced. In their position as spiritual leaders they should be enlightened, but mostly, and at best, they are as confused as their flock. At worst, they are guilty of the most heinous and unimaginable crimes in the history of mankind that they perpetrated in the name of God.

Their business of religion is big business. The church in Rome is the largest landowner in all of Europe. In the USA they own the Consolidated Edison utility company and department stores in Chicago. They are one of the largest, investors on Wall Street. During the pedophile cases in the USA wherein members of the clergy had molested young boys, the plaintiffs sued the Boston diocese for $30 million. The church pleaded in mitigation of the claim that it did not have the resources or assets. Upon investigation by the plaintiffs attorneys however, it was found that the Boston diocese alone had $130 million just in property, and that valuation was at tax value, not at sale value which would be significantly higher!

Religion is big business. Many evangelists own T.V. networks, radio stations, land, buildings, art, private airplanes, fleets of vehicles, and trade in financial instruments. They mislead us all when they proclaim that they alone know Gods will and path to salvation and that they hold the key to redemption.

The TRUTH is that the only key they hold is to their safe deposit box.

There is nothing in the world from which we need to be redeemed! God does not need redemption. We do not need saving unless it is to save us from religion.

The notion that we are sinners in need of salvation is a common assertion by many religions.

Another assertion they make is that we are doomed unless we subscribe to their specific faith and their interpretation of Gods will for us, whatever that may be.

This sad exploitation continues to wound and damage many people. Much unnecessary fear and pain are produced especially amongst the poorest and least educated peoples of this world.

Even they are required to tithe to the church in order to save their mortal souls.

Religion is legendary for promoting separation by calling attention to people's differences and by promoting elitism within the flock.

In the radical extremism of fanatical religious doctrine, bloody violence, hatred, division amongst brothers, genocide, rape and war are the consequence of these self-proclaimed emissaries of God.

The record of atrocities that mankind has perpetrated in Gods name is inscribed with innocent blood throughout history.

Religion has done the greatest disservice to our Divine Father. God is One with each of us totally and equally, without judgment or precondition of ethnicity, color, religion, belief or any other qualification imaginable.

One of the most ancient Hebrew prayers is an affirmation and cornerstone of professing the faith. No service is complete without this proclamation.

In the ancient days in medieval Europe this prayer was banned from being recited and congregations had to insert it surreptitiously in the liturgy. It is a powerful and beautiful affirmation in its simplicity and in its strength.

It proclaims, "Shema Yisroel Adonai Elohainu Adonai Echud". "Hear Oh Israel, The Lord our God, the Lord is One". Many rabbis would say that this is an affirmation that there is only one God, and by extension it may be inferred that the Hebrew religion is the true bearer of Gods covenant with Abraham and the Hebrew people, that of mono atheism. Whereas this may be interpreted as an affirmation that there is only one God, I would propose that as in many esoteric matters there is a duality of meaning.

I would infer that, "Hear Oh Israel the Lord our God the Lord is One" has another meaning.

That meaning is the message of this book. That message is that the Lord is indeed One.

God is one with all that is, and all that is, is the One!

We are not proclaiming how many gods there are, but rather that we are proclaiming the *essence* of what it means to be God. It is not a question of *how many* gods there are, but rather a statement that this is *what* God is. God is *One*.

So when we proclaim that the Lord is One we are affirming that all that is, is one, without separation between faiths, species, peoples and philosophies.

They all belong to Him.

The One is all that Is.

As one would plant a thousand varieties of roses and rejoice in the uniqueness of each one, so is our human diversity a source of pleasure and beauty in the world. Through us God experiences pleasure in the diversity of human existence.

Would we deny God the sublime pleasure of His human experience?

How small we are in our thoughts, how far we have yet to go in our evolution from violence and savagery!

o Any religion that denies the spirituality of human beings of another faith is based on FEAR

o Any faith that would purport to be the sole interpreter of the mind and will of God is based on FEAR.

o Any thought system that claims to be the sole source of salvation is based on FEAR.

o Any religion that preaches hurt, humiliation, war and the rejection of another human being must of necessity be based on FEAR

o Any religion that claims to be the only true faith is based on FEAR.

o   Any religion that omits to preach UNCONDITIONAL love, acceptance and respect for all of humanity is of necessity be based on FEAR.
o   Any religion that does not recognize the inherent equality of all expressions of faith is based on separation from God.
o   Any religion that has a desire to proselytize must inherently view itself as superior to other faiths and in doing so it promotes separation which is Fear.

The only redemption we need, if indeed we need any form of redemption at all, is deliverance from the Great Illusion of our separation from God. Remember, God has been around a lot longer than theology.

Brooks Atkinson, an American essayist once noted, rather cynically, "I have no objection to churches so long as they do not interfere with God's work"

The above guide is useful in evaluating the message of any place of worship, and I would choose that as my criteria before I would entered any congregation and felt comfortable.

There are many universal churches today that promote spirituality, as opposed to religion. I would say that as long as you can find God within your faith, or your particular place of worship, and whatever practices work for you, carry on and enjoy!

All rivers lead to the ocean; what does it matter the route they take?

God wants us to come back to our senses.

God wants what we want for ourselves. If we are honest and listen to our heart, what we desire is the best of all things sacred. These sacred things are:

UNCONDITIONAL LOVE
TRUTH from Spiritual realization
WISDOM that comes from a knowing of ones inner-self
COMPASSION for all life and charitable deeds towards others
HAPPINESS as an inner reflection of our true self
HEALTH
SECURITY in the knowledge of who we truly are
ABUNDANCE of all manner of life's blessings

And all things that is a reflection of your highest thought about yourself and does no harm.

You already have all the above, right now, within you. Just give up the Great Illusion. Start making out your wish list now!

There is no secret formula to achieving God realization that you cannot do immediately, without years of training.

To reach that space of inner peace you must go within.

This is the greatest teaching of all the sages and teachers.

To go within means to still the clutter of your mind and to be present in your body now.

One can study all ones life and read thousands of sacred texts.

I began this chapter with the opening sentence;

"In TRUTH the answer is so simple - you would not accept it. It is too easy."

Before I could present you with this *simple truth,* that you likely would have rejected, I had to accompany it with a complicated explanation, for such is our human nature that we do not readily accept the simple.

Our natural inclination is to say that there *must* be more to it than that. Therefore scholars will take this simple truth, which is the core of all spirituality, and they will create a theology around it. Then they will create a dogma and before you know it, they have created a religion with a multitude of texts and commentaries that it requires a university degree in comparative religions to understand it.

Yet to know what Christ, Buddha and Krishna were all saying takes just one breath!

Let your mind be still to the chatter of the illusion. *Don't strain. Don't train. Just be.*

Be still in the quiet of your body and your mind and know that God is within you, closer to you than your own skin!

To paraphrase the Buddha, listen to your own breath and be still. As you concentrate on the calm of your own breath in the here and now, know that in this instant in time all that exists for you is now. Do not think of the past. It is gone it does not exist. Do not think of the future, it does not exist. Your entire reality at each and every instant is right here, right now. All else is an illusion.

Therefore be in yourself now for that is where the ray of God light is shining to get in. Do not draw the drapes of consciousness with the useless chatter of your mind. It tries to remind you of all the worries you are supposed to have, used to have, or may have in the future. Do not block the light of God within you with meaningless thoughts. In this very instant, unless you are in a car heading for a precipice, there is nothing that can hurt you. There is nothing that you can do about the past it is gone, forget about it. Forget about revenge, past hurt, past failure and what might have been. Forget that there ever was a past.

When Maher Baba came out of years of self imposed silence he was greeted by a crowd who was anxious to hear what inner wisdom he had gained. He gave a big grin to the expectant crowd and said, "Don't worry. Be Happy", and he went back inside.

Buddha was asked for the secret to enlightenment. The crowd expected a long discourse from him. He replied simply that enlightenment is the end of suffering.

Since then people have spent their lives trying to figure out what he meant!

Your ego will distract you with thoughts of the past, yet your ego has no meaning in Reality.

Next your ego will remind you of all your problems. It will most certainly tell you that if you are not worrying then you are being derelict in your duties. Indeed many people identify themselves by their problems. They think their identity is tied up to their responsibilities, their problems, their illnesses, their jobs, the car they drive or their bank account.

Shut your ego out. Tomorrow is not here yet. Indeed the next hour does not exist yet. There is nothing to be gained in the present moment by listening to the ravings of your busy mind.

Be present right now in this very moment and feel your energy body beneath your skin. Feel the energy that moves your heart and sustains your body. Feel the stillness and power within your Divine self. And listen to the silence. Feel the harmony in the perfection that is you. Feel the love that created you and that sustains you. Be at one with the calm and be content in this moment. Trust that everything is exactly as it should be and that you are Divinely guided to be exactly where you should be at every moment of your life.

Allow the energy to build around you and feel it grow. Let it edge out control, that is subjugated by your ego. Let the energy replace pain and illness in your body with its warmth. Allow yourself to know that the same energy that directs a tree to grow or a mountain to stand also directs your growth.

Know that the force that created galaxies and causes the sun to blaze is also watching over you with infinite care and love. Close your eyes and contact the source of that love within you and embrace it.

Let yourself go. Just be. Let thoughts pass through you without meaning. Even as you gaze about you, have no thought or attachment to what you see.

In just being, there resides the infinite. *Don't strain. Don't train. Just be.*

Release all thoughts of consequences and worry thoughts about what will be. Trust in the essence that directs you and know that you will be exactly where you are meant to be at all times, and that you will know what to do, therefore give up attachment to worry. You will be safe and all that you need shall come to you. Do not concern yourself with the how and the why.

Practice being in the now at all times. Practice giving up attachment to the outcome. Practice giving up your attachment to worry. Just be in the moment. All of creation exists in the moment. Every creature just is. Watch a bird or a squirrel, or your pet. They exist totally in the present. Watch nature and see how the trees and plants bloom and go through the seasons just by being.

Do not forget that you are part of nature too.

Our natural state, before we invented religions, was to be at one with the seasons, and to accept the cycles of the earth, the courses of nature, the ebb and flow of life. Like a willow bending in the wind just is, we accepted our part in nature.

This is spirituality. Learn to be with yourself in quiet and peace and you will hear the voice of God and you will feel His presence directing you, always for your highest good. Know that the techniques and ability to be God conscious does not depend on years of practice. All you need to know is already within you. This is Gods gift, given to you in pure, unconditional love. You can do it now. This is where you can find Truth, using the gifts that are yours here and now. They were given to you even before you were born, ready for you to use at any moment you desired.

This is the essence of religion. All the rest is ceremony.

That, then is the answer, the *secret simple Truth.*

—

Un-creating The Illusion II

So'ham, "I am That." You should have this understanding: "It is God who is meditating. All the objects of my meditation are God. My meditation itself is God." Swami Muktananda (Indian Mystic)

To overcome the illusion of the world we have created, hold these thoughts constantly in your mind: All creation is filled with Love and Divinity. Nothing can exist where the Divine presence is not. The Divine moves through everything, everywhere, including you. Nothing can replace the Divinity. The illusion blindfolds us and prevents us from seeing this fact.

To really understand on a cellular level, with every cell in your body always keep in mind that;

God does not condemn, nor judge nor punish you.

The oneness of creation, God is within you - as you are within Him.

Creation is perfect - so you are perfect.

God will not judge what you perceive as imperfection in any way

You can do no wrong in the sight of God therefore sin does not exist.

Sin, judgment and guilt are the illusion you have created for yourself. This arises out of FEAR when you feel cut off from God.

God sustains His creation in perfect and unconditional love - knowing that you are an eternal and spiritual being, and one with Him.

When you overcome FEAR you will experience the perfection of who you are.

You are already free to enjoy the love, joy, enlightenment and grace of your connection with God.

In summary the whole situation can be summed up as;

You are God, and in your ignorance you have replaced Love with Illusion and Fear.

It is advisable to avoid certain negative behaviors:

When events do not work out the way you hoped in our world of illusion, accept personal responsibility. It is not God's fault.

Most people are caught up in negative behavior such as when they rage that they are being treated unfairly whether by the government, their boss, in relationships etc. This is when it is time to take responsibility for creating this reality. Accept the responsibility.

When things are going great and you have the thought that it is too good and it cannot last and that something will go wrong because it always does, be aware (beware) that you will create this happening.

You will create the situation that you most fear. And you will always be justified in fearing it!

One question frequently asked is related to the misery we see all around us in the world. Often the question is asked, "How can God allow such misery, especially where innocent children are concerned. Why are there terrible diseases and famines? Why are some children born handicapped? What have the innocent young babies done to deserve this?"

If reincarnation did not exist, life would indeed be ominous and randomly cruel. Indeed we would do well to question the purpose of life and lay blame on a cruel creator. However, reincarnation has the answer to this question. There is a purpose for every soul to have a specific experience. In order for one to reap the reward for past deeds, for better or for worse, makes this question less obscure and removes a random and vengeful God from the equation.

Without the balance of karma, western dogma teaches us that a soul that has sinned will not enter heaven. In the worst cases one is doomed to eternity in hell.

With the law of karma one has many cycles of rebirth and each cycle is an opportunity to learn and advance in consciousness. Through the power of our minds we create a life that gives us the opportunity to live a fulfilled life or otherwise. We have free will and the power to create our own reality and a restless mind or a tormented spirit will produce the experience of hell on earth.

It is mankind that has created poverty and disease on earth. Our feelings of separation from God cause our fears to actualize.

Consequently two things are happening here. First on the personal level, unconscious people often act in thoughtless and destructive ways. The consequences of the damage wrought in ones lifetime is addressed karmically. It may be they have a life filled with opportunities to redeem past actions and to grow spiritually. Conversely there are times where a soul takes upon itself suffering in order to commute the karma of their fellow man as an act of self-sacrifice and compassion.

The second thing that is happening is the low mindset of group consciousness that constructs the physical circumstances on earth namely poverty, disease, squalor etc. These are created by mankind and not by God.

Mankind creates reality and they can un-create the misery of the world if they chose to do so, including, in fact especially, ones own pain.

Once more we must see ourselves as Eternal Spirit and enjoin in awareness with one another to change the circumstances in the world that does not serve our highest good, and the good of the world.

Enlightened beings will elect enlightened leaders that inspire us. We want leaders that address the core issues of the quality of life. Enlightened leadership would seek the abolition of non- productive and wasteful use of resources. They would be peacemakers, environmentalists, and humanitarians. They would be concerned about using the abundant wealth of nations without the corrupting influences of paid lobbyists and donors. If you want to know the mindset of a country, simply look at their leaders. Countries get what they wish for.

Failure to act selflessly and with awareness results in thoughts of fear, the ultimate thought of fear being death. Pain, loss and an eternal restlessness of spirit and total fear of the unknown are the result of the disconnection from Source. Therefore we must be brave and seek TRUTH.

Many people fear loss and so they fear happiness - and they fear love - lest they lose this too. Love is part of the Divine creation, people frequently never learn to accept Love for fear that they will lose it. It is easier to suppress their feelings and to deny love and happiness in order to avoid loss.

There are individuals that create themselves attracting relationships that will never work. In this way they do not have to love completely. When loss comes, and it will, they feel justified in having suppressed their love so as not to get hurt. Self-sabotage patterns can run very deep and can be very complicated. Another thing is that every thought about the futility of love and happiness will create just that outcome. So the end result is that person's belief structure about love and relationships will always prove them right.

Needless to say, most people are unaware of these patterns they have created and how it rules their life.

We are conditioned to accept struggle and pain rather than to relinquish it in favor of a higher thought.

It is more difficult to relinquish control of their sabotage pattern than to accept a healing in its place.

Illusion sustains them and their belief system proves them correct time and time again. They build an ego and a persona around struggle and pain.

Struggle and pain is how they identify themselves.

I have met people who talk endlessly about their illnesses and difficult circumstances. Sometimes it appears to me as if they wear life's battle scars with pride like some veteran.

This is the image of themselves that they put out to the world.

They could never release control and accept love and compassion with faith and accept the truth that God has created within us all.

Hundreds of millions of people are stuck in delusion and they have a lot of brain washing to undo!

Another negative behavior is that of classifying people and ideas and events to fit ones own preconceived ideas about the world.

Labeling things according to race and culture, or as good or bad, typical of this or that, etc. is bigoted and anti-life. All that exists "just is" without attaching a thought or judgment to it.

This is letting go control.

One cannot control the outcome of events according to preconceived ideas. This is an illusion.

The consequences of which are frustration, resentment and rage.

This applies equally to personal as well as national belief systems.

The cost of not relinquishing control is that people create enemies. In their anger they create conflict. Spouses, children and relationships suffer and misery is spread to others.

Every negative outburst feeds into and confirms the illusion of others. Therefore the cycle of rage and frustration multiplies exponentially.

Picture the situation: the boss yells at an employee, he gets home and yells at his child, the child aggravates the neighbors dog, the dog bites the mailman etc. The cycle can multiply and is self sustaining.

Such fears and negative energy created by billions of frustrated individuals hundreds of times per person every day becomes part of the global psyche. The final result is an enormous cloud of dark energy waiting to go ballistic!

And it does.

Thought being creative - war, disease, famine, floods, disaster, violence are the inevitable outcome of negative energy forces.

Once again the universe has given us exactly what we have asked for. We have manifested our fears. And we are always right! That is the Universal Law in action.

Is it any wonder that so many people regard the world as a big mess? What are your thoughts about the world? How often do you hear people talking about the state the world is in?

These thoughts become a self-fulfilling prophecy. And the ego being what it is loves to be proved correct. We love to prove ourselves right.

We continuously choose to forget - out of fear - our Divine ability to create out of love and truth. Our true self is relegated to second place because they are so caught up in their illusion.

To escape from the illusion, however briefly, give up thoughts about being too busy for spiritual practice. Such thoughts are really saying that you have no time for love, happiness and compassion.

The wisdom inherent within each of us teaches that creation must serve us and not we it.

This means that we should create consciously and that we must not be at the affect of what we create. The use of creative thought must be honored otherwise our purpose in this world is wasted.

Bring your alignment as a spiritual being into focus - very clearly and in no uncertain terms and use your powers of manifestation for a higher purpose.

—

<u>Mutual Responsibility</u>

The salvation of mankind lies only in making everything the concern of all - Alexander Solzhenitsyn (Russian Novelist)

The negative attitudes that so many people display towards life affect all of us.

Bad attitude hurts every human being, every community, and every nation

Most suffer pain in some form every day. Whether one chooses to acknowledge it, suppress it or ignore it. We abuse ourselves and our bodies, our partners, our families, friends, co-workers and our environment. In turn, we ourselves are abused. Everyone has committed or experienced the pain of abuse at some time in one form or another.

We need to appreciate the holistic nature of the Eternal Divinity. Whether one is a beggar or the President of the United States, to hurt one is to hurt all. One cannot injure another without causing damage to oneself. Likewise, one cannot hurt oneself without harming everyone.

When you harm another you diminish yourself, for we are all one. We are aspects of the same Divinity, linked through the One to each other. All outwardly directed anger and injury towards another is ultimately self directed.

What we do to another we do to ourselves.

To offend one is to offend all.

Abuse is not limited to physical and verbal attack. Often that which is unsaid leaves more pain than that which is spoken. When a feeling is expressed, that is verbalized, you release its energy. If the emotion is suppressed the energy remains unreleased and is directed inwardly. One can do a lot of damage by the silence of ones thoughts. If negative thoughts are continuously internalized, the energy can grow and the manifest in an illness of the body.

Thought determines your life experience. When you suppress your thoughts, you suppress life itself.

Sometimes by withholding acknowledgment of someone who deserves your recognition you negate that person and their accomplishments. Abuse, can be subtle in that it can be in the form of what is left unsaid.

The manner and the level of consciousness when you express yourself are always of *vital* importance. Vital comes from the Latin word vita as in vitamin. Vita means life. Therefore the manner in which you express yourself either affirms life i.e.: *vitality,* or it negates life.

The energy underlying your thoughts, whether you withhold them or choose to express them can be a positive or a negative pulse of creation. The human mind is unlimited in its ability to create. You have only to appreciate science fiction movies or children's cartoons to realize the creative range of the human mind.

Also consider how frequently life imitates art, such as in Jules Verne's nineteenth century novels of trips to the moon, and submarines, space travel and rockets.

There is also the dark side of "copy cat" violence, wherein the horror of a movie, created by the mind of a screenwriter, finds expression in a real life situation. The release of one Hollywood movie and one made for T.V. drama about urban snipers was put on hold during the real life Washington beltway sniper attacks. When a thought goes out into the world with intention it can manifest reality.

An aware being can see this type of linkage between apparently unconnected circumstances.

Here, in the physical realm, is the denseness of the physical environment. There is a delay between thought and consequence for most of us. Therefore the consequences of thought are not immediately obvious.

That is to say that the time between a thought and its manifestation into reality is not necessarily instantaneous. Therefore one does not readily associate the synchronicity between a thought and manifest reality.

When you hold a thought in mind constantly you empower it. The reality of the thought may manifest days or weeks, even months later.

If you store resentment in your body, feel depressed or suffer from anxiety or other feelings of being ill at ease you should process those feelings. You probably would not see the correlation between the dis-ease you felt last week, and the disease you have created in your body this week.

I know a man who had a beautiful wife whom he loved very much indeed. It transpired that she was attacked and she was brutally raped and assaulted. Following that traumatic experience, the terrified lady would not leave her home at all. The husband devoted much of his time attending to her and caring for her at home. He doted on her and had tremendous compassion for what his wife had been forced to endure.

Some time had passed like this, she being housebound and he taking care of her every need.

Quite unexpectedly, one day she turned around and told her husband that she could not stand the sight of him any longer. She could not bear to have him touch her and following on that she left him. He was totally devastated. The loss of his beloved wife filled him with tremendous grief.

At an unconscious level that he could not verbalize, nor admit, even to himself, the whole experience was a tremendous blow to his self-esteem as well as to his manhood. He felt that his virility was challenged and brought into doubt. He was filled with grief at the loss. Not only the loss of his wife, but also his pride and his masculinity had been undermined.

He suppressed his feelings of loss and inadequacy and suffered in silence. His pride would not allow him to break down and feel the grief and sense of loss of self-esteem. He bore his pain stoically, in silence.

After some time passed he developed prostate cancer and he had to undergo intense radiation therapy.

The correlation between his feelings of *dis-ease* stemming from the loss of his wife and the affront that he experienced regarding his manhood, led him to create *disease* in his reproductive system.

He produced an illness in the exact area of his body that represented to him that part of his manhood that had been violated!

Not all thoughts are directed inwardly in this manner. Choosing to direct thoughts of anger and rage outwardly can cause a very powerful energy release.

Such thoughts expand into the world of creation as a violent negative pulse. There, combined with billions of other similar negative impulses, they coalesce into a massive dark force.

Unseen, yet tangible to the senses, the "dark mood" spreads across the land, an invisible black shroud, creating tension and dis-ease in its wake. It is capable of upsetting the harmony of creation, it may manifest as earthquakes, floods and other "natural disasters". "Natural disasters" are neither natural nor disasters (Disaster is a judgment. Judgment is a human perception of events and is therefore ultimately not real).

The effect of negative energy on an individual is profound. Directed inwardly, it creates frustration and disease within body and spirit. Heart attacks reflect issues concerning the lack of love or the inability to receive love, cancers reflect suppressed emotions and the eating away of oneself from within. Directed outwardly negative energy manifests in domestic violence, rage, crime, wars, global epidemics and much more.

Mankind is a very primitive species. The demand for physical gratification without paying attention to ones spiritual needs, except in a very superficial way leads to very dangerous and destructive behaviors.

Power is still perceived as being outside of oneself rather than in the spirit of what one really is.

We need to be very aware and very careful about releasing negative energy as we learn about the power of thought. The power of creation lies even in a single thought.

Especially be-aware, that is, beware of letting thoughts sustain you in illusion or have a negative influence over you.

When I speak of thought sustaining us in illusion I must be clear about this.

The illusion has its own apparent reality.

Life is inherently neutral, but it can be perceived in any way we choose to perceive it.

To us it appears real until we learn to see through the manifested illusion of our thoughts and our endless cycle of reactions to our thoughts.

What are pain, love and human experience save that which each of us, alone, as individuals experience in a unique way in response to our thoughts about it.

To overcome the negative illusion we must choose the middle path. This is the Buddhist way.

At each extreme is illusion. When we are out of balance and we concern ourselves about the future, we have anxiety. When we dwell in the past we suffer from regret. In the present is the neutral aspect of oneself.

Truth exists only in the present moment. Here in the middle, between the past and the future is the middle path that the Buddha enunciated. Here neither our past experiences that form our egoist perception of ourselves, nor the vague future that holds nebulous hopes exist. In the present is neutral territory in which we are able to stop and contact the love of the universe within ourselves. Here is where we truly are. "I am that I am" or in the Vedic teaching, So'ham, "I am That." "That" meaning All That Is, i.e.: God.

God IS. God is only in the here and now. God never refers to Himself as "I was what I was" or "I will be what I will be."

"I Am" is the now. That is the source from which all life springs forth, from the Now. The eternal Now. Not the was nor the will be, but the Now. This is the middle path.

The sensitivity each has of their personal life experience, needless to say, is unique to each.

It may be similar to that of another, but each person's thoughts and life experiences will ensure individual uniqueness. We each experience in a way that is unique way to us.

We manifest our individual experience. We are its creators. Always we create in the here and now. Eventually, that which we call the future, will be the here and now and we will experience the result of our thoughts.

The present is the future that you dreamed about yesterday.

The physical world is a slow motion movie. In the timelessness of the dimension in which God creates, thought manifests immediately. There is no delay between the thought and the result.

In our slow world of time and space, we have the experience of seeing the gradual unfolding of life as it evolves from thought into form.

It is sad that the largest part of mankind does not appreciate this unique God given gift.

Indeed, most are not aware of it.

The consequence is that we, as a species, fail to see not only the gift of our creation, but we also fail to see the synchronicity of our lives in relation to our thoughts in our physical world..

Occasionally a nation shifts into a mass delusion and the power of synchronism can be awesome!

The Germans as a result of their desperation created Hitler. The desperation was the product of FEAR and the futility felt in post World War One German society. Like so many of us today, Germans in the 1930's did not accept responsibility for having created the reality of the prevailing condition in their society.

Germans searched for a cause that was responsible for their circumstances that lay outside of themselves. National pride and arrogance (ego) barred their looking inwardly and taking personal responsibility. The idea took root in the national psyche that the foreigners in their midst were to blame for their situation. This idea of enemies within expanded until it encompassed all people that were not Aryan and who did not embrace National Socialism (Nazism).

Consequently Communists, Jews, homosexuals, even Gypsies and anyone who opposed the Nazis were regarded as traitors! Rage at these groups became manifest. (I have discussed the power of rage as it relates to manifesting war and negative behavior).

Jews were their primary targets particularly due to their apparent collective powerlessness. Being politically marginalized, they had centuries of history of victim consciousness. The reason for the Jewish collective manifestation of disempowerment is worthy of further discussion and consideration - and has nothing whatsoever to do with their punishment for alleged biblical sins or any other such nonsense!

Germans embraced FEAR and hate consciousness on a truly massive statewide scale. So powerful was this negative surge of energy that the German national consciousness manifested and took solid form in the space of a few short years in the 1930's.

The force of their collective negative energy created Hitler, the Final Solution, World War Two and the Holocaust! National thought into reality - is very powerful at this level.

In this way all reality is created for better or for worse (I use these terms relatively - for in truth there is no good or bad, only what is).

Mankind could just as well create greatness if they utilized this power for the conscious good of society. They could manifest a Jesus in every city! Nations should realize that they should create with the strength of conscious purpose for love and Divinity.

They should be willing to Un-create that which no longer serves their sense of higher purpose for society.

Individuals must accept full responsibility for their thoughts, their creation and how they choose to relate to their creation. They must take responsibility that they "own" their thoughts and they must use them judiciously and with Grace, Love and Wisdom.

No one is a victim, except for our being victim to our own thought process!

Only we are responsible for everything that we experience. We manifest our own destiny.

Ones thoughts about something are also their reality about that thing.

You can change your reality when you change your thoughts.

We are all mutually responsible for the highest good for each other.

There are no victims in society just creators and co-creators of events – for both good and bad (relatively speaking).

Never loose sight of the fact that we are creative beings. That our purpose is to create but not just according to our whim but rather to a higher vision. That which we have created we can also un-create - and all of it ultimately is a very realistic illusion - but definitely an illusion nonetheless!

The creative mindset at this time is currently manifesting in a new model of mutual global economic interdependence that is making consumers aware of the conditions of the third world laborers who produce the products that wealthy countries consume.

There is an increasing intolerance in the affluent countries for human rights abuses and the exploitation of labor. This is very encouraging to see and is a cause of hope for the future.

I believe that as we move into a new paradigm of mutual respect and global community, the consciousness of the planet will shift dramatically.

The Internet and satellite communications are two of the most far-reaching innovations that will change the world in ways we have yet to comprehend.

Governments can no longer operate with impunity and are increasingly being called to account for their actions and human rights record. The intense media watch and the instant communications of the Internet have created a global community. The actions of a government directed against its own people will not go unnoticed or unpunished.

Two world-changing events are the Gulf war and the war in Kosovo.

The Gulf war was a live television event. The first war to be fought on T.V. We saw the immediacy of military actions in such a way that Western leaders had to fight a war with minimum allied casualties from the fear of loss of public support! This was amazing.

As recently as the Vietnam war the US Government controlled the media and prevented the citizens of the USA from realizing the true scope and horrors of the war. Hidden was the Agent Orange defoliant outrage. Hidden was the Mai Lai massacre. The war was carefully edited for public consumption back home. It took a long time before the horror reached home and the anti-war demonstrations of the 1960's erupted in public outrage.

In Yugoslavia and Kosovo, we saw a military action taken by President Milosovic, a sadistic dictator, bent on the "ethnic cleansing" of the Albanian minority from his country.

It is remarkable in that NATO and the Western Alliance reacted to this situation out of moral outrage and not because of a direct threat to themselves. Their intent was to stop a human tragedy from occurring in Europe.

The message is that human rights are spreading beyond our own borders and that the world is losing its tolerance with dictators.

The Internet has truly shrunk the world. Even as bombs fell in Belgrade, I was getting emails from a family in Belgrade asking for our prayers for peace. The enemy is no longer faceless or foreign. They are our cyber neighbors, and they are hurting. No amount of government propaganda can make them a faceless, evil empire. They are no different than you or I.

I was chatting with them as they as ducked American bombs. We were just human beings praying for peace even as our governments waged war!

The more that the global economy becomes the global village, we will increasingly realize that we are a small human community of brothers and sisters on a fragile planet spinning in the cold of space. Wars and conflicts will be ever harder to prosecute once we affirm that we truly are our brother's keeper and that we have nothing to fear from them or they from us.

A very meaningful product of the global village is the integration of the global economic structure. Corporations today are truly global. The cross- pollination of multinational corporate holdings has created conditions where no country is an island. Investments and banking flow effortlessly via satellite across national boundaries. This is the financial and economic lifeline for countries moving into the global economy of the new millennium.

Trillions of dollars of investments flow in every direction pursuing economic opportunity.

Mutual funds, investment bankers and investors are voting on the stability of governments with their dollars. In effect, an investor in the USA may have a stake in the political stability of China or Pakistan. The international investor has a vested political interest in the countries in which he is invested.

He is a virtual voter. He votes with his money, and this can be a great deterrent to governments and industries engaged in social mismanagement and human rights violations.

Many times a foreign investor's financial vote is of greater value to a government than those of its citizens who vote at ballot box!

This is a remarkable turn of events. The economic and political stability of a country as well as its human rights policies can affect its politics. It is increasingly more difficult for regimes to act unilaterally without it affecting world opinion.

Investors have a low tolerance for putting their money in unstable regimes! The immediate accessibility of the world-wide-web creates an instant information source that no amount of censorship by a dictatorial regime can curb. Likewise, regimes can no longer keep their own population ignorant and deprived of news.

With knowledge comes strength. The masses living under intolerant regimes will become aware of issues concerning their government and world opinion. They will directly experience the economic impact on their lives created by their government. The level of tolerance for repressive rulers will diminish when people demand the freedoms and economic benefits enjoyed in other countries with whom they trade and communicate with.

The apartheid government in South Africa was crippled by international sanctions brought about by mainstream public pressure from overseas and disinvestments. An oil embargo and the withdrawal of international investor funds crippled the South African economy. The economy shrunk, unemployment increased, rampant inflation depleted savings and created economic stagnation. The population demanded that the government change in order that South Africa could rejoin the community of nations.

Future dictators in this new world will not find international acceptance of their actions. If they wish to take their countries forward they will be forced to consider world opinion at a grass roots level, because overnight billions of foreign investment dollars will simply evaporate and they will be economically hamstrung.

No regime is immune to international pressure for any length of time.

Multinational companies are sensitive to political pressure and are aware of the necessity in maintaining a good public corporate image. Shareholders like you and I, and mom and pop next door hold tremendous influence.

Nike, the maker of athletic apparel, is a case in point. The public disliked the fact that Nike paid their spokesperson, Michael Jordan, more than they paid all the laborers in an entire Vietnamese factory! Furthermore the reported conditions in the factory coupled with reports of abuse by management outraged US investors. Public pressure coupled with the threat of a consumer boycott forced Nike to raise wages and improve working conditions in its factories globally, not only in Vietnam.

Corporate responsibility has positive spin-offs for the rest of the workforce in a country that is not employed by a multinational corporation. Once conditions at the Nike factories improve, workers at other corporations in those countries will demand similar improved working conditions from their employers. In the meantime, corporations such as Nike, with improved employee benefits and conditions will hopefully attract the best workers and create a loyal workforce. This has tremendous cost benefits to the corporation in return.

As the workers lives improve, they will also be future consumers for Nike apparel and other consumer products. In this way wealth is created and everyone ends up winning.

The Internet also spawned the World Trade Organization riots in Seattle, Washington. These were immediately followed and supported by similar demonstrations in Paris and London. This grass-roots man in the street protest was over alleged secret deals and negotiations being conducted by major international corporations and governments behind closed doors.

The perception by the public was that these secret negotiations would lead to trade deals being made that would affect the environment, workers rights, and exploit resources and human beings.

These WTO meetings were seen as draconian and sinister because they were conducted by powerful people and held in great secrecy.

The upshot was that trade unions and the press look likely to be represented at future WTO meetings. Public intolerance for secret deals and exploitive labor practices is increasingly putting pressure on governments and companies engaged in such practices to be more open and public in their dealings.

Nike, an icon of exploitive labor practices, now publishes a list on its website of all its suppliers internationally in an effort to afford monitors easy access to names of foreign factories possibly suspected of labor abuse. Nike would probably not have done this were it not for the pressure of conscious human beings who are no longer willing to tolerate human rights abuses by multinational corporations.

Several other multinational corporations have since followed suit and have published lists of their suppliers as well.

The world is indeed moving in the direction of global responsibility. At least at the level of the common man. And this is what will force change in the end. Corporations like Nike are not faceless entities. The workers, managers and directors that run these companies are the good people who are your neighbors, the parents of your children's friends, your golfing buddies, and the person sitting in the pew next to you on Sunday. They must be held socially accountable for all their activities. This means worldwide and not only in the hometown.

Jeffrey M. Solomon

<u>Chapter Twelve - Energy As The Source Of Life</u>

If you knew how meat was made, you'd probably lose your lunch. I know - I'm from cattle country. That's why I became a vegetarian. - K.D. Lang (American Singer)

Energy

*The universe begins to look more like a great thought than like a
great machine - James Jeans
(English Physicist)*

Creative energy in the sub atomic level cannot be broken down.
Like light - it can be dissipated but never destroyed.

Even energy released in an atomic explosion is dispersed but not
destroyed.

Remarkably, the latent energy contained in a few tiny atoms,
when released by the splitting of those atoms, results in an atomic
explosion of enormous intensity. One researcher from the atomic
bomb project in Los Alamos, upon seeing the first atomic explosion,
exclaimed, "I see God", (He was correct. Each atom of creation
contains within it the power of God).

If a few atoms have such incredible potential, imagine if you will,
the awesome, Divine power, contained within the atoms of an entire
mountain. By further visualization consider the power inherent in a
star such as the sun. Imagine the power contained within the stars in
our galaxy, the Milky Way. Soon you will be overwhelmed by the
unimaginable power within the billions of galaxies in the Universe.
This is the mind of God.

It is beyond comprehension. Like trying to envision nothingness
or infinity, it is beyond our ability to comprehend.

This should bring into focus a fraction of the immense power of
the Being that we call God. (But not His entirety by any means!)
When you think of God as a fatherly figure with a long white beard,
stop and consider the true awesomeness of this Being. It is no wonder
that in Hindu theology that aspect of God that is the creator,
(represented by Shiva), is also the same aspect that is the destroyer.
Ultimately the act of creation and destruction are one and the same. It
is the transformation of Divine energy from one form to another.

The study of energy defies analysis.

Energy manifested as light behaves most peculiarly as both a
beam and a wave simultaneously!

This duality defies physical explanation. How can something
display two different attributes at once? It defies logic. Our imperfect

senses tell us that if light is traveling as a beam, that is, in a straight line like a laser beam, it cannot at the same time be rolling along like a wave in the ocean!

Yet light, incredibly, does just that. Depending on the experiment, physicists can prove that light both travels as a particle beam and as a wavy, roller coaster of particles.

The conclusion is that the mere presence of an observer affects the outcome of the experiment. This presupposes that there is a symbiotic link at an energy level between the observer and that, which is being observed.

This further infers that the desire of the observer for a certain result will create the expected result!

Quantum mechanics, that is the physics of Einstein, proves empirically that thought is creative.

This is an outstanding dynamic to come to terms with and one that defies our sense of reality.

Ask yourself what is defective - our sense of reality or the behavior of light beams?

We know that the mind manifests energy through the thought process.

How is this energy creative? How does the material world manifest from thought?

Thought in the form of energy is released by the mind of the thinker and it flows out into the universe. There are some people who are like radio receivers, they are able to pick up the thought transmissions of others. Some may call this sixth sense psychic ability.

Because energy is indestructible, one could, hypothetically, tune into thoughts from the past.

We can take this idea one step further. Time is relative, that is, all time past present and future exists simultaneously as one. Therefore all that was, is, and will be, simply IS.

Therefore a psychic can also be prescient or clairvoyant, which is exactly what many are.

The ability to see the future depends on the sensitivity of the receiver to tune in to the subtle energies around them.

Energy also attracts like or similar energy like magnets that are attracted to each other. When energy builds, the atoms of similar form may attract and coalesce. The united mass becomes increasingly powerful.

(Remember the earlier description of your atomic body looking like a galaxy composed mostly empty space?)

Unformed energy is very sparse and not defined by any particular form. As the mass of like energy accumulates it forms into a denser energy accretion.

Do you recall my analogy of energy being a form of psychic steam? Energy emanates from the Universal Source. Similar to humidity it is light and invisible. As humidity rises it coalesces and it condenses and forms vapor and then finally water droplets. At this point the humidity, once invisible evolves into steam and then into water. Its substance changes into progressively denser form.

Similarly energy accretion will manifest into a tangible mass.

Sometimes, one may walk into a place and feel a "good vibe" or a "bad vibe".

This is the consequence of thought "vapor" created by the people there. It is present even when nobody is there.

The positive energy of a sacred place where people have prayed for years as well as the pain of dungeon where people have suffered is tangible to most of us.

Few people can walk into a former Nazi concentration camp without feeling the despair and heaviness, even though the events that occurred there are long since past. The walls and the earth cry out. Similarly, in a very holy site one can sense the peace and awe.

This demonstrates the ability of most of us to feel psychic energy. Psychics are people who are more sensitive receptors and are able to discern finer vibrations than most.

Hospitals often have an air of despair. Hospital caregivers frequently report feeling depressed. This is often due to the negative energy inherent in hospitals where fear and death is played out daily.

Workers who take care of the elderly are particularly prone to depression and have shorter careers as elderly care givers than care givers in most other fields. It is no wonder. Surrounded as they are by the "death urge" of elderly and dying people is a very powerful form of "psychic energy attack".

There are techniques that clear the energy of a ward and a building and protect one from psychic attack.

Working with the subtleties of energy work is a field of study in itself. Every caregiver should have some knowledge of the techniques for dealing with energy and psychic attack.

There are Reikii techniques, the Lords of Karma process developed by Diane Stein, energy balancing routines, and many other forms of cleansing.

Dealing with negative energy and energy body cleansing should be a crucial part of the training given to qualified caregivers.

As is often the case, healers get involved in caring for others and neglect their own well being.

Energy workers and those in the healing arts should cleanse their energy bodies as fastidiously and as regularly as they take a shower, and even more so!

My partner, Sharda Collard, has done incredible work and training in this field. I owe much to her for my understanding of the use of energy, its forms, its use and its misuse. She has taught me the many forms of energy manifested in illnesses and how to move pain and sickness through the body for healing. She has learned to sense energy blocks, psychic attack and defense. Consequently she routinely works with people from all over the world, healing, shifting energy blocks and consulting.

Mental energy blocks sabotage ones ability to go forward and to see clearly ahead. Such energy blocks are capable of undermining your well being and can affect your health and performance and ones ability to function as a healthy being.

Many large corporations consult with Sharda with amazing results. A group that has created an energy block within a corporation can literally destroy a company. Fragmented leadership, low morale, internal conflicts, a lack of cohesion and sound strategy are symptoms that precede the fact. It is incredible to observe how many business problems stem from the energy contained within a given situation. Managers see and try to deal with the results of the un-shifted energy. This is akin to a doctor treating the symptoms rather than the disease. As long as the underlying problem persists there can be no resolution.

The cause of every business problem originates in the thoughts and feelings of the employees as individuals and also collectively as a team.

If the team is not acting positively and in synergy the results for the corporation can be fatal.

Sharda is attuned to the energy world and the subtle use of energy. This is useful in gaining knowledge, instruction, karmic release and awareness. I highly recommend that anyone who is serious about self-improvement take a reputable seminar in personal relationships and self- awareness, such as those that Sharda does.

Negative energy is molasses of the soul. Light attracts darkness. In darkness the higher self or soul is attracted to the healing properties of light. People with a lot of darkness attempt to suck in light from an en-lightened being and anyone that is lighter than them.

At one time or another everyone has had the experience of being in the company of someone who leaves him or her feeling drained and exhausted.

Negative energy clings to ones energy body.

The process of the accrual of energy from thought into form is the process of creation.

This procedure that manifests what we truly desire may also be used negatively to harm others.

Every thought is creative and we should be aware of the power of our thoughts.

All energy originates from thought.

The origin of all thought is the Mind that sustains the entire universe within Its' thought.

This Universal energy that originates in a Super Mind that we call God, sustains you and I every minute of the day.

This is the Nature of mankind.

Light and Energy

Consciousness....is the phenomenon whereby the universe's very existence is made known. - Roger Penrose (British Physicist)

Modern man may scoff at ancient societies for their belief in sun worship.

We do so at our own peril.

The question arises whether these ancient people had knowledge that we are just now beginning to understand.

The Mayans of Central America were highly developed in mathematical and astrological science and with a calendar yet unequaled in modern science for its accuracy.

How can we belittle them by imagining that they thought the sun itself was god?

These are people who charted planetary orbits and who predicted solar eclipses and astrological events a thousand years hence. At the same time Europeans believed that the world was flat and that the earth was the center of the universe.

What the Mayans did realize is that all sources of energy are from the One Divine Mind. The Mayans knew that the energy of the Mind, the energy of fire and the energy of the sun are all one. A cup drawn from the ocean holds the essence of the sea yet is apart from the sea, so all energy is from the One Source. This they knew.

Ancient people acknowledged this Source, using the symbolism of the sun. This is similar to the Christian use of the cross to symbolize the Christ, and as such it should be respected.

Christians would be offended if we judged them as worshippers of wooden crosses.

It is the Divinity, represented by the symbol of the cross that represents their faith.

So does the sun represent the Universal Source of energy as a symbol, and not as the deity itself.

Modern mans haste to dismiss Mayan and other "primitive" cultures as having nothing to offer us has caused us to dismiss much non-Western and ancient culture to the realm of mere historical curiosity.

Our arrogance has caused us to mistakenly dismiss sun-worshipping societies as primitives who regaled the sun as god. They were, in fact, far more learned than we generally give them credit for.

The Maya and many other sun-worshipping cultures knew that the sun was not a god per se.

They realized then what we are just beginning to understand now with the advent of modern science.

The energy from the sun in the form of light is the closest thing to the direct energy of God that we as physical beings can experience with our five senses.

The light from the sun is a manifestation of Divine love. It is direct creative energy, and it is the source of all life on earth. From this energy the source of breath itself originates.

Without the sun this planet would have no atmosphere, heat or life.

They understood the single source of energy and that ultimately all energy must return to that source. Sunlight is the physical manifestation of that Source energy. The sun not only gives life-sustaining energy it also gathers and transmutes spent energy and returns it to the source such as in the decay of matter. Therefore the sun is perfect as an instrument for spiritual purification, vision quests and the spirit journey.

Anyone who has been to the ocean will be aware of the charged energy of air at the sea- side. The sea is the earth's most natural reservoir of Divine Light. It absorbs the radiated energy of the Divine Light and stores it in its atoms and molecules. The result is a life affirming ionization of the air above the ocean. Plant life and phytoplankton are able to convert this energy into the basic building blocks of life on earth.

The sea is a prism reflecting the energy of the sun into the atmosphere and thereby charging the planet and the atmosphere with life. It is revitalizing. Older people are naturally drawn to the coast, though the reason they give may be far different from what they unconsciously intuit. They feel better. It is that simple. The sun and charged air particles are filled with prana or life source energy. Water is a magnet for retirees because it is a magnet for vita-energy.

The water that we draw for drinking contains toxic and corrosive chemicals, primarily chlorine and fluoride. Both of these are extremely toxic and can cause cell damage and cancer.

Chlorine gas was used as a chemical weapon during World War I to kill troops in the trenches. Its use has since been banned.

It is highly desirable to remove these chemicals for the sake of our energy bodies.

One should filter water or else wait several hours before drinking water in order to allow chemicals such as chlorine to disperse. Water should be set out in sunlight so that the chemicals in it can break down and to enable the water to reabsorb the prana or life force energy of the sun.

Harsh chemicals such as chlorine diminish our life force.

One way to do this is to collect several large glass containers, such as those gallon containers used for fruit juice (or cheap wine), and to have several gallons of purified water on hand.

Whatever we take into our bodies should be done with awareness and consideration as to how fresh it is and how closely connected it is to the source. The closer our food is to the source the greater is its vitality and life enhancing qualities. Therefore raw vegetables are closer to source than, say, cooked food, or meat.

Organic food is preferable to that covered in chemical poisons and fertilizers or that has been genetically modified.

In India there are yogis who have renounced food and drink completely. They sustain themselves on the energy (prana) of the breath, that is the light source itself. Not using their body for the eating, metabolism, conversion and storage of energy from plants, they are able, through breath alone, to sustain themselves in perfect health.[*]

The energy of the atmosphere permeates all. The Hindus call it Prana, the Chinese, Chi, and to the Japanese it is Ki.

---

[*] In Australia, there is an amazing lady named Jasmuheen. She has pioneered the art of living on light. Her Cosmic Internet Academy at www.selfempowermentacademy.com.au has further information on the subject of "Breatharianism", the art of living on light. Jasmuheen, herself is reported to have not eaten or had anything to drink in years. Many of her students apparently have also achieved this state.

The closer to the source of the Divine ones energy intake, the lighter is ones energy body. In this state these yogis are very closely connected to their higher selves while living in the physical plane. Every minute of their lives is one of conscious connectedness and Divine bliss.

A friend of mine, in his 70's, did Jasmuheens program for six weeks and reported himself to me to be fit and in excellent condition. He gave up due to social commitments and family considerations.

The source of life is energy. Energy is in the sun, without which there would be no life at all. Life consumes energy and the atomic building blocks of the universe, atoms, are energy.

The energy in a tree or an animal and a human is identical. Everything shares this one commonality. Every living thing also shares another thing in common, the need to propagate.

Energy is the most basic force fundamental to creation, indeed it is life, nothing less.

Energy is the only indestructible force known, being of the mind of the One Source, it is to the Source that all energy ultimately shall return.

Fossil fuel sources such as oil, coal, and natural gas owe their amazing ability to impart their energy to the stored sunlight that they possess from what was once living matter.

In the case of fossil fuels the stored energy is released from the sunlight of millions of years ago. When alive, the living algae, plankton and plants absorbed the radiated solar energy and converted it, via photosynthesis, into life sustaining energy.

When they died they decayed and yet somehow the energy within them remained. The energy did not die. Why is this so?

Notwithstanding the transmutation of the plant matter to coal or oil, is it not curious that the entire living organism did not decay into nothingness when it died? The almost miraculous process of transmutation from one state to another is nothing short of wonderful.

Consider the source of the energy. The energy originated as eternal and indestructible energy millions of years ago. Today it is still alive and intact in the form of the fossil fuels that we burn. The energy from the flow of God is eternal.

When we combust it, it will transmute yet again. The energy returns to the light from which it came. Gasses are also released and residual charcoal and ash deposits remain that contain the transmuted atoms of eternal energy within.

Hydrogen, one of the simplest and most abundant gasses in the universe, contains sufficient energy to power a vehicle. The non-polluting by-product of hydrogen combustion emissions is water.

The closer to the Original Source energy is, the closer it is to light. Further from the light source, the heavier the energy is. Therefore in splitting an atom, we have a source very close to light and a tremendous energy is released. Coal and oil is heavier, and is more removed from the light and is a less efficient source of energy.

To become heavy, the energy transmutes from Source energy, into light, and then condenses into succeeding heavier manifestations in a reverse of the burning or destructive process described above.

We call this the power of creation!

Let us look again at the energy body of man at the atomic level. We would see an enormous mass of energy and atoms, a veritable galaxy of light and fire and energy, swirling in fantastic synchronicity. In truth we look like the Milky Way, forms of blazing suns, swirls of atoms, photons, electrons, all vibrating and shining in an electrical field of gravity resembling the shape of a person. Through the limitations of our senses we see a solid body.

The soul is an even lighter body that exists at a different light frequency. Certain light waves in the short and long wave frequencies are invisible to our eyes. We cannot see infrared, ultra-violet rays, x-rays, gamma rays, or most of the light spectrum. The soul light frequency is invisible to us. Nevertheless we rely on our eyes for our understanding of the world around us.

We even say that seeing is believing.

What a misguided notion this is.

We should rather affirm that believing is seeing!

How little we truly see!

The process of creation in the physical world continues. Plants convert sunlight to energy in order to grow and reproduce. This is very close to the light source of energy.

Animals and humans derive their energy in the form of metabolism, that is, by converting the stored energy from plants when we eat them.

Plant eaters are one step further removed from the light source than the plants themselves.

Fruit and leaves eaten by a herbivore allow the creatures to absorb the solar energy second hand as it were.

Having digested the energy in the form of nutrients, the animal stores the converted energy in its own body and excretes the rest. The excrement being composed of atoms still contains energy. This dung can be used to fertilize plants and it can be burnt in cooking fires because of its stored plant energy.

Furthermore, the dung being a by-product of vegetable matter, is one step closer to the energy source than carnivore waste.

Cow dung is far less toxic then human and carnivore waste.

In third world countries it is not only used for fertilizer and fire kindling it is also used as a mud for the floors of huts as well as a stucco on the walls.[*]

Both the plants and the cows have taken Divine energy from the sun and transmuted it into life sustaining energy. The difference being that the plant is a step closer to the original pure energy. Solar energy

---

[*]In modern factory farms, animals and poultry are kept in pens and are fed a protein mix that renders their excreta toxic. This protein mix consists of the ground up body parts of animals that does not get used for food or other products. Much of the U.S. meat supply comes from cannibal cows and poultry! An outcry was raised when it was reported that in Los Angeles thousands of stray dogs and cats were destroyed each week. Their corpses were then sent to animal rendering plants, converted into animal feed, and ended up in the domestic food chain. In Britain,, diseased cows ended up in the protein feed mix. The disease, called mad cow disease survived the rendering process and was transmitted to healthy animals. People who ate this meat contracted the human form of this disease resulting in some deaths and the ban of British beef exports to other countries. A large portion of the British herd had to be destroyed.

The USA employs similar feeding practices and US beef was the subject of a boycott debate by the European nations. This threatened a trade war between the USA and the European Union. The US government insisted that US beef exporters have unrestricted access to the European market. The Europeans were concerned about the indiscriminate use of antibiotics and growth hormones used by US factory farms. The object of this use of drugs is to accelerate the growth and maturity of an animal, thus shortening the time it takes to bring an animal to market weight.

is not the actual Source itself, and is only a manifestation of that Source.

Hence solar energy is heavier than the Source Energy.

Consequently, in the process of plants metabolizing solar energy, a by- product is excreted from the plant in the form of a poisonous and corrosive gas called oxygen. Fortunately we need this gas to breathe. This plant waste product therefore contains life-sustaining energy!

How wonderful is the balance of creation!

Plant excrement being a gas, is lighter than dung excreted by cows. This is so because plants are closer to the source of energy.

An organism that lives on light, that is Source energy, is the purest form of life.

Life forms that exist on pure light and air are the closest to the source of Divine energy and the have the lightest vibration field. Those that eat plants and fruit are heavier life forms. Herbivores assimilate Divine energy close to its source from the photosynthesis of sunlight to energy that has occurred in the plants that it eats.

Plants therefore are our food connection to the Divine source of energy.

Plants also serve us in other ways. As a by-product of their activity, through photosynthesis, they produce the oxygen in the air we breathe and they remove toxic gasses from the atmosphere.

Trees, and rainforests in particular, are the lungs of this living, breathing planet.

Thus it is that plants transmute solar energy through osmosis and they supply us with energy.

They give us an edible form of energy and fossil fuel energy and in their excreta by way of oxygen.

Our bodies being composed of energy, albeit a much denser form than pure light, are nevertheless light bodies. The lighter our bodies become, the closer our attunement with the Divine and our higher self or soul. When we meditate, we draw in the light and strengthen the link between the Divine light and us.

Whatever we take into our bodies in the way of food and drugs is critical to the building of our light body and our level of higher consciousness.

Every decision we make concerning what we ingest and breath affects our consciousness.

The next level of energy absorption relates to the carnivore. It is substantially more heavy than the previous two levels of absorption, namely photosynthesis and herbivores.

The original source of energy, sunlight, gets transmuted and diminished downwards through the food chain and grows ever denser in the process of transmutation.

In consuming the flesh of a herbivore, such as a cow, we find that the energy is many times denser and far further removed from the light source from which it originated. By now it bears little resemblance to the foundation from which it originated. Although flesh eating is the third level of energy absorption in the food chain, the multiplier effect of energy dilution in the transmutation of the Source energy is hundreds of degrees removed from its original purity.

Flesh is highly toxic as evidenced by the excretions of a meat eater. In the case of man, the toxic ingestion of the flesh of a living creature, is not only difficult to digest it is the source of numerous health problems, from digestive cancers, to blood diseases, blocked arteries and heart disease to name but a few. Other diseases are ancillary to eating meat, such as bacterial and microbial diseases. (See the next chapter "The Price of a Cow")

This is no surprise considering that the pure vitality of the sunlight has journeyed from a plant through the digestive tract of a dead animal and is now being consumed third hand through the human digestive system.

Perhaps the biggest drawback of eating animals is the spiritual alienation of a person from the prana, or Source of life.

The death energy within the corpse of a dead animal is stored and imprinted in its blood, flesh and cells. When one ingests flesh, they take into their body this highly negative energy of the death throe and in turn store it in their own body at a cellular level.

At the point of death the creature releases large quantities of hormones into its bloodstream such as adrenaline that is designed to help them survive trauma and shock. These are assimilated into the human body. There is also the death consciousness of the creature to consider. We know that we create our own reality, therefore at some level of consciousness a creature that dies has created its own death and the person who eats it is taking death consciousness into ones body. This is anti-life behavior on the part of the person who eats meat. It is a flagrant disregard of their own body much like smoking or doing drugs.

You are what you eat.

If taking in death energy sounds extreme consider this. Caregivers, who work in old age homes, are familiar with the phenomenon that frequently when one patient dies, usually two more will die shortly thereafter. If there is a fourth death then another two deaths will follow.

At an energetic level, people exchange energies all the time. In any type of group or social setting, our auras, or energy bodies interact with each other and we take on other people's stuff.

Another common phenomenon is that in a very close environment women will begin menstruating in synchronicity with each other.

What is even more startling is that nurses in the aged homes are prone to shorter life spans, suicide and depression. The professional drop out rate is also higher in this area of nursing than in other branches of the profession. This is no surprise. If one is around the energy of people who are in their death urge, it affects one very intensely in their body as well as their psychic energy. Unless one does a lot of energy cleaning and release, this negative energy will remain in the body because energy as we know is indestructible!

When a meat eater takes flesh into his body, it is therefore no surprise that aggressive tendencies are accentuated when compared to that of vegetarians. Fighters, footballers and people engaged in contact sport boast how they eat great slabs of meat almost raw. This will enhance their aggressive tendencies. Aggressive behavior is negative, anti-life and therefore stems from fear not love.

Is it any wonder that the fear / aggression emotion is accentuated in people who eat meat? A diet of meat contains the chemical as well as the psychological death urge of a dying, terrified creature!

Blood conveys the nutrients, hormones, proteins and enzymes through a body to all its constituent parts. When a dying animal releases fear hormones such as adrenaline into its body, it is carried in the bloodstream. It permeates the flesh of the creature. Eating the blood of an animal, such as in rare meat, is particularly awful.

313

There are many primitive cultures that require a warrior to drink blood. The Masai of East Africa drink a mixture of blood and milk. The blood is drawn out of the neck of a live cow and is frequently drunk straight from the animal. Some hunters eat the raw liver or heart of an animal that has been killed so as to take on the attributes of that creature. In extreme cases, such as the warrior headhunters of Borneo, they eat the body parts or brain of their human victim.

In the Jewish dietary laws called "kosher" or kashrut, the prohibition against eating blood is very specific. Indeed, meat eating is discouraged to some extent.

Animals that are non-herbivores are considered unfit to eat. Furthermore animals, in order to be kosher must chew the cud and have split hooves. This, by definition excludes pigs, horses, most deer, all reptiles, etc.

Hunting animals for food or otherwise is prohibited for dietary and humane reasons.

However, if one insists on eating meat then the law is very strict and precise. The animal must be expertly slaughtered so that the jugular vein is cut and the creature is drained of blood. Then it is opened up and inspected by the expert slaughterer.

If the animal shows any signs of disease, such as growths, cancers, lesions, lung disease etc. it is rejected as un-kosher and it goes into the general, non kosher meat supply for general consumption.

The meat that is used and that is deemed fit to eat ("kosher" means fit to eat) comes only from the fore quarter of the animal. The hindquarter is riddled with veins and arteries that are very difficult to remove from the rear of the animal, so this too goes into the general meat supply.

The remaining flesh that is deemed fit to eat is then salted and soaked in water, and drained on a sloping board in order to allow the blood to leach out. This is done so as to fulfill the prohibition against the eating of blood. Finally it is well cooked, not rare, to the extent that no blood remains in the meat.

The sages of the ancient Hebrew law clearly recognized the spiritually degenerative effects of, and the inherent physical dangers in, consuming flesh!

They prohibited the consumption of all carnivorous creatures such as sharks, snakes, critters of various sorts and any animals that scavenge such as shrimps, and shellfish. All are considered unclean.

The list of edible creatures is very short and quite specific. Hunting is prohibited as causing needless suffering to an animal, and the killing method would render it un-kosher.

Within the flesh of any creature, energy is not as pure as that from sunlight.

Energy within flesh is fragmented and contaminated by the enzymes, chemicals, hormones and the very consciousness and psyche of the creature itself.

When eating living flesh one creates an immediate disconnection from the Source of Life.

Flesh is dead matter.

The uncleanness of meat, its density and lack of lightness creates a violent and fearful intelligence or awareness in the person that eats flesh.

Bear in mind that all thought is pure energy even those of an animal.

In all creature's bodies thoughts and fears are stored energetically at a cellular level, the same way that sunlight is stored in fossil fuels that originally were plants.

It is easy to see the connection and how the consciousness of the animal is transferred to the host body that consumes its flesh.

When meat eaters ingest the bacteria and toxins contained within flesh they should also consider that modern factory farms inject huge doses of antibiotics, steroids and growth hormones into the animal as well.

Many of these chemicals are banned for human consumption, but they find their way into our body via meat.

The primary consideration of the modern factory farms is to increase an animal's market weight and to accelerate its growth to maturity in the shortest time possible. The faster the animal grows the shorter the time one has to care for it, the larger the profit. Consequently animals are being raised and sent to market in increasingly shorter times. In some cases the growth and the development of animals is half their natural biological rhythm. This is completely against their natural law and growth process. This

315

chemical soup of animal flesh, hormones, steroids, antibiotics and drugs is metabolized in your digestive system whenever you eat meat. It is carried to your bloodstream, organs, glands and of course your brain. Your nervous system, brain synapses, glands and organs are bathed in this chemical cocktail. This is believed to be the reason why our children are developing adolescence at increasingly younger ages. They are driven to premature maturity by their diet! After all it makes sense. If animals fed growth hormones mature in half their normal time, and our children consume this meat, it makes sense that our children are being "factory farmed" as well. That is to say they are what they eat!

The blood of modern man on a modern diet filled with chemicals from his diet and his environment is a mucky chemical soup cloudy with the death consciousness of animals, fat, cholesterol and narrowed arteries.

Blood should be a stream of life, crystal clean, free of pollutants and sparkling with light and energy.

The fragmented flow of energy in a polluted body disrupts the communication with your energy body or higher self (soul) and ultimately with God. Reality is a harder goal to achieve when the channel is blocked. It is like trying to dialog with someone who is drunk or spaced out on drugs. Their sense of reality is distorted. They may imagine that they are lucid and they think that they are making perfect sense, to others they are incoherent.

Does this not describe what I have been saying all along?

One creates an illusion of reality and they believe that illusion to be real.

Is this not similar to what a drunk or a drug user believes and experiences?

We create illusions too, only without drugs.

Drugs are so powerful that the user creates worlds within worlds. That does not presuppose that he started off from the correct world in the first place.

The drug user shows us is how easily the mind can be affected and turned into an instrument that creates illusionary states of existence.

Therefore a healthy body is a precursor to a healthy mind and a healthy state of awareness.

If the vessel is sound we can sail the sea of illusions to the shores of Truth.

The atoms of the energy body in its natural and unpolluted state should crackle and sparkle with light and power like the miniature galaxy I previously described.

Instead people contaminate their bodies and their cells become aged and deathly and the energy body becomes fragmented.

This is not our natural and normal state. Yet we have come to accept it as so without protest or query.

The activity of eating meat is a toxic one that is very hard on the body and it prematurely ages it.

A healthy person who is in touch with his or her feelings and higher self is clear and intuitive. Pollutants in a body serve only to suppress ones Divinity and to cut one off from their true source of well-being and glowing good health.

Observe the healthy glow of a newborn infant to appreciate the radiance that surrounds a healthy energy body.

Those who are disconnected from the source of Divine and pure energy often experience life like a faulty electrical connection. The fragmented energy connects in fits and starts through the clogged connections within the body.

Without the connection to his or her true self, a person will have periodic spurts of well being between bouts of heaviness of mind and body.

Fear, moodiness, anger and aggression with a susceptibility to illness, sadness and a feeling of not being present are symptomatic of a compromised energy system. Sleep may be fitful. An overall feeling of lethargy, heaviness, cravings to eat, binges and helplessness may be interspersed with feelings of well being and self-empowerment.

This is the body fighting itself to maintain energetic integrity. The electrical connections are connecting sporadically as one vacillates between states of being and connectedness.

A feeling of malaise is common. Usually, by the time of adulthood one no longer has feelings of complete well being, which is your natural state. One gradually comes to regard the state they are in as normal. One may become more susceptible to illness and be prone to bouts of moodiness or aggressive behavior. The use of social drugs, such as caffeine, alcohol, and nicotine all heighten the state of lassitude and suppress the light within.

The precursor to such feelings is frequently precipitated long before people become aware of the negative thoughts and originates from blocking the light of their own bodies.

Ones death urge precipitated by negative thought processes, suppression of aliveness, and unreleased frustration cause illness. Long before you become ill, the groundwork for ill health has been prepared.

We know, through the works of such noted authors as Louise Hay and Carolyn Myss that illness is the result of ones negative thoughts manifesting into physical reality.

The cause of the negative thoughts may, to some extent, be the result of the imbalance of the energy body and is aggravated by self-abuse as a result of what you put into your body.

We know that diet and stress play a major role in the disease process.

At a superficial level doctors attribute illness purely to the physiological manifestation and chemical consequences of high cholesterol, chemical preservatives, sugars, salts, dyes and other agents used in food production and the deficiencies of a modern diet.

Doctors are starting to realize that the healthy well-adjusted body (light body) is far more resistant to illness. The study of how the energy complexity of a body is affected by diet and life style will show that the body is prepared for defeat and illness from birth if not sooner.

Diet combined with mental well-being is very important.

Children need to have self-esteem and know that they are perfect beings from an early age.

Thoughts about oneself are formed at a very early age, starting in pre-birth and these early thoughts manifest ones reality.

Therefore the energy body needs healthy nurturing in both spirit and body from the time of conception onwards.

During the course of the average American life, one will have eaten thousands of pounds of dead fish, chickens, cows, pigs, and other living creatures. They will take in untold quantities of death energy released in the moments of trauma prior to the demise of these creatures.

Death, decay and chemicals in addition to the death trauma itself of the dead animal accumulate in the body. Recycling energy from dead flesh is not conducive to good health or of creating a lighter, purer human energy being.

The average person is in effect a burial ground for dead animals.

This is conducive to the decay of ones life force and it serves to block the pure light and clear energy of love and connectedness to higher self. In this it also hastens death and depletes the quality of life.

Ingesting flesh is not the only dietary thing people do to their body that distances them from the Divine Light.

They remove themselves from life by eating processed foods. Today foods contain all sorts of "safe" additives in order to prolong shelf life and to add flavor, color and eye appeal. Food contains dyes, chemical preservatives, processed fats, starches and sugars as well as pesticides, hormones and chemical growth stimulators. This is all a part of the mainstream diet.

Fruits, in addition to pesticides, fungicides and chemical fertilizers, also have wax substances on their skins to preserve shelf life. Anyone who has tried to remove this wax from an apple skin knows that it is impossible to do.

The U.S. military is proud of its latest accomplishment. Meals ready to eat that will not decay for up to five years!

We don't need a foreign enemy to kill our youth the government will do it for us.

These foods are so far removed from the healthy source of light and natural food source as to be unfit for human or animal consumption.

Companies like Monsanto Chemicals have genetically altered plants, called GMO'S, so that plants manufacture and produce poisons within their cells to kill insects and to resist herbicides. These pesticides and herbicides are engineered so that they are produced in the plants own cell structure as part of its genetic makeup.

These *Frankenfoods*, as they have been called, in the case of Monsanto are designed to be specifically resistant only to Monsanto's Roundup weed killer.

Farmers planting these seeds spray their fields with Roundup weed killer and only Monsanto's seeds survive. This insures that farmers are locked in to Monsanto for their seed supply as well as for their herbicides.

They are banned in Europe. The USA threatened trade reprisals against the European Union if they did not allow the free import of Frankenfoods into Europe!

Famine stricken countries such as Zambia in Africa even refused to distribute US food aid because it contains genetically modified grain!

Here in the USA there is no way that you can avoid eating them.

Such is the world of corporate influence peddling in America.

The majority of grain and soybeans in the USA today are genetically modified. They are in everything from bread and breakfast cereals, and processed food products, to the animal feed in the meat that you eat.

The long-term consequences of eating food with genetically implanted toxins capable of destroying life forms such as insects has yet to be studied on human beings.

There is no logical reason to suppose that it is benign.

There is every reason to suggest that, as information becomes available that corporate lawyers will likely suppress it.

Oprah Winfrey was sued by the cattle industry in the USA for making disparaging public comments about the health value of beef. They lost in court and the industry embarked on a huge advertising campaign to promote beef consumption!

In the meantime, over 70% of the soy and grain produced in the USA are genetically altered in some form. This affects countless off the shelf food products. It is also used in livestock feed, so the accumulated effect of Frankenmeat and Frakenfood may take years to materialize in the American human population.

Based on past mistakes that the chemical industry has made, it took decades of prolific use of the pesticide DDT before it was found that the poison accumulated in the body.

It did not disperse or degrade. As an animal ate DDT tainted food, the pesticide levels in its body kept increasing until the creature died, or else it was so toxic that if another creature killed and ate it, the predator died!

Thousands of species of birds went extinct or nearly so, including the California Condor, the largest bird in the USA, and the American bald eagle.

The poison accumulated in their bodies from eating smaller creatures that had been exposed to DDT. Eventually they were unable to reproduce. They laid eggs that were infertile or whose shells were so fragile that the embryo was unviable.

Processed foods are also a terrible abuse to the body.

Combined with other abuse, to which people subject the body, this further suppresses their aliveness. The added use of alcohol, stimulants, smoking, over the counter medication, prescription drugs such as Prozac, tranquilizers, hormones, illegal drugs, anesthetics, chemo-therapy, plus smog and pollution, all put the body under tremendous strain.

The result, depending on your level of consciousness and the nature of your chemical diet, that is, the substances that you expose yourself to every day, is that you may feel so far removed from your spiritual connection to God that one feels spiritually abandoned.

Of course you will *feel* disconnected. (In truth you never can be, you are always connected), but in your physical and mental state, you will experience disconnection.

One blocks the flow of awareness with every lifestyle choice they make that is not in accord with ones spiritual being.

When deep separation is felt, the mind tries to rationalize ones life but at the purely physical level and ones feelings are dulled to any sensitivity of the spiritual source of being.

This is a very frightening and bewildering state to be in. That is when the lower animal instinct for the survival of the body kicks in. In this state one can kill another without conscience and remorse. One can kill oneself.

It is no wonder that there are such high numbers of dysfunctional parents and children. Entire neighborhoods and cities can be dysfunctional.

It is a testament to the strength of our bond with God, and Gods love for us, that we still have a sense of spiritual awareness and humanity.

Even without awareness of God connectedness this does not mean that God has abandoned you or judged you.

No matter how disconnected you may feel, you are always a perfect child of God.

Your physical body may be in denial of that fact, however your soul is perfect and longs for you to find your healing and your way back to your divinity.

To achieve healing, one needs to forgive oneself and to see oneself as perfect, no matter what you have done or are currently doing. The start of the process is in forgiving oneself of past ways and of working towards healing your connection to the Divine.

The Light will be waiting for you always in total love and to welcome the return of your dear soul back from the darkness of the illusion and to Light.

If you choose not to seek reconciliation with your higher self, your senses will always be blunted towards feeling or realization of the spiritual source of your existence.

This can be a terrifyingly dark place to be. Unfortunately certain institutions thrive on attracting people who are immersed in the dark. The military, security agencies and some churches and hate organizations attract souls bound up in darkness. They seek to break down ones sense of self.

The void created by suppressed spiritual awareness is replaced with the credo of the organization.

The manifesto of such organizations is inevitably based on fear, racism, xenophobia, paranoia and suspicion. There is always an external threat to ones well being that the candidate can focus his attention on. As the Course in Miracles says, there is no need for defense unless there is fear of attack.

All thoughts of fear are caused by our separation from divinity.

It is interesting to consider that those in charge of national security are arguably the most fearful beings in our society!

In the realm of spiritual darkness life cannot make sense. Therefore people create false realities or illusions to help them to make sense of their fears. Madness reigns and the perception of personal helplessness prevails. Circumstances appear to be spinning out of control and a feeling that no one is really in charge may predominate.

Mistrust even of ones own senses, guides the critical thinking process

In this condition it may appear that there is no love in this world, and joy is nowhere to be found. One may feel confronted all around and reality feels disconnected. In this illusion of despair and paranoia, a person cannot hear the voice of the Father calling His beloved child to emerge from the dullness of a mind out of control.

Whatever we eat and think, all we have ingested both physically and mentally is either supporting or suppressing aliveness. What was once was a perfect baby, reflecting all the Light and Joy of the Universe, has grown ill and distant in his adult madness as he separates from the One who loves him still, and who awaits his return with love and compassion.

Psychic nightfall is the darkest of all illusions. Psychic night can be the longest and darkest of all illusions.

In the psychic nightfall you must call forth the child pure and innocent that is still you.

Call upon the child deep within to remember the bliss and innocence of the calm where love, light and joy prevail.

<u>The Price of a Cow</u>

In real love you want the other person's good. In romantic love you want the other person - Margaret Anderson (Scottish born biologist and writer)

The United States is the largest grain producer in the world. We produce enough to feed the entire world.

o   38 000 children die of starvation and malnutrition every day, one child every 2 seconds
o   20 000,000 human beings will die from malnutrition this year.
o   Livestock consumes 70% of the US grain production.
o   64% of US cropland is used to produce livestock feed. 2% is used for fruits and vegetables.
o   If Americans cut their consumption of meat by a mere10%, 100 000,000 people could live on the land, energy and water resources used to grow livestock
o   To produce just one pound of beef takes 16 pounds of grain
o   One acre of prime land can produce 250 pounds of beef - or - 20 000 pounds apples, 30,000 pounds carrots, 40 000 pounds potatoes, 50 000 pounds tomatoes.
o   It takes 78 calories of fossil fuel to produce 1 calorie of beef protein - or 2 calories of fuel to produce 1 calorie of soybean protein.
o   In California, the number of gallons of water required to produce 1 pound of beef is 5214,
o   or - Tomatoes, lettuce and wheat 23- 25, Apples 49, Oranges 65

The actual cost of squandered resources is not the only cost to mankind. Animal farming takes a heavy toll on the environment.

o   One third of original cropland has been permanently removed from production due to erosion
o   35 pounds of topsoil is lost for each pound of feedlot beef. It takes nature 200 - 10000 years to make one inch of topsoil

o   30% of earth's landmass is suffering desertification. The annual loss of land due to desertification on earth each year is 52 million acres.

o   The main causes are: Overgrazing livestock (there are about 3 head of livestock for each person on earth) Deforestation (mainly for grazing livestock), prevention of reforestation (the livestock chew on saplings and bushes)

o   125 000 square miles of rainforest is destroyed each year.

o   1000 species of flora and fauna go extinct each year due to destruction of tropical rainforest (About 25% of all medicines are derived from plants)

o   25 % of South American rainforest has been cleared for cattle production.

o   Amount of beef the USA imports from South America each year $300 million pounds

o   The value over 50 years of burned and cleared cattle ranching rainforest is estimated to be $2 960 per hectare compared with $6 330 of virgin forest.

o   European animal farmers received $120 billion in 1990 subsidies. Surpluses were dumped in less developed nations, economically damaging rural farming communities and social structures in those nations

In addition to the soil degradation there is a tremendous cost in terms of air pollution

o   The average US beef eating family of four requires the burning of 200 gallons of fossil fuel each year to produce the beef. This releases 2 tons of carbon dioxide into the air each year. This is almost as much as the annual output of the family car - 2.5 tons annually. One steak is equivalent to about a 25mile drive in a typical American car.

o   About 33% of all carbon dioxide emissions in the atmosphere are from the burning of biomass.

o   Cattle release methane gas when they pass wind, which they do continuously. About 100 million tons of methane gas is released annually or about 1 pounds of gas per 2 pounds of beef. This is about 20% of the world's total. Methane gas is a major contributor to global warming.

Then there is the problem of waste.

o   In the US cattle produce about 230 000 pounds per second. A 10 000 head feedlot will create waste equal to a city of 110 000 people.
o   50% of the US groundwater is polluted with agricultural pollutants such as pesticides, fertilizers, herbicides, soil runoff and manure. The amount of water pollution attributable to agriculture is greater than all the municipal and industrial sources combined.

How does diet affect our health? Here are a few of the many disorders related to diet.

o   68% of disease in the US is estimated to be diet related. Diseases which are preventable or can be improved by a low fat non animal diet are: Arthritis, Cancers of the Breast, Prostate and Colon, Constipation, Diabetes, Gallstones, Heart Disease, Hypertension, Hypoglycemia, Kidney Disease, Obesity, Osteoporosis, Ulcers, Food Poisoning, and Strokes.
o   US physicians receive on average about 2.5 hours of nutritional training in a four year medical school.
o   The most common cause of death in the US is heart disease which costs the US about $135 billion annually to treat. One person is stricken about every 25 seconds and one-person dies every 45 seconds. There is a 50% chance of the average American male having a heart attack.
o   The risk of heart attack for the average American vegetarian male is 15%
o   40% of cancers are estimated to be diet related. About $70 billion is spent in the US annually on treatment. Women, who eat meat daily, compared to once a week are about 4 times more at risk of breast cancer. A similar figure applies to prostate cancer in men.
o   The average bone loss of female meat eaters at age 65 is 35% compared to 18% for vegetarians

o   Beef is the food most likely to cause cancer from herbicide residue. Only one animal in 250 000 is tested for toxicity. Female meat eaters mother's milk has a 99% chance of having high levels of toxic chemical residue compared to 8% vegetarian.

o   55% of antibiotics used in the US are fed to livestock. The percentage of Staphylococci infections resistant to penicillin rose from 13% in 1960 to 91% in 1988 primarily as a result of the routine feeding of antibiotics to livestock. 80% of livestock and poultry will receive drugs in their lifetimes. In 1991 63% - 86% of milk samples contained Sulfa drugs, tetracycline's, and other antibiotics.

o   33% of inspected chickens were found to contain salmonella bacteria. 75% of federal poultry inspectors said they would not eat chicken.

* This information is excerpted from Thom Hartman's book "The Prophets Way" and is sourced from the Pulitzer Prize nominated book "Diet for a New America" by John Robbins. Thom Hartmann advises that Further information is available from EarthSave - 706 Frederick Street - Santa Cruz - CA 95062-2205

Jeffrey M. Solomon

Chapter Thirteen - Consciousness

You cannot surrender to God without accepting unconditional love. -
God (Universal Deity)

The Linear Nature of Consciousness

We call the unconscious "nothing," and yet it is a reality "in potentia". The thought we shall think, the deed we shall do, even the fate we shall lament tomorrow, all lie in our unconscious today. - Carl Jung (Swiss Psychologist)

The consciousness of modern man has discarded the ancient accepted principles incorporated in human consciousness.

Since the Age of Enlightenment mankind continued the pattern of the previous two thousand years of life in a blinkered state of awareness. He is now starting to emerge. Man is becoming aware of his delusions concerning himself and society.

The Age of Enlightenment, so called, was ushered in approximately with the age of Newtonian Physics, and later Darwin and the Evolution of the Species. Western man started, perhaps as far back as Leonardo Da Vinci to question the classical Church dogma of existence. However scientific query and enlightenment can reasonably be said to have truly commenced around the late 17th century in Western Europe with the age of scientific inquiry, the subsequent French and American revolutions and the re-birth of the ancient Classical concepts of the Republic and the rebirth of democracy.

For almost two thousand years preceding this, there were Dark Ages. This was a time of physical servitude to the church and bondage to the nobility. It was a time of mental darkness as the flame of learning went out in Europe. There was a complete lack of individual rights. The light of truth and discovery faded in the West.

The concept of individual thought, enlightenment, expression or freedom was anathema for centuries. Even the privileged nobility had no spiritual independence even insofar as their personal thoughts were concerned. To disagree with established Church dogma was heretical. Even kings who fell afoul of the church had to swiftly recant their views or face the risk of losing their crown and very often the space on which to wear the crown!

The church thrived in this climate of repression and it kept the population at large steeped in superstition, ignorance and fear. In so doing, the Church by inculcating ignorance insured both a compliant flock throughout Europe and the uninterrupted flow of revenue, land holdings, power through the infallibility of the papal office.

Central to this ideology of the Church was the installation in the general population of the fear of God and the threat of eternal damnation for sinners. In this regard, the ministers of the Church set themselves up as God's own representatives on earth with the power to absolve sins, usually for a fee, as well as the sole arbiter of Gods divine will.

The Church of Rome demanded total subservience from a docile population that was kept dumb and intimidated for the greater glory of Rome. God was not a god of love and light but rather God was a deity to be feared. Ones every thought and deed was judged and almost nothing a person could do was deemed good enough to gain entry to heaven. Only the church as Gods sole emissary on earth could intervene on your behalf and absolve you of your sins. The Pope was the infallible word of God on earth. The pope's will was Gods will under a doctrine of the infallibility of the pope. The pope's church was His church, the pope's word His word. Ones admittance to heaven depended on the hierarchy of bishops, cardinals and priests of God's self appointed emissaries.

Thus it was that the power of the individual in every aspect of life was subservient to the church.

Given the atmosphere of the Age of Enlightenment at the time of revolutions in Europe and America, science was embraced as the new great enlightening liberator. Scientific discovery would set mankind free and unshackle his mind.

Over the past three hundred years, science has indeed fulfilled one promise and has liberated individual thinking. People's ideas about themselves, the universe and society are all open to inquiry and exploration.

The Church still dictates about issues such as birth control etc. The tyranny of the papacy has faded though it is not dead yet.

The church still clings to faded hopes of past glories but no serious thinker can possibly embrace the idea of God as vengeful or judgmental. It is ludicrous to imagine today that the church is the sole arbiter of Gods will or that the path to God requires an intermediary in the form of a priest, or any other societal representative in order to obtain Divine Grace. Individuals are free to seek the light of God in any way they now choose.

People have for the most part withdrawn the absolute power that they originally accredited to the church.

Yet man still is not free.

Freedom implies that we should be free of fear. Fear is the great illusion that hides our light.

I would like to look at the current state of our society to see if there is a trend to indicate if we are moving to a higher state of consciousness or not.

What is the current state of personal empowerment?

It is now in the hands of a new god in the form of corporate states.

Global corporations have developed into massive corporate undertakings in every field of endeavor such as multi-national drug companies, global telecommunications, world wide media companies, financial institutions, computer companies and so on.

A secret cabal called the World Trade Organization now controls the new power structure for the new age. This is the age of globalism and a New World Order.

The power and influence these titans of commerce wield over governments and public policy has an affect on our lives that are unimaginable. In the USA 80% of the national wealth is accumulated in the hands of less than 10% of the population, with a large portion of that in the hands a few dozen families of the mega rich. The wealth of Microsoft chairman, Bill Gates, at about $80 billion exceeds the gross national product of the majority of the member countries of the United Nations!

This state of affairs has certain similarities to that which existed in the world during the Middle Ages. The power of the feudal lords and the church has transferred into the hands of a new aristocracy, namely, the corporate CEO. The One World Economy is at hand, ruled by a few dozen super powerful corporations in each country.

Individuals, as they did in the Dark Ages, have again disempowered themselves, and their freedom. This time they have handed it to the government, which in turn is the servant of the super wealthy and the special interests of mega business. In line with this, new legislation will restrict access of citizens to information under the

Freedom of Information Act. It will also provide for severe penalties to anyone who releases information to, the press or academics.

Vice President Dick Cheney, (a former CEO of Texas energy company Halliburton Co.), is currently being sued by the Congress of the USA for refusing Congresses' demand to divulge the minutes of a secret meeting that he had with oil company executives. Congress believes that the meeting is critical to National energy policy and perhaps to the policies of the Bush administration itself.

In terms of the new secrecy policy, Cheney can claim immunity from Congress under the pretext of National Security.

Synchronicity is a strange and wonderful thing. The Universe always provides. Here is another example of something turning up to support one when you are in tune.

I had earlier written the above about Dick Cheney's links to big oil business and last night I was reviewing and editing this section.

I am going to digress at this point to tell you about this synchronous event, after which I will return to the issue of the impact of the proposed secrecy policy on everyday people.

Today the St Petersburg Times presented me with an article. Front page of the paper, November 21st 2002 that reports the following.

Halliburton Co. (Cheney's former company) and Hunt Oil Co. have close ties to the Bush administration and are two of the largest contributors to the George Bush - Dick Cheney administration.

These two oil conglomerates are seeking administration support for $900 million in public financing to build a pipeline in Peru through *one of the world's most pristine tropical rain forests!*

The Camisea project, as it is called, has provoked outrage and opposition from environmental groups and even some members of congress. Scientists have deemed the region in pristine condition with a *wealth of unique, unidentified species.* The project follows on a trip Bush made to Peru in March 2002. (Now the Universe is showing us *why* Dick Cheney, even under a subpoena from Congress, is not telling Congress about his earlier meetings with these companies!).

The following quotation from the St. Petersburg Times may well be restricted in future, under the guise of National Security, if the security bill passes.

"Under federal regulations, projects receiving backing from the Import-Export Bank of the United States and the Inter-

American Development Bank must pass rigorous reviews to insure that they will not threaten rare natural habitats. (Emphasis is mine)

But according to the *Washington Post,* officials reviewing the Camisea loan applications, who asked not to be identified, say the project is proceeding despite warnings that it may run afoul of international environmental standards".

Even reviews commissioned by the developers themselves have concluded that there is destructive erosion, landslides, spills, and unauthorized pipeline diversions, and the clearing of too much land.

In the 1980's Royal Dutch Shell Oil prospected the Urubamba River Region and 5 million acres of Peru's Uyacali Basin. Shell agreed to avoid contact with the indigenous people and to cut no roads in the region. Nevertheless in their wake poachers invaded the previously impenetrable jungle, harvesting rare trees and wildlife. They introduced influenza and whooping cough and other diseases that killed 40% of the indigenous tribes!

Since then, in 2000 the Texans have moved in, pledging to adopt Shell's social and environmental program. The consortium led by Hunt Oil has carved large swathes through the jungle exceeding 50 feet in width in places. Erosion and landslides have rendered pristine waterways muddy and unusable for the indigenous people for drinking and bathing and hunting. The scar cut through the forest is a mud pit becoming deeper and cratered from erosion and rainfall. Deforestation, illegal poaching, habitat loss and contamination of headwaters are already an irreversible fact. There is a significant decline of fish and game populations.

The Inter-American Development Bank is considering part of the $900 million loan applications of the Hunt Halliburton consortium. Their environmental project reviewer, Robert Montgomery, has played down the disaster in progress, "If they have had past bad actions and they are willing to improve, we have to take that into consideration".

Jon Sohn of Friends of the Earth said that, "the connections are obvious …Hunt and Halliburton were involved in their (Bush and Cheney) campaign fundraising, in their transitional policies and in Vice President Dick Cheney's secret energy plan".

The U.S. representative to the Inter-American Development Bank is a Hispanic Bush appointee, Jose Forquet, who is an "elite donor" who raised at least $100 000 for Bush's 2000 campaign.

Separately at the Export-Import Bank that is considering the other part of the $900 million loan, Phillip Merrill, Bush's nominee to run the bank, is another major Republican Donor and a friend of Dick Cheney and his wife, Lynn.

Ray Hunt, whose son is Hunter Hunt the Vice Chairman of Hunt Oil Co., was appointed to Halliburton's board with Dick Cheney's Backing. President George W. Bush named Ray Hunt to the Foreign Intelligence Advisory Board after he raised money for Bush Snr. in 1992. In 2000 Bush Jnr. Tapped Ray Hunt to chair the Republican National Committee's Victory Fund to which Hunt gave $20 000. The Hunts gave at least another $460 000 to other Republican campaigns. The Hunt companies and their employees and spouses gave more than $1 million to the GOP since 1995. According to the Hunt Oil Co. website, Hunter Hunt is listed as "Bush's primary policy advisor responsible for energy issues".

Regarding the impact of the new secrecy law on private individuals, here is one person's story.

Once again, this is pure synchronicity having been broadcast today, the same day as the St Petersburg Times article appeared about Hunt Oil.

I never listen to the radio when working however I felt compelled at around noon to turn on my local Public Radio Station.

Once again, in editing my notes about the secrecy laws this broadcast came at precisely the moment I was working on this topic. If I had heard it in my car or in the bathroom it would not have found mention in this book! Believe in magic my friends.

You may argue that this secrecy law does not affect law-abiding citizen who has nothing to hide.

You are wrong.

On November 21st 2002 Public Radio program Democracy Now aired an interview with a lady.

It seems that in the wake of 9/11 the FBI compiled a list of terrorists and individuals that may have come into contact with the terrorists. This list includes hotel staff, schools, car rental personnel, bank employees and any place where suspected terrorists may have

335

come into contact with ordinary citizens. The FBI released this computer list to airports, banks and various public service companies in the hope that they would be alerted the minute that someone on the list appeared on the database and that the FBI could be notified.

The FBI lost control of the list. It was copied and passed on from bank to bank, financial institutions, car dealerships, and soon it was turning up in South America and Asia. By this time the list was outdated for the most part except that real terrorists knew that they were on the list.

By this stage the FBI could not update the list. It was spread worldwide. Those that had any form of innocent contact with the terrorists did not know that they were on the list.

One of these innocent people was the lady that was interviewed. It seems that every time she flies she is stopped for a full security search. She is usually stripped searched, made to undress and is frequently humiliated in the process. When she asks why she is stopped at every check in counter, and frequently a second time at the gate, she is told that the computer has randomly selected her!

In another example, a man inserting his gambling card into a slot machine at a casino in Las Vegas triggered a security alert!

Twenty-two Federal agencies have been merged. This includes all the departments of the military, FBI, CIA and all secret agencies such as the Secret Service, the INS, Customs, Transportation and Coast guard. One man, Tom Ridge, appointed by the President will head all. The absolute power that is concentrated in the executive office of the President is beyond anything that the framers of the constitution could have imagined.

Public ignorance and public tax funding of the activities of clandestine organizations such as the CIA and FBI, National Security, Secret Service etc. is beyond question. Citizens are asked to accept in blind faith that the decisions made by these secret organizations is in the best public interest. Until recently we were not even aware of the existence of certain covert agencies.

J. Edgar Hoover, former head of the FBI and one of the most powerful men in the world at that time, had dirty files on every politician, political activist and celebrity in the United States. Hoover used his office to gain personal leverage over politicians. He had entertainers blackballed by the entertainment industry if he suspected them of being Liberals and Communists. He even had files on the presidents under whom he served, and used this knowledge to consolidate his iron grip on power. For decades Hoover was indeed the power behind the presidency in the United States, using Machiavellian intrigue and scandal to further his personal agenda.

The power that Hoover had is but a fraction of that of the new Leader of the Department of Homeland Security (Tom Ridge) will have. President Bush called the passage of the bill, "A historic and bold step to protect the American people".

The position of Leader of Homeland Security itself rings ominously similar to that of the Reich fuehrer (Homeland Leader) in Nazi Germany. It was the Reich fuehrer Heinrich Himmler (a convicted war criminal) under Adolph Hitler who commanded the notorious homeland secret police, the SS. With their infamous totenkopf (deaths head) insignia, they had authority over every branch of the military, its officers, and government departments and of course the infamous death camps of Europe. They were responsible only to the Reich fuehrer himself.

As you read this, and in the knowledge that we create our own reality, stop and do a reality check.

What is it that this nation is manifesting? Do we have an Imperial American desire for world domination? Are we becoming an intolerant nation?

Consider whether this is the manifestation of Fear in the national consciousness.

Remember that the need for defense is an illusion in the face of another illusion, the Fear of attack.

Let me continue.

Information and military projects such as the research center at Area 51, is shrouded in secrecy.

The government has posted signs indicating that it will shoot its own citizens on sight if they enter this secret area. Indeed, the very existence of Area 51, in spite of books and television documentaries about it, is still officially denied! This is our elected official's at work.

The citizens of the USA, having bought the official line of "secrecy being necessary for national security" and have empowered the so-called "government of the people, and by the people", to hijack power from the people.

The current buzzword is National Security. Information is shared on the basis of the need to know. Many times the president of the United States is excluded from the inner knowledge of so-called secret skunk works that are clandestine operations performed by the various secret organizations in the USA.

In the name of secrecy, radiation experiments on civilians and convicts have been carried out. Nuclear fallout experiments bathed unsuspecting communities across the country in the 1950's for the purpose of government research. Chemical warfare agents have been tested on our own troops in the 1970's and 1980's. Thousands of classified projects are hidden behind the net of national security.

What we do know is that the individual is no more empowered now than in the past, and hence the popularity of conspiracy shows such as the X-Files on TV and the Art Bell show on the radio.

One reason for the popularity of these types of shows is that the broadcast media is largely controlled by the same multibillion organizations that influence national and international policy. These are the "king makers".

Control of the news is vital in maintaining a docile and confused population. The less that is reported in the mainstream news and the more that fringe elements report on conspiracy and cover ups, the easier it is for the powers that be to ridicule such fringe reporting as extremist minority propaganda.

Mega business is involved in the education system. It requires that our school system be designed from the top down to provide a conservative and homogenous labor force commensurate with the consumer base required to purchase production and for the efficient flow of goods and services. So whereas we turn out a prodigious supply of technicians, marketers, lawyers, accountants, designers, physicists and the like, which keeps industry and government supplied with the means of production and mass consumption, personal happiness has not resulted from increased materialism.

Certainly and unarguably we are better off than people in the Middle Ages were. Yet in terms of empowerment modern society has yet to become empowered.

Clearly the level of paranoia in government and the level of consciousness has not improved.

Indeed we have created a World Trade Tower catastrophe on 9/11 that has taken us backwards in our evolution. We have spawned the need for attack and defense and a right wing xenophobic government that reflects our fears. We are quite possibly in the process of giving up our freedom.

True personal freedom is our birthright if we only had a truly enlightened society. When will the self worth of every individual be honored? Where is the awareness and time in our lives that allows us to be feeling human beings taking personal responsibility for our lives?

Where is brotherly love?

It is not taught in our schools.

This should be the direction for our society in the new millennium!

Here, as "Trekkies" would say, is the prime directive.

Power must be returned to the people and be used by the people for their betterment, enlightenment and mutual care.

In the transition from serf to citizen, individuals still have not reclaimed their personal power, because they have never considered self-awareness as a valuable goal worth pursuing.

Not once in the past two thousand years has any society embraced spiritual values, without discrimination, and honored the worth and growth of every individual. Not once has society taught high values in school as the prime lesson in life above mathematics and reading or anything else.

It would be preferable to create a desire for universal peace and tolerance in young minds, rather than churning out spiritually challenged consumers who are grist in the mill of global corporations engaged in the exploitation of mankind and competition for earth's resources.

To begin, we must first consider the child and then the adult in an holistic sense as a multifaceted being, each of whom is miraculously interconnected with every other being and life form throughout the entire range of life on earth. The interconnectedness of all human beings and all life does not stop with this thought. We must see our entire planet itself as a whole, holy and conscious life form, interdependent across the universe. To approach the world with reverence and awe is the highest thought we can have.

And yet it does not end here. We must embrace the notion of the interdependence of all life and that of planets across the universe. Beyond this we must see this connectedness extending inter-dimensionally and thus the interrelatedness of all things and all matter in the world of the five senses and beyond. Then you will see the I AM presence throughout the grand scheme of creation. You will know the magnificent oneness of all things in the universe as it exists in the here and now. Truly experience that we are collectively the entire universe, multidimensional, and one. With this realization, children could not grow up behaving in the ways that big government and big business behaves. And the people would not accept it if they did.

We will know at the deepest level the true meaning 'to hurt another is to hurt myself '.

This concept, however appealing, is not easily marketable as long as individuals remain disempowered, confused or unconscious. In other words, as long as one is a slave to three dimensional reality and ego, the fear of moving into a new paradigm, coupled with the fear of the unknown, will supersede all other considerations.

Government, being the incubator of fear of attack, greed, ego and paranoia, will most certainly resist when it feels threatened.

Government cannot regulate self-awareness. Therefore the established hierarchy cannot control you. The self-actualized being does not give energy to the mind games and egos of the powers that be. There is no model for control when a person has no personal attachment to the outcome. Self-awareness challenges the power of government in ways that they can have no answer to. Government currently is a law unto itself. We know that the charade of elections and democracy is just that. If you have read the preceding passages in this chapter you will acknowledge that government is the playground for a privileged few. It makes no difference which party is in control nothing ever changes. That is why the American people turn out to vote in such low numbers. The guys who own the ball get to play and they decide the rules.

And the American public does not own the ball. They don't even know where the playing field is!

Government has many hidden agendas, secret projects, deceptive practices which undermine the rule of law. We see this over and over again.

Admiral John Poindexter, the man who gave us the Iran-Contra scandal is a master of defying the rules. He was convicted in the Iran-Contra affair on five felony counts of Lying to Congress (perjury). Destroying official documents. Obstructing a Congressional Investigation. The conviction was overturned on appeal.

If you or I were so much as late paying a bill we could not even get a credit card!

Today Poindexter is back with a master plan to control the entire U.S.A. He is in charge of running the Total Information Awareness Project.

The Total Information Awareness Project is part of the new Department of Homeland Security. It is the creation of a huge database on every person in the USA.

Every time you use the phone, or visit a doctor, purchase medicine and rent a car you create a computer record. When you buy an airline ticket, have a judicial matter, use your credit card, surf the internet, send an E-mail or a fax, make a financial transaction, get a mortgage, write a check, apply for a passport etc. you create a computer record. The Total Information Awareness Project will draw all these records into one consolidated database on you! Government wants to have the ability to electronically track your every move right down to the Internet sites that you visit.

Government is arrogant in the treatment of its citizens. Nations treat each other with contempt, fear and xenophobia, and they extend this same attitude to all that they perceive as a challenge to their power including its own citizens.

The financial, military, industrial complex realizes that a public kept in fear is a public that can be exploited. Fear is presented via the media in diverse ways such as fear of foreign, economic and military threats, job security, legal threats, racial tension, disease, and loss of cultural identity to foreign influence, and the list goes on. If there is a human fear, the government and media will find the means to exploit it. That is why in the wake of 9/11 Americans are willing to sacrifice their personal freedoms and give government huge sweeping powers in return for the vague promise of Homeland Security.

Power once given is never relinquished peacefully.

The powers being handed to the Administration in America today have no comparison in the Western world unless we look to the former Soviet Union or Nazi Germany as a model.

Fear keeps the individual in society working, consuming, and supporting the status quo by voting for politicians that promise to protect them from perceived threats. Fear sells insurance products, political agendas, labor compliance, and fear even sells status symbols.

Financial success and power primarily determine the measure of ones importance and social standing. Status symbols such as homes, vehicles, clothing etc. are the status symbols of society.

What one has is more important than what one is. This becomes the societal expression of who you are and how you are defined.

The fear of losing status is a powerful aphrodisiac that fuels greed.

This state of affairs must, of necessity, lead to competition and not cooperation within society.

From the first day of school-children are programmed to be unthinking and accepting. They are encouraged to be placid in their acceptance of the status quo. Conformity is encouraged and rewarded. Who they truly are as great spiritual beings has no place or recognition in the system. Nor is this of value to the marketplace or government.

The result is that we have a flat line mentality and a flat line society. People have exchanged the authority of religion with that of the military industrial complex, in a flat line of consciousness unbroken since the Dark Ages.

One form of personal disempowerment has replaced the another. Personal power has been handed over and relinquished to authorities who have no moral imperative to represent the people in the first place.

Personal empowerment is no more real today than in medieval times, although the freedom to be a consumer has created the illusions of both personal empowerment and freedom of choice.

We are out of control as a consumer society.

The only freedom of choice you have is the brand of washing powder that you buy.

This false sense of freedom, this limited expression of choice is enough to send millions of consumers into shopping frenzies. Shopping is a form of release. The ability to choose in a visible and consequential manner is a powerful yet illusionary drug for the masses mired in this form of self-expression.

True empowerment is when our multidimensional soul consciousness is given full recognition and permission to define who we are in our full glory of being.

If people would only realize who they truly are, they would see that they are so much greater than their conditioning. Once you gain self-realization your entire perception of power and government shifts. Your priorities change. Your sense of awe finds expression in life itself.

You are greater than any church allowed you to be. You are a multi-dimensional holograph of Divine Will manifest. You exist across galaxies beyond time and space. You are eternal and timeless. Buried beneath your ego and social conditioning, beyond fear and repressed memories is a being of pure light. It is you.

When humankind is consciously aware of Self people will no longer emote in linear consciousness.

<u>Ten Signs of Spiritual Awareness</u>

A deep conviction that all just is, and it is perfect.

A desire to act spontaneously without fear and with certainty that all is well.

An ability to be present in the now and to enjoy the moment.

A willingness to forgive oneself unconditionally without judgment.

A willingness to forgive others as we forgive ourselves, without judgment.

A detachment from conflict

A detachment in interpreting the actions of others

A detachment from worry

A feeling of joy and safety in all situations

A feeling of love and acceptance towards all persons and all things

—

The Non Linear Nature of Consciousness II

Do not hate or hurt anyone. Make friends with everyone, For your own Self exists in every face. -
Kabir - (Indian Saint)

What is non-linear consciousness?

To know the nature of something you need to understand its opposite. To know hot, first understand cold. In the physical world the duality of knowledge is what enables us to comprehend our experiences.

Therefore first understand the linear in order to know the non-linear.

When we know what we are we can realize that which we can become.

Currently, the majority of mankind is living a linear existence, a flat line of awareness of self.

This flat line awareness has as a basic attribute, a horizontal perception of time, self and history. Hence consciousness is likewise flat. This is expressed as a reactive personality in an individual and as a reactive society when extended to the psyche of nations.

The progression of linear events inevitably follows a story line consisting of an incident, a reaction to the incident, a consequence, followed by another reaction. This sets up a chain of occurrences or events to which one is forced to continually respond in a knee jerk reaction to things as they happen.

For example, John insults Scott. Scott reacts with aggression, they may fight and each attempts to win and control the outcome of the situation. The hostility is never resolved. There may be feelings of guilt, enmity, fear, aggression, pride and ego followed by resentment.

There is never a winner, except in a very superficial and narrow sense. The source of the aggression is never erased or commuted. The fight is not resolved in a true sense. The outcome is beyond the control of the two of them because the karma is not balanced. Forgiveness has not been genuinely offered or accepted.

This is the pattern of human history. Northern Ireland is an example of a feud that has existed for centuries in a reactive and linear consciousness in the Irish mentality. No amount of linear thinking can control the final outcome of this dispute. Only genuine forgiveness offered and accepted by all concerned, along with a willingness to seek cooperation rather than confrontation will effect peace.

Mankind perceives its history as a long chain of events and consequences that produce results, frequently unanticipated, such as the armistice between Germany and the allies after World War One. The conflict was never resolved at the heart level (spiritual level). There was no forgiveness or rapprochement. Therefore peace was never in the heart and mind. This led to a further chain of events requiring response ad infinitum culminating in a Second World War.

This model exemplifies mankind's powerlessness to control it's destiny while at the same time it is under the misguided and futile belief that it is in control of its destiny.

After 10 000 years of human civilization since the first towns appeared, we have believed that we can direct the outcome of human actions. If we have not got it right yet what makes us believe that our present way of thinking works? One definition of insanity is to repeat the same behavior over and over again and to expect a different outcome! This is linear consciousness.

Books have been written on the history of man. Universities study political science and history, yet politicians and professors alike have never been able to predict the outcome of a given series of events. Nor can they, for the law of karma, (some would say chaos theory but this misses the point entirely) does not know the bounds of linear thinking. And as the Eternal Law is the True Law, any physical attempt to mold circumstances or to control the outcome of ones actions, has no place in the True Law, and hence must by very definition be an illusion and is consequently doomed to failure.

Unless you understand the karma to be healed by your actions and the karma being created anew by them, you can never, through five sensory, three dimensional perception ever be in control of your life much less any of the outcomes precipitated by the course of your actions.

One can only react blindly to situations and hope to create a given result that may or may not work, or that may end up as a compromise or possibly result in total failure. Frequently short-term results, such as the armistice in Europe after the First World War, have unforeseeable long-term consequences.

The final outcome can never be foreseen when action is taken in the name of ego and power and all you are spinning is an illusion.

The analogy of the butterfly whose wings cause a tiny ripple in the air current that magnifies into a wind which then intensifies into a full blown storm on the other side of the world, comes to mind.

The consequences of mindless and unconsciousness acts cannot be underestimated.

Apply this logic to your life. How many times have you started something, such as a relationship, a job, an enterprise, with the best intentions and the consequences or outcome have been very different from what was initially intended?

This is what I call the Titanic effect! The linear consciousness, having launched a course of action can never perceive the final destination of its actions.

Back in the 1960's, the hippie era, I passed by my teenage sister who was looking at herself and her new slacks in the mirror. In an innocuous remark as I passed I said

"Hi hippie"

Thirty years later she confessed to me that she thought that my remark was directed at her hips, which unbeknown to me, she was extremely self-conscious about. Soon thereafter she started dieting, became anorexic, her grades slipped, her self esteem took a beating, and in short she messed up part of her life. Now, twenty-five years and two marriages later, with her personal life having been a roller coaster, she is finally coming to conscious terms with her place in the universe through spiritual awareness and growth. She is gaining awareness of herself as a karmic being rather than a victim.

This is a good example of the unforeseen consequences of a mindless act, or the Titanic effect.

Another example of the Titanic effect in motion is exemplified in an excellent TV series of a few years ago, called Connections, shown on the Learning Channel. In this series one can follow the progression of historic events resulting from the invention of something through all the consequential and unforeseen ramifications of the occurrence and the subsequent implications of its invention.

For example, prior to the Industrial Revolution, fabric weaving was done on looms, by hand.

That is until a device called a Jacquard was invented. This was a belt with punched holes and fitted with pegs, (much like those metal cylinders in wind up music boxes that plunk out a tune). The Jacquard device caused the loom to raise and lower in a set pattern, endlessly repeating a weave automatically. This greatly speeded up the production of fabric and England became a world center of fabric production.

The amazing thing is that no one could guess that this punch hole loom of the industrial revolution would be the inspiration and forerunner of the computer punch card a century and a half later! The result? Space travel and the Information Age.

Still further down the line, no one foresaw that the limitations of the punch card would lead to a space saving device in which dates are reduce to a two-digit code. This led to the Y2K computer crisis, in which many essential computers, it was feared, would not recognize the change of the millennium! Had the world's computers crashed as some had predicted they would, it may have created one of the greatest cataclysms in modern life and all industrial production from oil to telecommunications and missile defense being disrupted.

Such is the Titanic effect on linear consciousness.

Linear consciousness is like putting life on autopilot. If things go well one may be inclined to attribute this to "luck".

Should things go poorly, the blame rests on circumstances beyond ones control, or "bad luck."

There is always a reason to be found in circumstances beyond ourselves as to why things do not go as planned. Chance events or other people may be blamed.

A non-linear thinker will tell you that nothing happens without meaning. There is no such thing as coincidence.

Even something as innocuous as the particular server you get in a restaurant has some meaning.

Linear thinkers, programmed from birth and through school, attach no importance to the seemingly trivial and meaningless. They also rarely attach much significance to the important stuff either!

This mindset leads one to feeling helpless and ineffective in a world out of control.

Thus people tolerate corrupt governments, war, poverty and personal disempowerment simply as the way things are in this world.

No wonder then that men look to the drug Viagra as a means of reviving diminished potency. Do you think for one minute that sexual impotence is unrelated to feelings of impotence in ones life as a whole? (Ask Bob Dole who lost to Bill Clinton in the Presidential race, and who is a spokesperson for Viagra).

To be a non-linear thinker you must look for the synchronicity of events in all levels of life and society as a whole. It is important to take responsibility for everything in your life, the good and the bad, and realize that you alone manifest all that happens to you. In doing so you must come to the realization that the crooks we have as elected leaders and to whom we have relinquished our power, are products of our own creation. If you shrug and say that all politicians are dishonest, then what you believe, will be true of what you get.

We need to teach our children and empower them. Neither the Church nor science can empower them for us.

Inasmuch as the Church would have once been our salvation in days gone by, today science attempts to fulfill that role.

Curiously at the turn of the twentieth century, it was a popular concept among many scientists that science had almost solved all the riddles of the universe. Some scientists even proclaimed the end of scientific endeavor and that there would be nothing more in the universe that required understanding!

Today we may well laugh at this incredible notion, yet we are only a few decades removed from this popular belief.

Today, we know of worlds in the atomic and sub atomic universe that were unimagined a hundred years ago. Remarkably, this time, the closer science gets to the origins of life and the cosmos, the closer they are drawing to the ancient spiritual knowledge and teachings in mankind's oldest texts, especially Sanskrit teachings of the nature of the creation. Through quantum physics we learn once again of the universal stuff (energy) of the universe, the relativity of time and space and the influence of the observer on the observed (creative manifestation).

In becoming spiritually aware we can begin to understand that there is a vertical way as well as the horizontal way of thinking and experiencing. In fact there is the global way of thinking, in which our thoughts emanate from us like a bubble or globe in every dimension, interacting at many levels of reality beyond our untrained and limited awareness. I would say that we do not think horizontally or vertically but rather holographically. There are perspectives without end and multiple dimensions to our concept of reality, which reach across time and space.

The interest in metaphysics continues to grow and soon the desire for self-awareness in mankind will reach a critical mass. No longer are we content to passively accept the status quo. Our higher self cries out for equal rights and equal time. We must evolve our society, science and leaders. We will explore the meaning of life beyond the limits of our five senses.

Becoming thus empowered, we shall recreate our lives and our society according to the Universal Law. It will not be enough for a slick lawyer to argue the fine point of law according to legal definitions in a casebook. The law will be simple. "For every action there is an equal and opposite reaction." The law of karma is impartial and absolute.

And whether we like it or not, that which we sow, we shall reap, without regard to the legal definition of sowing or reaping! No fancy lawyer can get you off the reaper's hook.

Mankind will come to understand in the core of its being, in our foremost awareness, that everything we do, think, say or cause to happen, will create an imbalance of universal energy. A debit or credit in the Universal Ledger if you prefer, that will bring to account all of our actions and thoughts. The negative will have to be balanced by the appropriate positive energy to prevent the effects of any act or acts from having repercussions on oneself.

This is the law governing all creation. It is simple, non-judgmental, impartial and eternal for all people, all nations, worlds and universes without end.

It is not a question of whether you shall reap what you sow, only a case of when. For in the Eternal Law, it matters not whether you reap in this life or the next. You cannot argue for a lesser sentence nor can you die and leave the debt unpaid.

Time, is not linear, as our senses would have us think. Albert Einstein showed us that time bends and curves, speeds up and slows down under the effects of gravity. In the case of a black hole, time ceases to exist at all. At the speed of light time is constant.

The universe does not share our five sensory perception of time. That which requires balancing will be balanced.

The Universal Light is the source of all faster than light travel. For example, most people have heard of cases where two people, apparently psychically attuned are aware of each other's emotions in the same instance. There are many documented cases, such as a wife knowing that her husband, who is hundreds of miles away, has had an accident in the exact moment it occurs.

The instances are numerous of such phenomena, however they are usually relegated to the level of curious anomalies. There are quantum physics experiments that show atomic particles behave as if time and space do not exist. Their behavior suggests that they are unbounded by the laws of time and space, and that communication between particles exist at a level or dimension that is not restricted by the familiar laws that we take for granted.

Universal Law demands a universe in balance. The positive and the negative are in balance.

If a particle "A" which is linked to a particle "B" is destroyed, then particle B will simultaneously disappear in the very same instant, without regard to distance or time. This unique cosmic balancing act is done instantaneously, not at the speed of light, but instantly at the speed of thought. The only thing that displays synchronous behavior of this magnitude is thought, which being instantaneous, is not being bound by the physical laws of our three dimensional science.

It would be ludicrous to think that the Divine in manifesting and sustaining creation is limited by the speed of light. He would wait 4000 million light years for His will to manifest at the far ends of the Universe if He were limited to the speed of light! Thoughts are instantaneous. Our thoughts are likewise instantaneous. Thought, therefore is an energy that is not limited by the laws of time and space.

Light does not travel in a straight line. It bends around planets under gravitational influences. This can even slow light down.

Using this principle, if a vehicle is to go from point A to point B that is a thousand light years away, the quickest way is to bend space and time. Imagine that points A and B are two points at the opposite ends of the galaxy light years apart. Now imagine two points on opposite ends of a sheet of paper. If you fold the paper in half so that points A and B are now touching each other, then the space between A and B is negligible!

This is not magic. It is within the Universal Law as well as within the theories of quantum mechanics. Time and space are relative. All things exist at all time, simultaneously.

Time, past, present and future are all in the now. It is our distorted five senses and our illusion that places time and space in a linear manner.

Therefore when we use linear thinking we do not see all of our "selves", that is, all of our lives and incarnations as existing simultaneously. Nor do we realize that we can affect our total karma, past, present and future from all lifetimes in the here and now.

In this state of being, the law of karma, one should realize that which graces you today, may be your reward from any of your incarnations and vice versa. Think of it as a bank to which you make deposits and withdrawals.

Misuse of the grace you receive could create the opposite effect if you are unconscious of the value of the gift you have received.

Therefore we should always accept the goodness in our lives with gratitude. Gratitude is an essential attitude. We should act with awareness that we add to the universal store of goodness through our conscious thoughts and actions. We do this by doing that thing which is always of the highest thought in any situation. If we fail to act in this way to all situations and at all times then we lose the opportunity to advance spiritually in that moment. This creates an imbalance of energy that requires the lesson to be repeated as many times as necessary until we have redressed the karmic imbalance.

Such it is for all people and all nations.

That is why it is futile and self-defeating to hold a grudge or to seek revenge over a situation. That is just the ego wanting to exert itself. The highest thought is to look for the lesson you have been given with that state of affairs and to be in gratitude and forgiveness.

In other words, do not launch the Titanic effect. That is the ego of man out of control applying linear thinking that we know has not worked in 10 000 years. What makes you think that it will work for you today? Become instead a non-linear thinker.

This is not an easy thing to do by any manner or means. Perhaps the easiest way for you to be conscious of your response and actions at all times is really a very simple device.

When you are confronted with a situation in which gratitude and forgiveness are the furthest thoughts from your mind, pause before re-acting (re-acting = re-enactment or acting out again what you have done in the past that never worked the first time and never will in the future). Remember that the definition of insanity is re-acting the same pattern of behavior over and over and expecting a different result each time. It does not work.

Pause your thoughts before you re-act an old pattern and ask yourself, *"What would love do now?"* Then proceed on a brand new course to produce a different result.

If your ego is too active choose to do nothing until the heat of the moment is passed and then in the light of conscious awareness choose to see that you are innocent of what anybody else is feeling and how they choose to react. You are only responsible for how you act. Let your actions be guided by your highest thought of who you are as a light being.

Realize that in order for all of mankind to grow in consciousness and to evolve, non-linear thinking is an essential prerequisite towards conscious awareness.

One can begin today with Intention and the power of being in the now. Now is the very moment in which, no matter what ones past life has been, you can create yourself anew. Now is not a re-action (re-acting = re-doing the act or repeating the same action) it is a *brand new action.* i.e. cre-action = creation. Practice envisaging yourself right *Now* as the greatest, highest expression of yourself that you can possibly imagine and create a new you. Now is the only time there is. The past is of no consequence and the future only represents unconfirmed fears and uncertainty. The only thing you have with certainty is this Eternal moment of Now. Now is the beginning of the realization of all your dreams. This is the time in which all your dreams are created.

Value your intention, this determines your thoughts that determines the quality of your words and actions.

The energy you put out into the universe, whether from love or from fear, (positive or negative) will be returned to you in much the same degree and measure. In fact the universe is more than fair inasmuch as the love you put out shall be returned to you in greater measure, whereas fear is returned measure for measure. Such is the way of Divine and unconditional love. We can all practice such giving of love.

Therefore, understand whether in the life of man or nation, there are no coincidences. Every happenstance is an opportunity to create for the positive or the negative and every thought and action is bankable in the universal account.

Whenever you meet someone it results in an energy exchange at many levels including at the soul level.

Our responsibility is to be conscious of this energy flow and to make every interaction a holy encounter that proceeds from our highest possible thoughts and actions. A brief and seemingly meaningless encounter, such as with a server in a restaurant, may present an opportunity to release some small amount of past karma with that soul or to create light for that person. You have the opportunity to express yourself anew as a non-linear person in a familiar situation.

In your interchanges with others be aware at all times to avoid confrontations of the ego. The negative consequences are not worth it. Mentally step outside of confrontation and remind yourself that they are in linear mode and are launching the Titanic effect.

You, on the other hand, are not responsible for how they are choosing to behave. They have their karma to work out. You are innocent in this moment. You can ask your soul to speak to the other person's soul. Ask for the highest good to come out of this exchange. Bless them, look for the lesson being presented to you in the moment of Now and mentally ask for the release of yourself from this situation for the highest good of all concerned. Avoid unconscious re-actions!

The Universe sends you only teachers and opportunities to grow and to expand your light. Following what love would do now is your surest guide at all times.

The Course in Miracles says that we are never presented with a problem in which the solution has not already been offered. In most cases the solution is love. Returning love in the face of hate is one of the highest thoughts we can display. It is a true sign of self-awareness and self- confidence.

A non-linear thinker is aware of the options available, as an alternative to re-acting the old movie script that has never worked in the past and assuredly will not work in the future.

Achieving a multidimensional, non-linear, consciousness requires a constant state of alertness and presence in the eternal current moment – the eternal now. A person must be engaged in active awareness of his or her thoughts and actions at all times.

Life is a play. One should mentally step back to observe themselves acting their role. Play with the dual awareness that even as you are acting you are, in that moment also scripting the play. You have brought every situation upon yourself, so it is very helpful to step out of the situation into the moment of now, and engage the dispassionate observer within yourself so as to view every situation without emotion. Practice detachment. Detachment does not mean removing concern or empathy. It merely means that you be conscious on both levels of what is occurring. By being conscious on both levels you step out of the linear into the multi dimensional world of non-ego.

In this state you act with clarity and compassion but without investment in the outcome knowing that you are always being directed on the right course.

You must also be aware that you may frequently be presented with unhealed situations in your life. They may occur in various guises with some regularity. You must resolve to recognize them for what they are, an opportunity to heal yourself so that you can go forward and on with your life.

To advance and go forward on the spiritual path you must recognize and release the issues that have affected you all your life. This must be done consciously and alertly.

Asking God to take over your life, or seeking spiritual ascension without dealing with your old patterns is an impossible task. Admittedly many ascended masters have gone through just such hardships in order to attain spiritual mastery. However, pain and suffering are not prerequisites to mastery.

Your responsibility to yourself in order to avoid "spiritual madness" as Carolyn Myss has phrased it, is to be constantly alert to the meaning of the lesson in the moment. In so doing one follows the path of highest good and alignment with the universe. This allows you to flow and to be self-empowering.

The energies invoked in attaining spiritual awareness are not compatible with the crud and debris that one brings along with old thought patterns. In Rebirthing terms we say that one must heal ones case.

In truth you must go to the next level of consciousness and this implies your being aware of your case when it arises. Then use the opportunity, when your case does come up, to seek the lesson in each occasion as it is being presented to you, and use it to grow in spiritual stature.

Frequently, spiritual acolytes believe that meditation, ceremony, healing circles and channeling as well as various other activities will lead to their spontaneous release of old patterns.

This is not so. The light energy you are invoking will clash violently with the darkness inside of you and all your unhealed issues will continually surface and confound you.

Commonly, perhaps more often than not, energy workers, healers and spiritual students will be faced with all manner of "bad luck' situations. Issues over relationships, money and conflict arise with regularity in their lives. Certainly the spiritual path equips them with the necessary attitude to face such challenges. Nevertheless, one cannot help but notice the high proportion of difficulties so many people who are seeking enlightenment have to face in their material lives.

They need to be aware that being spiritual is not sufficient to create a joyous life if one does not deal with the material issues in a material way by bringing their level of consciousness into the problem solving equation.

Putting out living energies as you do, with your every thought and action is like giving birth to children. You are responsible for your energy. And like one's children, it reflects who you are.

The Universe is not going to clean up your mess. Only you can do that. Calling Light into a messy situation does not clean the mess it adds further complications to what you have failed to deal with in the past.

Calling in a Higher Power is a declaration to the Universe that you are ready to take on more. Certainly you can ask for Divine assistance, but you must be willing to do the work at the physical level. It's all too easy to romp in the esoteric world of spiritual

Disneyland. You chose to be in the physical world when you incarnated. The physical world is how you have chosen to experience your life lessons. Your job is to be present in this, your chosen world, and apply your spiritual principles towards your physical growth. This requires extreme diligence. Diligence means awareness of yourself and your personal issues. Diligence means seeing the play of life around you and confronting life head on and untangling the webs of past failings. It requires that you challenge your weaknesses and shortcomings and create strengths in their place. All the while you are coming from a place of spiritual awareness. That is consciousness of the now. Being present in the moment. Aligning yourself with the strength of Light and seeking, no, not even seeking but knowing, that you can manifest that which is for the highest good. Knowing that which is good for you is good for everyone when your motivations and intentions are well reasoned and honest.

Conscious awareness also implies your acceptance of your own power plus your willingness to use your power courageously. Thus you acknowledge the Divine Universal Energy within you as the being the same as that within all creation whether living or inanimate.

Acceptance of this truth requires acceptance of yourself as indivisible from all that you perceive. Acknowledge the connectedness of yourself to All That Is, and by extension acknowledge the sanctity of all life forms, and ultimately acknowledge the earth as a living, conscious life form deserving of your supreme love and respect.

The earth and the sun together are indeed the mother and father of all life on this planet. Do not view the earth as less than a nurturing and respected parent. It is itself a life form. It is not to be conquered, strip-mined, burned, deforested, polluted and abused.

It requires respect and nurturing. Through the earth moves all life energy and life consciousness, and it, in turn, moves through you.

Non linear awareness requires that you accept the oneness of all within the Divine Universal Energy, and awareness that to harm something in any manner is to harm oneself.

Realize that "All That Is", is one Universal soul. Multifaceted, pluralistic, but ultimately One. All waters running into one ocean. You are one glorious drop of that sea in which all exists from the One Source. You are of that sea, inseparable from it, manifest in your own

357

unique way, but never removed from its essence. Thus collectively we have a universal connection to each other and a responsibility to everything. In loving all, you love yourself too. Love, along with two other factors is very important. These factors are forgiveness and gratitude.

Forgiveness of ourselves and of others is important, for when we forgive others they are raised up and so, by extension are we all raised up.

A non-linear society, knows that every action reflects upon themselves for better or for worse. Develop awareness and control over your actions. They shape your reality and that of the society in which you live. Learn to choose how you wish to experience your life and how to choose your highest level of consciousness by being alert in the now. Understand that the physical world is not the only reality. You can truly transform every facet of your life when you think and act in a non-linear fashion.

With regards to the soul, you will achieve an awareness that you are much more than your body. Indeed your soul itself is but one aspect of a larger self-soul. This soul is having many dimensional experiences, of which this life is but one. Your actions reflect not only on this worldly experience, but also on your greater soul. The good you do will reach many levels of consciousness and many dimensions of time and space.

Failing to see your greatness beyond the physical level is like looking at life through the inverted end of a pair of binoculars, and concluding that what you are seeing is all that there is.

We know that the physical body is composed of a dense form of light.

The atoms, which make up our bodies, are light energy, and pass through many layers of density prior to taking on the attributes of the physical plane.

Each level is an energy vibration level unto itself, and each lighter plane, or dimension, is a step closer to the Universal All – that is God.

To exist at the consciousness vibration of the Universal All, or God, requires raising ones awareness and energy state from the linear to the non-linear and thus to a multi dimensional consciousness.

In this state, you will perceive events as a related and interlinked set of circumstances in which coincidence has no place, luck and unpredictability is non-existent.

This is the first step to true empowerment.

The next step is to create a government and society run by conscious people who are aware of the energetic force of their actions on both people and on the whole planet. Such a society should hold no prejudices, should celebrate unity and honor of all life forms and revere the earth.

A society governed by such people would not be based on fear or mistrust of others. The idea of gaining advantage over another is abhorrent. To be in service to mankind is the highest aspiration. There should be universal cooperation, not confrontation.

Spiritual and karmic responsibility should be taught in our schools and imbued in the character of our children for the sake of future generations.

An enlightened society would not tolerate control or gaining advantage over others. It would not deny the oneness of all nor deny the Universal Truth. Mankind would understand that to be in denial of Truth is to be in a state of delusion. This they would know is the dark path of fear, psychosis, xenophobia and a return to the conditions in which we currently live and have labored under for thousands of years.

To the Mayan Indians our great cycle of ignorance has existed for 25 000 years, and is calculated to end in the year 2012.

In the ancient Sanskrit records there is a similar long period called a Yuga. We are currently in the Kali Yuga, or Dark Age. The ancient Hindus also date a Yuga as being 25 000 years in length, and the end of the present Yuga, according to Hindu cosmology is now drawing to an end!

It can be no coincidence that both the Mayan great cycle of 25,000 years and the Hindu Yuga of 25,000 years both conclude at almost the same time.

As this Dark Age draws to an end, we will see a great level of confusion among the military industrial government complex.

These people are the most xenophobic, greedy and fearful individuals on this planet. Theirs is a world of duplicity, mistrust, control and Machiavellian intrigue. They hold tremendous power over mankind. Their activities have enormous ramifications for our planet, and their sense of responsibility is severely diminished in the face of the delusion and illusion that they have created.

We should not underestimate the danger that the military and industrial complexes of nations pose to mankind. Theirs is a world of intrigue. They operate at a level that when measured by the common physical world standard of illusion, is filled with duplicity, espionage, conspiracies, power brokering, greed and manipulation. It is unto these people of the military industrial complex that the citizens of linear society have relinquished their power, just as they did to the Church in ages past.

Our power has been handed to technocrats and bureaucrats whose lives are so far out of synchronicity with the Universal Law they are out - laws.

To evolve, we must understand that the fear generated by this clique of outlaws, who represent a tiny fraction of the total population, is transmitted to the larger population via the media that they control.

Their message also permeates the workplace, which they command, and it is endemic in the school system, that they have created. This state of affairs is a huge illusion and it creates a negative karmic debt for all peoples as well as for our planet.

They maintain control by creating fear. They create perceived threats to our well being as a nation and to our continued existence and it is this activity that is a real cause for alarm. As the universe speeds towards change, third dimensional thinkers such as these will have a great struggle ahead in maintaining their sense of identity and balance. This poses a potential risk to all of us.

A negative thought structure of this magnitude must be balanced. What we fear most we will manifest. In other words, in reality, we will have to pay for the negative energy we have created in the form of all the lies, wars, hatred, violent thoughts and acts that our government and society is putting out.

This much is an inescapable fact. The only way to negate the negative is to manifest the positive - immediately.

Failing to act now in a conscious way, means that we will keep borrowing and living beyond our karmic means.

In the 20th Century we have had two world wars, several mass genocides of civilians as in Germany, Cambodia, Rwanda and Bosnia. These have been horrific wars. Vietnam saw the unprecedented use of earth destroying chemicals and the random spraying of a poison called Agent Orange defoliant that destroyed huge swathes of Vietnam.

There are hundreds of millions of randomly scattered landmines which, decades after the conflicts in Asia and Africa continue to blow the limbs off children.

The Gulf war saw the introduction of tactical nuclear weapons.

In a barely publicized event, the material that the USA used on the tip of armor piercing projectiles contained a form of uranium that heated and exploded its way through the armor of tanks.

This material is radioactive, and it may well be that the illness known as the Gulf War Syndrome is the partly the result of radiation sickness caused by the exposure of US troops to contaminated dust from the use of these weapons.

It took forty years and the Freedom of Information Act for the US government to even acknowledge that it tested nuclear radiation on the civilian population of the United States. And it took twenty years for them to admit having used deadly Agent Orange in the Vietnam War.

Do not expect the truth about the Gulf War to be known for many years to come.

Added to this mess are the clandestine activities of corrupt world leaders, plus hundreds of spy agencies such as the CIA, FBI, Secret Service, the old KGB, Mossad, MI5, etc. Every country has one or more secret organizations operating outside of the law and beyond public scrutiny, under the guise of national security.

Not even the president of the USA and our lawmakers are fully aware of the activities of these agencies. Nevertheless we are asked to blindly trust them as they go about their business. We know that they cannot be trusted. Historically they have lied to Congress, they have plotted against political adversaries and they have power to act without the control of our lawgivers. J Edgar Hoover ran the FBI for decades as his private power base. He kept files on all the presidents, politicians, entertainers, rock stars, as well as millions of files on every political and trade union organization and its members. He used the information contained in his files to blackmail whomever he pleased, including presidents and politicians. For years, J Edgar Hoover could be said to be the power behind the throne in Washington.

Such clandestine out-law organizations are one of the prime reasons there is world wide national insecurity.

There are predictions of a global calamity of catastrophic proportions. One can refer to the Bible, Hopi Indian predictions, Nostradamus, the Maya predictions, Edgar Cayce and thousands of modern psychics. Almost every culture has such a legend of Armageddon.

When one views human actions, and those of nations, not in terms of the mystical, but in real terms, in terms of the Universal Law, we can see that we have created a situation that requires a solution.

The scale can be balanced without a devastating human calamity.

The way to do it is to become conscious and to resist the linear impulse which is to create and live in a reactive and unconscious society.

We must return to the spirit that we will only find within ourselves - not in organized religion. Organized religions are much of the time, a part of the problem and not a part of the solution.

Perhaps we need a new Universal religion based on egalitarian principles embracing all humanity.

Such a religion will focus on self-empowerment of the individual and the recognition of the Divine nature within us all.

It would embrace all the world's great teachers whose message is universal love and tolerance. There would be no dogma and no myths of a vengeful God. There would be no hell and angels of death, just personal responsibility for ourselves and all our brothers and sisters. It would be a faith that empowers mankind.

Religion must uplift the spirit and seek truth and knowledge and not be based on fear. It would be a faith that acknowledges the highest in the least of us. A religion without symbols and without adversaries, and one that is based completely on seeking Truth, Simplicity and Unconditional Love.

A religion based on a God that has no needs and therefore does not demand that we approach Him in fear or in guilt.

A religion based on a God who is a friend and not a judge.

A religion that rejoices in the Divine with songs and hymns and thought wherein everything without exception would be seen as a thing of beauty and spirit.

A religion that demands no set form of expression, save that which flows from the joy of self- realization of our own Divinity and our oneness with Creation.

The flow of power within would be celebrated and not relinquished to a priest to act on our behalf.

A religion in which we take personal responsibility for our own lives and for everything that happens in our community without blame or exception.

A religion in which we take mutual responsibility for each other. The supreme acknowledgment being that we are one soul. I am you and you are me.

A religion based on unconditional forgiveness of everyone and ourselves and unconditional gratitude to God within with whom we are one and with whom we are equal.

A religion that sees reverence in everything and consciously acknowledges everything as being Divine in nature.

A religion in which the concept of sin does not exist, only the need to do right according to the principle of unconditional love and universal veneration.

A religion of music, song, nature, fire, water, food without slaughter, dance, lightness, introspection and intellect and continual striving to know the Divine by every loving and reverential means possible.

A universal religion based on the heart and spirit and the depths of our expanded non-linear consciousness.

Such a movement would shift power away from politicians, users, abusers and losers and create in the spirit of mankind such an awakening as to counter balance the negative condition with the positive, for the greater good of mankind and the planet!

We also need to overhaul the education system as a priority. The notion of not allowing religion in school is fine. But we are spiritual beings, part of the divine and one with the universe. Is this not, at the very least, more important than what we are as biological curiosities?

Therefore we need to teach our children that they are divine, that they can do no wrong and that every act of love is a blessing on themselves and all mankind. Is that a terrible thing to teach? Is it not what we ourselves already know in our hearts to be true?

It is the children who will inherit our karmic debt. (The sins of the fathers shall be inherited by the children even unto the seventh generation; - Bible). Are we not obligated to teach our children to be strong, loving and forgiving people?

We begin by acknowledging that our children did not come to us by accident.

There are no accidents and no coincidences. We agreed at a soul level to be their parents, as our parents, in turn, did with us. The purpose of which is to fulfill a lesson, have a specific experience, or mitigate a debt. Those who fail to do that in this lifetime will repeat the lesson in the next until they erase the debt and they have learned their lesson. If they fail, because they are in a linear and unconscious way of thinking, they may continue to increase the debt, having an ever-larger issue to deal with later.

Clearly what is needed is that we all start accumulating positive energy in the love and joy account as soon as possible, even if we have not yet attained the level of awareness to understand the full implications of what our actions mean. Do this not from fear, but from a desire to change and grow, and out of a desire to become more tolerant and reverent towards life.

From such an attitude of simple willingness, your life will change, and your growth will come even without effort!

The soul is where reality dwells. The physical being is the transitory illusion given to fear and selfishness.

From an early age, we should inculcate in our children that they are great and eternal beings on a mission to serve, enlighten and to raise the consciousness of mankind.

Teach them that the primary goal of their existence is reverence towards all life forms and to honor all, and in so doing to honor themselves. They are to seek the conscious connection from their physical bodies to the soul and to bring the Universal Love into the physical realm. The highest purpose is to raise the human species to a greater level of evolution and more purposeful and consciously directed destiny.

Children should learn to regard fear as the illusion that it is and to become fearless. Children should be taught to avoid confrontation and separation from one another. Thus they will realize God consciousness, universal awareness, love and healing. Cooperation is the first concept they must learn.

Teach them, even as we ourselves learn, to release their ties to the accumulation of material possessions. When goodness flows out, then goodness shall flow back in abundance - to each according to his needs and lessons in this lifetime.

Reverence, is the second concept that children need to grasp. Learn to walk this world with reverence and wonder at the bio-diversity of the planet and its wondrous beauty, for our thoughts reflect our own soul therein. Approach all beings with reverence, for the Holy One resides within each.

Learn the sanctity of life, the joy of forgiveness and the wonder of love without condition. This is how the Divine manifests. Know that we are one soul, split from the Divine Universal Oneness, yet complete in our unity with the Divine. You are a drop of Divine nectar drawn from the Divine Ocean. You are everything the ocean is, within the one drop.

Manifest your destiny in Divine Love and in accordance with the Universal law for the highest good of yourself and consequently our species and planet.

Do all these things and they shall evolve into Divine beings on earth, in oneness with the All and like the All, capable of everything, even miracles!

Jeffrey M. Solomon

Chapter Fourteen - Who Created God?

Your idol is shattered in the dust to prove that God's dust is greater than your idol - Rabindranath Tagore (Bengali Poet)

<u>Playing In The Mind Of God -Conclusion</u>

Nature is the art of God - Dante (Italian Poet)

Imagination is not governed by the law of cause and effect.

That which we conceive in our imagination is unbounded by any form of restriction. Yet we ourselves are limited.

We understand that we are born of parents, who themselves had parents, and so on. There is a line of ancestors, each a cause of the following generation, and each generation is subsequently the effect of the previous one.

In the material world, the law of doing one thing in order to produce a specific outcome is paramount. That is, we create a cause in order to produce a desired or an undesired effect.

Imagination is not bound by this law. In our minds, and indeed in our dream state, we can imagine anything, unbounded by physical laws. We are unlimited in the directions that we can imagine, dream, think or even hallucinate. The mind is totally free of any restrictions.

On the contrary, in our physical lives, we think and act only in terms of the law of cause and effect.

This is the cause of the Ultimate Illusion.

We experience all, even the universe, as a cause and effect.

The cause is God; the effect is what is.

All that exists is in the mind of God as a thought. You and I are a thought in the Divine mind.

We perceive God as being subject to the same laws of cause and effect that we see operating in all of our physical reality.

This is a lie mankind has constructed.

We subject God to our limitations. Our religious institutions, and the whole structure we have of perceiving the Divine in whatsoever form we personally take to imagine it, are wrong.

We see the Divine cosmos as a cause and effect. Our saints and teachers, who are also human, are subject to the same human misperception.

If our saints and teachers have seen beyond this misperception, and most have, they have not been very successful at communicating this clearly to the masses.

The fact is that when we ask ourselves the Ultimate Question, the one unsolvable riddle of the Universe - *"Who created God?"* - We find that the question cannot exist!

God is *not created*, because God is not subject to the laws of cause and effect.

God Is.

God always has been.

All else in the universe exists only as a thought in the mind of God.

In our human imagination, we can create whatever we want, free of time, unbounded by space, and not subject to cause and effect. Randomness is the key.

When you dream, there is no requirement or cause to the mental experiences you process in your dream world. What you do in your dreams, likewise, has no effect. That is why, to our minds, which can only relate in terms of cause and effect, dreams are illogical. We try, upon awakening, to restructure the memory of a dream into a logical sense of order based on causes and their effect. Dreams simply do not fit the cause and effect straightjacket or mold.

Notwithstanding this, we, as tiny thought bubbles in the mind of God, are subject to, or we subject ourselves to, the law of cause and effect. We cannot wrap our limited minds around the concept of life being anything other than a series of events and circumstances that follow on from a preceding cause, which in turn was the effect of yet an earlier cause, ad infinitum.

We need the sense of continuity. Our minds cannot deal with randomness, indeed simply being in the now, and not drifting off into the past or the future is a tremendous mental effort. We are always looking at what was and what will be in order to make sense of what is.

Yet what is, is all there is.

All the rest does not exist at all, it is an illusion that we create in order to avoid being here, now.

God is beyond this illusion because He is the thinker. In thinking, time and space do not exist for Him.

Time and space is the creation of our minds thinking in terms of cause and effect.

We are the created, therefore we exist only in the mind of God.

We are inside His head. There is no "out there" for us, only the "in here". This, then, is our misperception. All exists "in here" Inside the mind that is God.

We are an imagining of a Mind where time and space, cause and effect do not exist.

That is why the Universe is eternal and infinite. The mind has no limits.

We seek the boundaries of the Universe because we think linearly in terms of time and space, cause and effect. There can be no limits to the mind. Therefore the existence of a place that is the beginning or the end of the universe cannot exist!

God is both outside of us because we are within His mind, encapsulated if you will. He is also inside of us because the stuff we are made of are His thoughts.

All of the exercises in this book have been a demonstration of your mind, how it works, how you perceive and how you create illusions.

The greatest illusion is that you exist in the physical realm.

God creates the universe in His mind that He may experience it.

That's it. Period.

In one sense we are a game. We are created to play in the mind of God.

That is what God does. He creates. In His mind.

We are His toys, His amusement. We can no more hurt anything or anyone because we are merely a thought creation. We exist in a world of illusion, restricted by cause and effect. None of what we see, do, or experience is of any consequence in the larger scheme of things, either to ourselves or to God.

No doubt we are amusing to observe. However, our littleness, our insignificance, is hard for us, and especially our egos, to accept. So we have created egos to remind us of how important we are.

But who are we important to? The answer is, we are only important to ourselves.

Most of us cannot remember, or never knew who our great grandparents were, or who our ancestors were. Their lives are as if they never were. Their lives have no consequence to us, nor shall ours be to future generations. Even if you were to be another George Washington or Jesus Christ it would be of no importance.

What has become of the great kings, scholars and thinkers of the ancient times? Do we know anything more than fragments about the lives of the greatest men of ancient Greece, Babylon, Sumeria, Egypt, Central America, China, or India?

We know even less about any great people in the time preceding these civilizations, say about five thousand years ago. Their lives are as if they never were. And so it is. All is the illusion of existence.

In the scope of the physical our lives are fleeting and inconsequential, our achievements meaningless, and our perception of reality is an illusion.

The thing that is of consequence, indeed the only thing of consequence is that we are this speck of cosmic energy in the Divine mind of God.

That is also why we can never know the nature of what God truly is. He is not out there awaiting our discovery in a place called heaven. He is not limited by our perception of reality, a reality that does not exist.

Indeed the only place we can find Him is within ourselves, for we are "of" Him.

We are just the shadows on the film of His mind, thinking that our brief exposure on the screen is reality. When the frame changes we are gone, save that we are not forgotten within the mind of God. Like all thoughts, the energy is eternal, and in that sense, being part of the Mind that created us, a Mind unbounded by the restrictions of time and space, cause and effect, we exist forever.

The order that exists with mathematical precision in the universe is the product of the Divine Scientist. God is a powerful mind of sublime science and mathematics. His thoughts are orderly and creative and structured. Therefore He has created a mind-universe in which we exist and perceive structure not randomness. Even though the underlying principals of existence arise out of chaos and randomness.

This means that chaos and randomness exist alongside structure, beyond the limits of our present science, and certainly beyond the limits of our senses. Out of this chaos arises the structure and perfection of the thought that is our perception of the world.

Indeed, many realities may abide side by side in the Mind of God. Whether we perceive them or not is unimportant.

What is important, is for us to understand that the Mind that created us has no physical limitations. Nor does the number of realities or dimensions or levels of structure within this Mind have any limit.

To create an analogy; In computer terms, you and I are a file on a site called "earth.com.".

We are on a website full of links to similar websites.

There are also many websites, some on unconnected servers, to which we are not linked. We know nothing about the existence of the other websites to which we are not linked. Those servers that are unconnected, have there own separate web to which we can never link.

One cannot begin to comprehend the unlimited mind in which we play, therefore we employ reductionist tactics.

Mankind reduces God to manageable proportions, a superman with human attributes, so that our mind can embrace Him. We limit Him to time and space, personalize and anthropomorphize Him.

Some groups, such as the Southern Baptists, issue pamphlets and calls for conversion on the holiest days of the Islamic (Ramadan), Hindu (Diwali) and Jewish (Rosh Ha Shona) religions.

They have called these religions misguided and dark, because they, the Baptists, claim to know what is really in the mind of God, and non-Southern Baptist religions are not a part of what's on God's mind!

All of this the ego does in order to give meaning to ones existence so that mankind can deal with creation and God at a manageable level.

The Truth is quite different.

You are simply playing in the mind of God.

+++

<u>Reminder:</u>
The whole visible world is only an imperceptible atom in the ample bosom of nature.
No idea approaches it - Blaise Pascal (French Philosopher)

Return to the opening chapter and review your thoughts about it.
Do you feel that you have grown on this journey of discovery?
Thank you for your trust and for allowing us to take this journey together.
With Love and Blessings - Jeffrey Solomon

****

Jeffrey M. Solomon

Book Two

Playing In The Mind Of God

Jeffrey M. Solomon

<u>Questions and Answers from The Higher Self</u>

To be conscious that you are ignorant is a great step to knowledge -
Benjamin Disraeli (English Statesman)

Jeffrey M. Solomon

<u>May the Force be with you</u>

We thought, because we had power, we had wisdom - Steven Vincent Benet (American Poet)

The Source of all wisdom is a force that anyone can tap into. By going within you will find all the answers to all your questions.

Knowledge can be communicated, but not wisdom - Herman Hesse (German Novelist)

I have chosen to create a book within a book of intuited knowledge. Some would say channeled information. I feel that my readers would find the experience interesting, and more so if you choose to tap in to your own inner voice and wisdom.

Within us at a soul level is a direct connection to our Higher Self - the God within us. It is that part of ourselves which is an eternal connection to the Source of All Being. When you "go within," in the stillness of your being is the core of who you are. This is the part of you that never ages. It is the energy with which you see and the power that sustains you in life.

It is that part of yourself that you have been trying to reach all these weeks. When you have stilled the chatter of your little ego and laid your mind aside, then you allow the "Greater You" within to emerge. This part of you has no concern with the physical aspect of who you are. It knows you for eternity in all your magnificence. It is connected to the Creator and the Divine plan that HE has for you. It is the part of yourself that sees only the highest purpose of your being - that wants only the highest good to come from all your experiences.

This part of you is the God essence within you. Its thoughts are yours and your thoughts are Its thoughts. Inseparable, It is the silent observer of your life and the Source of your true identity.

It waits in endless patience while you, at the level of your ego, make all the mistakes in your life, knowing that each step you take on the road is a step closer to self-fulfillment.

It is closer to you than your own hand. It is the Source of all wisdom.

The Course In Miracles states that God has placed the answer together with the problem.

379

Whatever problem arises in your life, the source of all wisdom, is closer to you than your own hand. Within lies the answer to everything.

Herein is the source of all wisdom and Divine Light within you, so close that you feel that you must look elsewhere for answers. Yet when you go within, the answers that you never thought possible arise from a Source of wisdom deep within the silence within you. The Source is intimately connected in Love to the entire universe with which it is a direct part, inasmuch as the cells within your body are a part of you.

From this connection within you arises All That Is.

We are all capable of reaching that part of ourselves. Here is the state of pure Being. One reaches this part of us in quiet and stillness. You must silence the ego that would defeat your attempts at bypassing it. It is to found in a state of stillness and calm wherein you don't train, don't strain, and just be. Be present in the moment and dismiss all thoughts of fears and anxiety. Just allow yourself to be and sink inwards into yourself without expectation. Dismiss all thoughts gently and let them wash over you. See yourself as a light shining from within your limbs, your body and your head. All thoughts are outside of your being in a mind that is not you.

Knowing that you are one with the Source, and that God is within you, your minds are one.

Here is a startling thought that you should embrace.

You are entitled to miracles!

The way you block miracles in you life is by being attached to your mind that projects your fears and your smallness through your ego, and so the light within you cannot shine through.

When you learn to stop the chatter of the illusion being projected by your mind then you can tap in to the Source within you and allow the power to grow and increase until it is the driving force in your life.

When you can tap in to the inner voice, the Source within you, then you can call forth the wisdom of the Universe. You can relate to this energy within you. And whether you call it your Higher Self, God, or Intuition it makes no difference because the connection you have with the All That Is, is nevertheless within you. This is the power you want to access.

When you "go within" as I have done, and which I have related in the following pages, you can have a discourse with yourself, and sometimes the answers will astound you with their wit, depth and love. This is set forth as a teaching guide for you, to show you the latent power that is within you as it is within all of us.

Here is guidance, in the form of questions and answers that I have received from my Higher Self. I present this in the form of questions and answers in the form of a dialogue.

This is not the only way to relate however many times the answers will come in a flash of knowing. When you really get clear you can channel your higher self when talking with others as many psychics may do, or as many of us do in times of stress when we set aside our minds and relate with a clarity and certainty of conviction which may not have been present in our minds a moment earlier.

In Love, I share it with my fellow souls reading this book. May the peace and the Joy of the Divine be with us all.

Understand that some of what you read herein may be repetitive however know that the TRUTH is one and all answers that elicit the TRUTH must of necessity lead back to the same beginning!

Also know that this is transcribed verbatim with minor editing for clarity. Therefore the syntax and language is closer to natural speech. The parentheses are comments that I have subsequently added by way of explanation. Some personal content has been removed for reasons of privacy otherwise the dialogue is unaltered.

o   **The one question I have is what is the biggest problem in this life that I may recognize it?**

The answer to the problem is separation. All of life (as we recognize and experience it) is an illusion. As long as you believe and trust in the illusion all problems will seem separate and real.

Lose the illusion - you lose the problem.

Therefore all your problems, no matter how separate they may appear to be are all the same <u>one problem,</u> they are not real. Therefore when you recognize that <u>all is nothing</u> - which all you have created is nothing, then you can take that nothingness and disregard it and the problems with it.

    o **Conceptually I can see that. But if you have a child that needs feeding, shelter, education, - in short if mankind has responsibilities, how can we ignore everything and still be a society? Will we not revert to subsistence living - like prehistoric man - with no science or technology?**

One can look to the spirit world to see the similarity. In the spirit world one can manifest anything from thought. Think of a nice house with a garden, music, friends, disease free, care free and with love and free of want. As you think so shall it manifest.

Mankind on the physical level has the same ability. The challenge here is that unlike the world of spirit, the physical world is more dense.

It takes more effort and therefore more faith to move the "stuff" of the physical world. The souls in the physical (world) are really some of the bravest souls who have chosen to come to the physical in order to learn some of the hardest lessons and face the toughest challenges.

It is not easy - however they need to be united on the planet in one vision of themselves as a community of souls - all one - for the same purpose and for sharing the same learning experience.

They need to unite their energies in harmony and cooperation and to shift - move the world in a great mental shift - towards manifestation - towards the light and out of illusion.

The whole world is already a product of your creation - it is apparently in a "mess" (in mankind's judgment) for two reasons.

1. Lack of harmony. That is common agreement (amongst people) of why you are on earth. What your purpose in life is and the lack of cooperation and common goals. This leads to the second reason that is the result of the first, namely:
2. Everyone is pulling in separate directions. The energy is fragmented and the results are scattered. Sometimes it is for the Highest good and sometimes not. This creates fear, and because there is a lack of purpose and uniform direction and a lack of common acknowledgment that all people are of the

same group of spirits who are intended to work together in harmony and cooperation.

The end result is uncertainty of purpose, mistrust and fear. That causes the masses to experience life as "out of control". That thought then generates fear, war, conflict and most importantly misplaced trust. (Trust placed in the wrong place, or in the wrong things. i.e.: lack of trust in who we really are. Trust placed in the illusion).

Because the group (mankind) is not in cooperation, individuals seek comfort in the seeming permanence and security of the physical (world), mostly in possessions, money and status.

(Materialism thereby substitutes for and confirms identity and status).

Hence the illusion deepens and the loss of self-identity as souls or spirit, the loss of God as the prime manifestation in your lives is lost - and so the more the dependence on illusion deepens!

"You can manifest the earth as it is in Heaven"

However, as I said the energy on the physical level is more of a challenge to move. In the spirit world, as you think so it is.

On the physical it takes group effort. This is the lesson and challenge of the physical; To be in harmony and cooperation.

And that leads to the highest spiritual ideals - trust and love of one another.

On earth as it is in Heaven.

You have the ability (to be highly developed) to reach your potential. You too, can develop to the level of being a teacher to others on all spiritual planes. But your job right now is to start small and grow in confidence knowing that I bless you - have always blessed you - and am always here for you.

If you want a simple thing, say a ball. On the spirit world think ball and it is there.

On the physical you are not always in such direct manifestation - though you can be if you develop yourself. Right now, think ball and a ball may come in to your life. Not necessarily - bang - in front of your eyes. Perhaps you find one in your garden - your kid or dog finds one - but ball will come to you.

The love of the Divine is manifest in the intention of the spirit of the people.

That is, in order to bring about a realization of the fullness of the Divine we must reach into the spirit being of ourselves and to project that outwardly to all mankind.

This truth is immutable. No matter how many times you say I love you and in how many different ways, the final intention never varies. So it is with this message.

o **There must be a better way to get people to realize self love and love of others. There have been thousands of saints saying the same thing for eons - the message is not getting through. It's frustrating for us. Over the billions of years – you would think that God would produce a technique - or a show of force to bring about love realization on earth?**

God is not in a hurry. Time is all he has! We have teachers and techniques use them! How human would you be if God just stepped in - controlled you like a puppet and made you feel love? You would not be here for the reason you chose to come to earth - it would defy the pact God made - with humans and God - to give you free will. The consequence of free will is independent thought and the ability to make choices - one of which is love - and how to learn and apply these choices. (If there were no fear we could not choose love. In order to have free will we have to have the choice of opposites. For example if we choose light there must be darkness. Hot and cold define each other. Opposites are needed to define each other. Without the one you could not have the other).

Imagine a planet, or people that do not have choices of free will - for that is the pact God has with them. They are completely spiritual - for they have no choice but to be otherwise - and their lives are very different to yours.

Their every action is a controlled one devoted to the praising of God and themselves and each other. No step is taken without careful consideration of the consequences - no thought made - no word spoken without careful soul searching and reflection on their part. Needless to say, their lives are spent in contemplation and reflection - very little activity takes place outside of meditation, save farming and gathering. Technology is shunned. It has no purpose when you spend your life in contemplation and pouring out good thoughts - love thoughts into the world.

Love is all there is. The rest beyond subsistence is superfluous. There is no greed, famine, disease and death is rare. Birth is a rare occurrence and takes place after careful consideration of all the consequences of two people uniting and the consideration of the needs of the newborn soul and the society into which it is being brought into.

This might sound awful to some and it may be appealing to others but that's a judgment. On such a world judgment would be unheard of!

Humans have free will. Always have had and always will.

A society based on total love may also sound like a total bore to human beings. Where does that leave us in our search for love?

To reconcile the two (free will and love) is our job. Free will and free love. I don't mean that salaciously. Love arrived at freely out of choice. That is our job.

On earth we have created many challenges for ourselves. I emphasize we - not God - God merely created the conditions for life on earth. Mankind has created everything else - such is our power to manifest. We are ultimately more God - like. And like God we can do all this plus be in a perpetual state of grace and unconditional love!

o   **Tie up is the topic of the next discourse.**

We are all tied up. We are tied up in ourselves as well as our illusions of life. Which is fine with God. God has no judgment - never has. But it is amusing to see how tied up we all are in our illusions. I wanted to say chasing rainbows - but that is more real than what we term reality! We are tied up in so many situations, relationships, business deals, plans and agreements - we don't have a knife big enough to cut the bonds - never mind cutting some slack - there is no slack - we are all too tightly bound.

If you put 10 % of your daily effort into trying to hear God - your payback would be 100% better life and reduction of stress.

(The emphasis is mine. I believe, in re-reading my notes, that herein lies a very strong instruction - of which we should do well to take heed)

385

Jeffrey M. Solomon

How many of you can get a better deal than that? Put down 10% and get 100% back. I can't offer you a better deal than that and I defy you to get better odds anywhere else!

Of course that means that in your 24-hour day - 2.4 hours or 10% must be given to God totally, fully, lovingly unhurriedly and unbegrudgingly. I will guarantee your life will be 100% better than it is now. Then you will see you how you can release your ties to this illusion that you spin around yourselves. Then God will cut you some slack!

(In giving time to God, we are really giving to ourselves!)

We already know (within ourselves) much of what I need to say - you don't need me to say it again. However I could go on forever - in a sense I suppose I do.

We need to trust more, don't be afraid to let go of the illusion, it no longer serves you. Trust in God (and yourself) that I will take care of everything. It may not be to your immediate understanding (or expectations) but it is always for your highest good.

So learn to let go, learn to trust, be brave and uncomplicate your life. Do everything with honor and with love and you will never have disagreement or disharmony.

When you do something with - or for - another, stop for 30 seconds and really take a good look at them. Take a deep breath and release all the resentment and guile and dishonesty from your body. See them as a soul and part of your being and do nothing to them, nor say anything that does not raise their honor and self worth. See it as your job to love and assist them. And if you cannot - release them and move on and do no harm.

Conduct all your conversations and relationships in this manner. Bring no conflict into yours or others lives - and by example teach others to do the same.

o **I wondered if God ever gets tired of creating. What I mean is that, as interesting as it may be - even doing the same interesting thing such as creation must eventually get boring after a few trillion years.**

Firstly, who says that a few trillion years is not just an afternoon break in God time, and then He goes off and has tea? Metaphorically

386

speaking of course. However who could get tired of creating? The problem is that we see God as "over there" somewhere sitting in contemplation and manifesting the universe.

This is incorrect.

Imagine a baseball game. Now I enjoy baseball - but God participates at a level even the players cannot imagine.

Not only is He every player, He is the ball, the mitt, every blade of grass and every pebble and the wind. God gets to be the bat, the ball and the field - even the shirt on the players back - and He can experience it all - and He is in every game everywhere all at once, even in a sandlot.

And while He is doing that He is also in every couple making love, and every drop of perspiration, every form of love, every animal, every drop of seed. God experiences that too, right down to the molecular level, while He plays baseball!

o **That thought brought me to a question about a heel spur that I had at the time. I had the thought that if there is no place that God is not, then at some level He must be in my heel spur!**

We are conditioned to seeing the body and hence something like my heel spur as something separate from ourselves - and definitely separate from God.

If you realized that He is inside everything and He does His creating from within, not from without, you would see that if you want to be healed, ask the God within the heel spur to stop being so.

It is better to talk to the problem rather than to see the source of relief outside of yourself somewhere.

This is the key to manifestation.

Realize that the God - the I - within everything can respond directly - it is easier than calling on a vague concept of God in some uncertain realm in time and space.

God is as close as the sweat in your armpit or the heel spur in your foot. Ask it to change, ask the God in it for relief, or to manifest in whatever form you wish.

The calling on the God within – is an inherent power within everyone.

(Personal note: I had been unable to run for the previous two years as a result of a heel spur I developed in my right foot.

My ambition at the time was to run a marathon. I went to a foot specialist and had cortisone shots soon after the x-rays showed the heel spur. I had orthotic inserts made for my shoes, and nothing helped. I was considering surgery for the past two years as I could not even be on my feet for long periods. However, the surgery was not guaranteed to work, and I was told that it probably would not help.

Six after this realization I took up running again. I started with a cautious run around the block and then I built myself up to twice around the block. Now I have been running / walking five miles three times a week with no pain whatsoever! The only thing holding me back from running the whole five miles is my lack of condition. Thank You God!)

o **When one hears the voice within- how does one know whether this is really God - or ones higher self, or even just imagination?**

It makes no difference - your higher self or God - its one and the same. If God is in every drop of sweat, every blade of grass - why should He be less in you?

You are He and He is you and you experience God, (or whatever name you want to call it) through yourself as God experiences you through yourself.

o **What if we desire a teacher like Babaji? What if we feel a need for the contact in a direct (physical) sense, with Divinity. What if we want to transcend this plane and achieve higher realms of consciousness - to be consciously aware?**

It is one thing to say these things and quite another to really want them.

To get the level of awareness you would have, you need to be informed - to know what you are getting into.

An enlightened teacher cannot accelerate your transition or growth for you, you still need to be willing. Perhaps they can transmute Karma and overcome psychic blocks. But are you committed? How will you know?

Read and study. Tune in to your higher self more, and let that take over. (Most people say they want spiritual enlightenment) yet are still very committed to the plane they are in and their illusion.

They spend their days (in illusion) - except when they meditate - they sometimes escape.

o **How can one overcome this illusionary state? How do we really move on and develop?**

Be at peace with yourself. See yourself as a spirit moving through an illusionary existence.

Try and see the light and love everywhere.

See people as spirits not bodies. Be in tune to the vibration of life all around you.

Pray for release from the illusion all the time - not just in meditation.

Learn from everyone - each person, soul, you meet is another lesson for you, another paving stone on your path. In this business of life you will meet many people on the path - learn from them. People tend to prefer talking to listening. Learn to listen.

o **What is physical immortality and is it a goal we should aim for. And what about our families?**

Insofar as it is a spiritual goal - aim for it. The result is not automatic.

The important thing is the journey not the destination.

The most desirable thing for you is to grow - if possible allow your family to grow with you - but they should not hold you back. Perhaps merely the fact that they have known you is enough energy for their souls to take in and to get them facing in the right direction. Some journeys they have to take alone - you cannot learn, or take it for them. All humans are on the same journey.

It does not matter when you arrive. Sometimes all a soul needs is a little orientation into the direction they should take, and then you, as the teacher, have completed the lesson they came to get from you.

If they prove eager, you can give them more - but never can you force the issue - in time they will learn all they need to know. As children they may need more playtime to be children, before the souls journey truly gets started. I have patience. You should learn patience too!

o   **Is there going to be a great destruction in the near future?**

It is possible. Not likely as long as the awareness of mankind can shift to be one with the earth and recognize the soul and life energy in everything - animate or not. Be guardians of your planet - not conquerors. Be a global family. Honor each other, honor the earth, and honor the God energy in everything. See yourselves as spirit first and body last and honor the Divine aspects of all creation - even the rocks - see the earth as a holy temple - all grand, all life, all aspects of creation as sacred.

View the planet as Temple Earth, a place of refuge and sanctuary in a cold and hostile solar system. You are the guests on this planet - she offers you safety, nourishment and love. Tread softly, honor her as you would a sacred shrine to which you are privileged to visit. Remove your shoes, speak in reverence and hushed tones. Honor every nook and cranny of her being.

Be humble, be loving and caring. Nurture her, respect her and be gentle with her.

As you would approach God if you were brought to a palace / temple in which you knew you would come face to face with God, so honor the temple of this world He has created.

Created for you to cherish and to sustain you. Be servants and guardians in this temple. Do not trample harshly over her, do nothing disrespectful, honor and cherish her and obey the rules of your visit to her, like the temporary guest that you are.

We all will gain much knowledge as we go. Our obligation is to teach respect of the earth by example, word and deed. Respect all people and life forms that you meet and this includes plants and bugs, fish and all creatures including the water rocks and air, for all is Holy and all contains Holy Spirit. When you honor this you honor God.

You are then in a state of Grace and Worship and that is how your lives should be lived. Not church on Sunday and sin all week. By sin,

I do not mean anything less than disrespect for your environment, your air, water, the insect, plant and animal life.

Do you think that the rape and plunder of this is any more acceptable than the rape and plunder of each other? It is not. God cares deeply and has unbounded Love for all that He has manifested. He has no lesser concern over a stick in a field than for a human being, for it is His thoughts, His Love, His energy that flows in all and sustains all.

How much more so then for the entire living planet which He so truly loves?

The earth should be honored and respected as a total living organism flowing with life giving creative energy.

Even the stones shall weep at her pain.

This is a statement of fact.

God feels the pain of every atom in creation and truly the stones do weep!

Mankind must honor creation at every conscious level. We must change our thoughts about what is real or not.

Our lives to which we have attached so much importance to are meaningless if we do not rise above our selfish illusionary existence into the Light and Love of the Divine.

This is our purpose for being on earth and nothing less. To rise up out of the illusion and to honor Divinity in every thought and action every minute.

Be an aware and conscious Being. Without that you have no honor and no purpose in being.

So learn this lesson and engrave it in your hearts. God needs no church, no temple, no worship unless you treat all of creation as a temple, and the honor that you show to all creation will flow back to the Godhead like no prayer yet devised by mankind. And blessings and enlightenment beyond your present level of comprehension will be for each and every person and thing on earth.

o **What are these things beyond our comprehension?**

We can become a race of Holy and Enlightened beings capable of Love and Joy beyond our imaginings.

391

We will be in such a state of Light and Grace that you will perform miracles as easily as God.

We are made in Gods image - not physically but spiritually, but we have not manifested the abilities inherent within us.

Like an apple seed has the potential to be an apple once it realizes its potential to be a tree - all the "image" of the tree and the fruit is within the seed that you cast away when you eat the fruit.

The potential you cast off is the miracle of what you could be!

Mistakenly, we believe that we are created in Gods image and therefore we believe that we are already complete.

You mistakenly believe that we have been given the earth to rule over and all that is upon it.

So we are vain in ourselves and despots over the earth.

The truth is that you will realize your potential when you plant the seed and grow into Gods image.

Before we do this we must prove to be worthwhile guardians of the earth and all that is above and upon it - animal, vegetable, mineral and gas.

When we raise ourselves up all manner of miracles shall we manifest - as gods - in His image.

There shall be no more pestilence or disease, no earthly disasters - no famine, just perfect joy and bliss as it was intended before man created the world of illusion and lost his spirit.

Then shall you and we co-exist in perfect awareness one with the other. (God and mankind as one)

As you grow and teach others and take them along with you and inspire them. Show them the earth and sacred sites. Show them how mankind has for millennia searched for his Creator in temples, pyramids and sacred spots - when all the earth is a temple!

His (mankind's) mind is the greatest of all temples.

Enter it!

Honor it!

Learn what it has to give!

Show how every tree, plant, rock is holy.

Teach how the holiness within you is the same holiness in the lowest grain of sand and (it is found) in the souls of every man, woman, child and animal.

Raise the awareness of people that even as they travel thousands of miles to witness the search for reality and God over countless generations and civilizations - that the search can only begin in their own minds - there they should speak to God and look for salvation and honor all creation.

Start with those who are drawn to spiritual growth. Out of that all others will come - even the skeptics.

The skeptics need it most. They have more invested in their little realities - Lawyers, politicians - some professions demand that you submerge your truly spiritual side.

The desire to be hard nosed, uncompromising, closed minded and shut down is part of the job description in many professions. To be otherwise (in the corporate world) is a sign of weakness!

This is truly funny.

Imagine being so afraid of your peers and so vain as to be concerned by their opinions of you that you deny who you truly are. (Here I got the mental image. The joke is that all these high-powered businessmen live in fear of one another and what others think of them. They all dress alike and keep each other in line. No one is willing to acknowledge the irony of the situation and so they all maintain the charade - like the emperor who had no clothes.)

What fear they live in!

Afraid of being "out of step" with all the other "suits" as they are colloquially referred to.

So constrained in their tight suits - or straight jackets - they fear that to show emotions - to have holy thoughts - to want to be spiritual - to love God. And to meditate and receive love is (perceived as) a human failing - it shows weakness!

So we have armies of severely depressed, fearful, "power people"

Can you not see the irony of this?

They think of themselves as smart, intelligent, even enlightened - but where is the original thought?

The dare to be different?

They live in fear of being out of step. So they are also out of touch with themselves, with mankind and with God.

They need to be shown that it is safe to be human. It's okay to cry, it's okay to give love, and it's okay to receive love. It's safe to be spiritual and to treat everyone with kindness and respect.

That corporate profits can still be earned with an enlightened attitude.

That success flows easier when love, honor and respect are present.

That concern for the planet is a safe place to be.

These are the people you most need to reach.

They are more stuck in illusion and fear than most of you realize.

They need love and nurturing and to be brought back to spiritual health!

—

o   **What is the meaning of to give and receive?**

Do you think that you exist separately from God?

Do you think that anything can exist separately from Him?

All of creation does He hold in His mind and in His hand.

Therefore you cannot exist independently of Him. In His thoughts are you united as one with all creation. In His thoughts about the universe so are you. You are as much a part of God as any part of His Being. So know that inasmuch as you and all creation are a part of the One so are you one with all creation and all are one with one another.

All is One.

All is nothing without God.

He is All.

Be assured that God could no more judge you defective than He could judge the stars, the sky or Himself as defective. All is One. That is the All of Everything. (the Bible says) "I am That which I am".

"Therefore, that which I am not, is not. Existence is within Me and without Me - is not". (I understood this last thought to be a dual message that on the one hand existence without God does not exist, i.e. it cannot be. And also that existence is both within God and outside of God simultaneously.

To hurt one another is senseless for you hurt only yourself. It is as if you would cut off your right arm for it offends your left arm. You can only hurt yourself and none other. (If we are all one, then we indeed hurt ourselves when we hurt another.)

You cannot hurt or offend God for He is timeless. He judges not and questions not that which He has created in perfection.

Should you hurt another you hurt yourself. You should learn this lesson at a soul and cellular level. See yourself as one with all and everyone.

When you are offensive to anyone in thought, speech, or deed so do you hurt yourself.

When you are kind towards creation, so are you kind to yourself.

Whenever you are out of integrity with your treatment of another - your words and actions though hurtful to another - reflect on you. It mirrors your mind. Your cruelty is a reflection of your cruel mind. The cruelty you would project outwardly from yourself is ultimately a reflection of what you are, and as such demeans you Even though you would demean another.

Your love of another and your respect towards all, mirrors your self love, your self esteem, and the surety of the confidence you have in yourself, knowing who you are and how powerful you are.

Powerful people have no need to show power.

A ruler or a state that has the power of life or death over his/it's subjects shows (it's own) terror when it misuses its power, and it will be hated. A merciful ruler is no less powerful, however in exercising mercy instead of force, it demonstrates true power and fearlessness.

It shows power and control over the abuse of power.

Anyone can abuse power. A powerful person knowing his power, shows power in restraint.

Not having to prove your power is a true demonstration of your confidence and power.

Therefore what you put out in the world is a reflection of yourself.

If you are weak you will show meanness, greed and abuse of others.

If you are powerful you will show compassion and love with no expectation of that being returned to you, for in your confidence and self-assuredness you do not seek the approval of others.

What you give is (given) unconditional and your reward is in giving, for from this giving comes your power and self-confidence. So will you grow more powerful.

So, when you give, give love, joy, happiness, and peace without condition or expectation of reward. Your growth will come from this as will your power.

As you give, so shall you receive, in humility, faith and (with) no expectation or selfishness.

And your reward shall multiply that which you given.

o **What is salvation?**

Salvation implies being saved. And yet if you are God and We are One, from what do you need to be saved?

Nothing can harm you. Your body is but dust. Your light is your soul that belongs to and is a part of God. So who but God can harm you? And why should God harm you for your soul is a part of Him.

Would God harm Himself? Would you cut off your nose to spite your face?

Truly you have need of saving, but from what or from whom?

Inasmuch as only God can hurt Himself, only you can hurt yourself. And, you may ask, why should you want to hurt yourself? Yet you do so repeatedly. Through a lack of awareness you see the world in competition to yourself. Life is not a win or lose game. Yet I have said to you give without expectation of reward, you cannot lose, only gain in power and strength.

Life is a win and win situation when you process all from integrity, selflessness and love.

The planet is not a challenge to be tamed or conquered. It is your home, your life support system. It lives by Divine blessing and love. Yet we do not honor this. We burn, consume and pollute.

We think that he who consumes more is better off. That piles of paper called money confirms status and respect because thereby you can consume more resources. A bigger house takes up more land, uses more timber and resources, consumes more water, power and materials, and this the measurement of status.

We abuse the resources of the earth and rise in status the more we consume.

Your car is bigger and so it uses more fuel, steel, etc. and so you rise in status.

This is not your purpose on earth.

From yourself do you need salvation.

It is you that would destroy and consume for lack of true values and understanding of your purpose in life.

Life is to enjoy each other. To practice simplicity, love of one another, respect for all and caring for all life forms, plant and animal, for the oceans and the air.

We should come back to the realization of ourselves as spiritual beings in physical bodies put on earth as protectors of all life and of the planet.

Honor yourself. Honor each other. Respect and nurture those souls, children, that into your care they have been entrusted. Teach them meaningful values. See yourselves as one with God and as truly Divine.

Know that all the illusions you create around status, wealth, ego, and competition with one another is an illusion only. The stress of this illusion makes you ill. This illusion you have created denies your sense of self worth and your values, you would deny the worth and value of others.

You sense only hopelessness, and despair and futility and you make yourselves sick. You create cancers to consume you. Heartaches destroy your heart. Headaches and pain to punish yourself!

Stress to keep you from truly feeling.

All sorts of guilt related illness are you willing to accept as your punishment for living as you do.

All your soul wants is for you to see the lunacy of your life, it is all an illusion. Come to your senses, leave the darkness and seek the light.

Therein is your salvation.

o **How is illness and pain is an illusion?**

It should be self-evident.

When one allows thoughts about yourself to constantly be in your mind, you will attract or create that situation for yourself. Whether the thoughts are positive or negative will determine what you attract and how you will be affected.

o **How does negative thinking create disease?**

Dis-ease.

A lack of ease. A lack of true joy for what you already have. A lack of true love for your purpose in life. A lack of unconditional peace in your life creates dis-ease within yourself. Medical science already knows that stress causes heart and artery disorders. Low self esteem causes emotional disorders, eating disorders and drug abuse.

Abusive behavior causes or results in various emotional and physical problems. You know that people who are positive, self confident, heal quicker after surgery or are prone to fewer health problems.

The only thing medical science has not acknowledged is that the same positive mental attitude that promotes quicker healing - when related to the negative, creates illness.

Lack of self-awareness, self esteem, self worth, bitterness, held in feelings, suppressed emotions, resentment, anger, frustration, all cause physical manifestations in the form of illness and dis-ease. Exactly which disease may depend on what your greatest fear is.

If you fear heart problems, then you may express your dis-ease via this means. A deep feeling of futility may cause an unconscious desire to die because that seems to be the only resolution to the problems one is facing. You may not even be aware of your longing to die. In fact your (physical) fear of dying may be so profound that you will do all you physically can to stay alive.

So you will be in conflict between an unconscious desire to leave this life of hopelessness and a profound fear of dying. A lingering disease such as cancer may be the result.

A lack of love and joy may be a cause of heart felt illness - the heart is in dis-ease. No love, no joy, no heartfelt positive emotions lead to heart disease.

So whatever your deep unrealized and unresolved thoughts and feelings are may lead you to related dis-ease.

Religion needs to get back to the earth.

Get in touch with yourselves as part of the universe.

The sky is your cathedral, the mountains the pillars and the plants my choir.

Join them. Celebrate your oneness with the all. See the plants and animals and insects as aspects of yourselves. See the wonder of the stars and know that you are made of the same stuff as them.

You will not find Spirit only in the buildings you erect in the name of religion. These are monuments to human ego. Better spend the money on the needy. Celebrate God (Life) everyday in the breath you take, see God in the leaves and grass or in the ant or bee.

Feel God in the dew and the rain and the breeze.

Sing out from your heart at the beauty of life and the love He has extended in keeping life flowing as in even a mustard seed.

This is a good step towards healing yourselves.

See yourselves as part of the oneness of the Great All.

See others as reflections and aspects of yourself.

When you meet someone, see them as yourself.

Greet them as if you were greeting yourself, for in truth you are.

Ask yourself what aspect of yourself are they showing to you and honor and bless them with a silent prayer of acknowledgment.

Send love to strangers in a silent thought.

Send love to people in your city.

Send thoughts of happiness randomly to anyone at anytime.

Silently greet people with the greeting "I honor the Divinity and Oneness of both of us".

Better yet - say it out loud!

When you shake hands, send an electrical pulse of love into the body of the other person and look them in the eyes as you acknowledge them silently with a wish of love or joy for their well-being.

You must realize that all experience is self-created.

In a world of energy, which all of creation is, there can be no distinction between yourself, a rock or the air you breathe, nor, for that matter, your thoughts about those things.

"All of creation is Mine and I am All".

Therefore in the thought creative process all originates from the energy of one Mind. These are the thoughts that have brought the universe into a state of being.

Although your senses may tell you that a thing is a gas, a liquid, or a solid, at an atomic level all is one.

The molecules, atoms and sub atomic structure contain the same energy - which derives from the power of Mind - Gods thoughts.

Nothing exists, save that which Divine thought energy has manifested, and all of creation is His.

Therefore as He holds the thought energy of you or a cow turd, to posit an extreme example, fundamentally you are the same - atoms composed of energy.

And the "emptiness" between atoms is also His thought and therefore Divine energy.

That where His energy is not - is not.

Divine energy is the All.

So know that insofar as you are energy, so are your thoughts energy. In this (ability to think and join thoughts) are God and you are the same and in this you have been created in Gods image, and not the cow turd in His image.

However, insofar as you exist in energy so do your thoughts, emotions, experiences, feelings, dreams and imaginations. You cannot see yourself as separate from your thoughts.

You would erroneously see yourself in one place and your thoughts in a second place and the world outside of yourself in yet a third place.

I tell you now this is your illusion.

Therefore that which you would see as separate from yourself is one with yourself and inseparable.

You are not "over there" whilst all else is "over here". All is here, now, forever in time and space.

Furthermore your sense of what is real and what is not, is an illusion.

Inasmuch as all matter is, at the sub atomic level, more space and emptiness than solid matter, therefore all that appears real and solid, is primarily composed of emptiness, nothingness, save Divine energy. (It is the emptiness that defines the being. A musical note is defined by the silence at its beginning and at its end. A room is not the walls or the ceilings. The empty space contained within defines the room. Therefore it is the nothingness that defines the something ness)

So your perception of reality if seen at the sub atomic level would show vast spaces of nothingness, with the occasional atom or particle floating in the void.

All of which is created from the Energy and therefore that which has a more dense or solid aspect to it, is the condensed energy brought into form.

But the nothingness and the something ness are one and the same.

So it is with you. And so it is with your thoughts. And so when your think, the energy can (and does) take form, and you can create your experience of reality.

The illusion is your perception of being separate from your thoughts.

The illusion is your perception of being separate from Gods thoughts.

And the illusion is your perception of having no control over your perception of reality.

Worlds within worlds do you use to delude yourself and baffle your senses.

As conscious beings that have feelings, you must integrate your understanding of awareness into alignment with this, which God has given to you.

You are neither the observer or the observed. You are both!

That which you observe is that which you are.

This means that you cannot blame others for what you are. Because to do so you would first have to set others up as outside of and separate from, yourself.

Then you would have to place the event outside of yourself, as something that "just happened" to you.

Then you would have to set up your response to that event as outside of yourself.

And, finally, the whole cause and effect would you see as a chain of events, separate from, and outside of yourself, in which you are the innocent bystander (or victim) and observer of events.

In truth it is one energy, one thought event of continuous, creative manifestation in which you and all parties and all feelings and emotions are one.

I know the difficulty you have in grasping this concept. When you consider that you have spent all of this lifetime telling yourself that you are separate from the world of experiences, it will take some time for you to integrate this thought.

You are the play, the script, the actor, the stage, and all the characters and you all are nothing save energy patterns in Gods consciousness.

Therefore, know too, that if your experience of reality is an illusion, so too is your concept of time. For all time exists simultaneously within creation. There is no beginning nor an end.

All of what was, what is and what will be, co-exist in time and space.

That you are in one time frame is an illusion.

Even as you are think, so are your thoughts in the past. That which you think you are, is no more, even at the moment that you think it.

And yet you hold on to that thought of what you are, and so you see yourself as what you would be.

For all your senses can know is the here and now - yet your mind would have you believe otherwise.

So you base your reality on what was, and not on what is. Such is how you perceive reality.

When you realize that all is one and yet all is nothing, you will lose your attachment to ego and hence all cause of conflict, suffering and jealousy. You will merge your consciousness with the Divine and experience Divine love, bliss, peace and happiness.

—

Eternal Law

The interconnectedness of all souls is the most important lesson for mankind to learn.

It is one thing to understand at an abstract and intellectual level that all of creation is from God, it is quite another to realize this at a conscious, everyday level.

On the one hand you must surely see that everything is Divine - without exception all of life must be honored and revered as holy.

On the other hand all of creation is one.

You as an individual cannot, cannot, cannot, be seen as separate from the whole.

The lesson of this is that every soul is a part of the one Holy Soul.

You are one with every living creature. Although your limited five senses will tell you that you are separate, your soul knows otherwise.

The import of this is that you delude yourself when you think that you are separate from the rest of humanity and other life forms. This is the illusion of your own creation because you do not listen to your higher self.

You rely on your very limited five senses for your truth about this world, and you ignore the voice in you head. You ignore your intuition. You fail to honor the more subtle senses and rely totally on your gross senses.

Some insects can see in the infrared spectrum and others in the ultraviolet. Can you?

Do your eyes see all? Can you see the perfume wafting off a flower?

Can you see the shapes in darkness and pinpoint your food source in the night?

How come, if you consider your senses so reliable, that a "lowly" animal can do this yet your eyes cannot?

Yet you would say that your eyes do not deceive you?

Is not the fact your eyes do not see all, a deception?

Yet you would base all your reality on what you see and set yourself up as a superior being because you have a mind?

Your mind only thinks it has awareness. It bases its conclusions on the input of faulty sensory input. It is deceived and therefore would interpret itself and its environment on partial and incomplete

403

information. And it would call itself complete and superior and deserved of ruling the world.

Do your ears hear the song of the whale across oceans of distance away?

Can you hear the ultra sonic sound spectrum?

We are more blind and deaf than seeing and hearing. Yet we would base all of our understanding of the world around us, and our place in it, on our half blind eyes and almost deaf ears.

Can you smell a flower from a mile away? A moth can smell its mate from several miles away.

Yet you would believe you are a complete being.

What of the radar sense of bats? Do you have the ability to find your way without eyes?

What of the echolocation senses of cetaceans - dolphins and whales? Can your ears and voice find your way in the ocean?

Yet you say that you are to have dominion over the earth.

Do you feel the currents of the magnetism of the earth? Lowlier creatures, as you would see them, fly by the earth's currents, sense earthquakes and storms.

Where is your sense of the earth?

Be not proud mankind, for the lowliest ant lives in greater harmony with his kind than you with yours. You need to know the soul of the ant, and work your way through creation from there onwards.

You must know without fail, in no uncertain terms, in so clear a sense, that all of creation is one soul. I cannot say this in stronger terms.

If we do not base every thought, every action, at all times on this awareness, we shall not evolve in consciousness. Mankind is at the toddler stage of growing up. Do not think that we can yet make adult decisions of import, such as our role in the world and who we are as beings.

We are yet to be spiritual children, if we survive as a species long enough to evolve.

We are all one creature, not individuals. Study the ant and learn.

When you see one person hurting another - do not think that does not affect you.

You are one with each other. The hurt done by one to another is a hurt done to all.

It would be as if your mind were to say that it matters not if you loose your eyes or an arm because that is somehow separate from yourself.

It is not.

Nor when you see any person as separate from yourself, it is not.

Nor any creature that crawls or walks or swims or flies, as separate from yourself, it is not.

The hurt you do to another will come back to hurt you.

This hurt will also come to hurt all mankind.

The love and care you give another will likewise come back to you and benefit all mankind.

Herein is the difference between doing love and hurt:

Love is the deepest aspect of the Divine.

The love you do advances the growth and spirituality of the world and yourself.

Hurt keeps you stuck in pain and negativity.

You must know that insofar as the law of karma, or cause and effect is concerned, that which you sow today, shall you reap. The day of reaping may be in this lifetime or in a later incarnation.

It makes no difference.

You can never know whether the beggar, drunk and diseased in the cold gutter, was once a prince who performed hateful deeds in a past incarnation.

Such is why the accumulated effect of hateful deeds increases the misery of the world from generation to generation.

Conversely, so does the loving deed create joy.

Never see yourself as separate from the karma of the world.

You are your brother's keeper.

What evil man doeth unto himself, shall befall all mankind. He that raiseth up the poor and the broken hearted, raiseth up all by his actions.

Such is the Eternal Law.

Do not judge, nor condemn, for the Eternal Law says that all must be in balance.

Each hateful action to another will incur a hateful action back to you in return.

405

Each act of compassion will likewise be rewarded.

Balance is the natural state of the universe. For every action there is an equal and opposite reaction. Therefore in the eternal universe it makes no difference when the balance takes effect in terms of the present lifetime or a future one.

Whatsoever you sow, shall you surely reap.

This law is infallible. It does not judge, it does not condemn. It merely is.

In our limited and imperfect sense of the world, we do have the ability to choose kindness over hurt and love over hate. We can choose to destroy other life forms and decimate their habitat. We can murder, rape and assault each other, and other nations and races. But know that the negative energy will be balanced, and none among us are so great as to be beyond the Eternal Law.

The promise of redemption is through honor and reverence of all life forms.

When we truly can see beyond our limited and imperfect senses, then we will start to revere the life force which is God in all creation.

We shall recognize that each and every soul is here to learn and experience from past lives and deeds, then we will honor who they are and try to help them. For when we help them, we help their karma as well as our own, and therefore that of all mankind.

Reverence for the holy mission of each soul in finding its way back to a state of Grace is our first step towards growing up as a spiritual being.

This is the way to improve life on earth - by knowing that All is One.

Only our weak senses, would have you believe that all are separate. Remember that we cannot trust our experiences for we have not in our five senses the equipment to make true judgments of any situation.

It is your soul that is perfect. You must learn to trust it. Let it speak through you. Follow your higher sense of purpose, for that is your soul's voice.

Always work from a position of the highest respect and reverence for everything.

Work consciously as your daily goal - to go out in the world and raise the good karma of the world for you and all you brother and sister souls - some yet unborn.

—

Instinct

We must integrate our light and dark (primal) sides.

When we do not recognize the connectedness of our thoughts, then we are fragmented as individuals. We need to create a depth of safety in our feelings about ourselves to allow us to go beyond the fear and the dark side (primal instinct).

This will enable us to grow with the confidence of who we really are.

People who fragment themselves and the two aspects / sides of themselves, put out the energy of fear. This is the primal or animal instinct.

An animal has a nurturing instinct and an attack / fear instinct.

The attack / fear instinct is primal and is always dominant and comes to the fore instantly a (fear) situation arises.

An animal can never subvert or control this instinct nor can it integrate it with the nurturing aspect of itself. In some domestic animals such as dogs, the primal instinct is suppressed because of the symbiotic relationship the animal has with its owner. Many instances of symbiotic relationships exist in nature. Some predator species such as lions will allow a tickbird to walk all over its body removing ticks. The reward for the animal is it gets rid of the vermin and the bird gets a meal! This does not mean that the lion is now a pussycat and anyone can walk up to it and pull ticks off its back.

With wild animals we are acutely aware to avoid close contact with them. Our fear of the irrational and unpredictable attack / fear side of their nature keeps us at bay from them.

So it is in humans who have not integrated the two sides of their nature.

People should understand the duality of their nurturing and their attack / fear primal natures.

Some people cannot control the animal attack / fear primal instinct without a reward.

For example, a dog will trade (control) its primal instinct for a loving, nurturing home in a symbiotic relationship with a human. If you abuse the dog it will become vicious.

It cannot willingly control its natural instinct to growl, bite or attack when it feels threatened.

Therefore its relationship is a trade of suppression of its primal instinct in return for a reward - in this instance a symbiotic relationship with its master.

Some people, in whom the primal instinct is still predominant, or is not well integrated in themselves, display a level of unpredictability that is often suppressed out of self interest such as what is in it for them to be pleasant in given situations. Such people are known to turn on others seemingly without rhyme or reason. They radiate an aura of edginess and display traits such as forced pleasantness or lack sincerity that we often can pick up and which makes us feel uneasy in their presence Even though we as yet have no reason to be wary of them.

In these people the fear of being alive reflects a darker side of their human nature.

The fear is always present below the surface waiting to come out in some unpredictable manner.

This we can sense, even though we may have no obvious cause to mistrust that person in an emotional sense.

In other people, the highest thought is to be in a nurturing / love mode irrespective of circumstances. We are quick to intuit this in people and are drawn to such people for their openness and warmth.

This display of a lack of primal instinct - is not possible with the primal instinct inherent in animals.

We need to work on eliminating the primal animal instinct of fear / aggression from ourselves.

The closer we can move towards allowing the love / nurturing aspect of ourselves to dominate who we are, then the closer we are towards ascending and transforming ourselves. The more we can master our love / nurturing natures the more God-like we become.

Only humans can do this.

The degree to which we succeed determines the level of spirituality we achieve.

This is the whole purpose of our human existence.

The domination of the fear and overcoming of the aggression and replacing the primal with the Divine is what the spiritual masters have achieved.

The need for ritual is Divine. Animals cannot construct ritual.

Ritual is a conscious affirmation of who we are and what we want to become.

It is an affirmation of our connectedness to the higher self and to Divinity.

The power of ritual is the empowerment it gives to ourselves as the performers of ritual.

Therefore our sincerity and intent is the real determinant of the value of ritual.

Reinforcement of the ritual increases the value and the intent.

—

Surrender

You cannot surrender to God without accepting unconditional love.

Once you accept unconditional love you have to release all negative thoughts and emotions from your life and give only love – unconditionally in every situation.

Never again can you hold thoughts of jealousy, hate disdain, rage, contempt or any form of judgment whatsoever.

Love does not judge. Nor does God. Without query or reservation.

As you give (of yourself) shall it come back to you and in this process do you release yourself from the illusion surrounding you in this life. The illusion of judgment and negative thoughts is manmade and not Divine in nature. Therefore it is not real. Love shall conquer all.

Surrender to Love and you surrender to the highest form that you can be, pure God essence. Never again could you harm or injure anything. In so doing you will advance your karma a thousand, thousand times, and the karma of the world and future generations will be greatly accelerated and purified by your single act of surrender.

(The act of complete surrender to love is similar to the powerful story in the New Testament concerning Jesus' surrender in love for the benefit of mankind. We can all do this act of surrender. And it is not a prerequisite to suffer or die in the process).

Jeffrey M. Solomon

God's creation is pure love.
Fear is the filter we place
Between what we see,
Which is pure love,
And what we experience.
This is the meaning of sin.

++

<u>About The Book</u>

This book is a journey into the mind that questions why it exists, why things are as they are, why things happen as they do and ultimately what is the meaning of life.

It is a simple book filled with anecdotes, stories and gifts of wonder. All the elements that make a journey pleasant and enjoyable.

This journey is one of discovery to find the immutable Universal truths that hold the key to reality and illusion.

It examines what these Universal truths are and how they affect your life. It unlocks the gates to your self-empowerment by harnessing the energy of the Universe.

In doing so you will see the wonder of the Universe unfold and you will find your own most important role in being the person that you are that goes beyond your wildest dreams.

There are practical exercises that you can do should you wish to use the material contained herein for personal growth and advancement.

This book is a gift to all people who have wondered about what it means to be human. To all those who want to know about creation and life and the Energy that flows through all things, yet did not know where to begin looking.

To anyone who is aware that life is a journey and would like a map.

If you ever felt that you were more than the image that you see in the mirror yet never understood why you felt limited, this book is for you.

This book will show you why you are already perfection incarnate.

The truth, no matter how it is stated, is eternal, immutable and constant.

You are that Truth.

Jeffrey and Sharda have established a spiritual retreat in St Petersburg Florida called Whispers. It is a secluded place of incredible harmony and peace from where they teach and encourage small groups to come. They also rent the condominiums on the property for those just wanting to spend time relaxing near the beach.
Whispers is on an Island in the Gulf of Mexico – called Treasure Island – and the dolphins play off the back patio.

Jeffrey and Sharda are available to host groups at Whispers or to travel and present seminars and trainings to your own group. Sharda in particular has created a specialty of personal coaching, particularly to business people, politicians and celebrities. She is regarded as one of the most gifted and life- transforming persons they have ever met. Her results in transforming peoples lives and coaching them to create truly inspirational, successful lives are nothing short of miraculous.

They also take fellow "travelers" on journeys to sacred places, such as Babaji's ashram in India, Peru, Stonehenge and Bali etc. If you would like to join a group or organize your own, - complete with trainings – they would love to hear from you.

They would also like to hear if you have had any life transforming experiences following your reading of "Playing in the Mind of God"

At the time of writing a new "Spiritual Website" is being constructed. It will be linked to the Whispers website.

If you would like to contact them or to be placed on a mailing list:

Whispers – 279 104th Ave Treasure Island Florida 33706 USA
Fax – (727) 363.1500
E-Mail jeffmsolomon@cs.com
www.playinginthemindofgod.com
www.whispersresort.com

About the Author

Jeffrey Solomon is a traveler.

Born in Johannesburg, South Africa, at age two he boarded the Union Castle steamship from South Africa to England and back. His earliest memory is crossing the equator and being dunked in water by the crew.

At the age of eight he boarded the first BOAC Comet jetliner with his businessman father to Europe. At ten the family went to America before returning to South Africa at age twelve.

Following his graduation from the Johannesburg School of Art and a brief stint in the South African Air Force, he worked for a few years for a wholesale watch importer. He took time off to travel alone around Europe before returning and eventually starting his own business at the age of twenty- five.

Over the following twelve years he built up his own electronics wholesale company and became an established businessman and one of the largest watch importers in South Africa. A member of the Johannesburg Chamber of Commerce, a respected member of the business community, he counted among his friends and acquaintances some of the elite of the business community. During this time he traveled the world, especially in the Far East and in Europe. His business interests took him far and wide to over thirty countries. With business interests spanning the globe he was on top of the world, constantly traveling and taking the time to explore new places at every opportunity.

In 1986 following German Bank speculation on the South African currency, the South African economy fell and the country fell into political turmoil. Having lost a fortune in the collapse of the economy, like so many young South Africans of that time, Jeffrey and his young family made plans to leave South Africa. Abandoning a privileged life style of BMW's and servants.

Facing an uncertain future, they departed South Africa for Omaha, Nebraska in the USA. There he opened one of the first sports bars at a time when the concept was practically unknown. During the following twelve years the business flourished. He also started a travel consultancy. It was around this time that he felt increasingly discontent and isolated from life.

He was invited to join a group that he had booked to India. Upon his return from India, one night Jeffrey had a dream. The experience of which shattered all his preconceived ideas of normality. In this dream, that appeared more as a vision of his life, he found himself pleading with God to take him from this world.

Upon awakening, he was so completely shaken and he tried to make sense of what had occurred. He passed into a spontaneous and deep state of meditation bordering unconsciousness in which he was literally taken to the point of death. In this state he could feel his hear beat slow, each beat clear and infrequent as his breathing faded. He saw the abyss between life and death and it would take just a small step to cross over. He realized that he was being given a unique opportunity to pass on consciously and a warm calm settled overcame him. Before him was the abyss, a line. All he had to do was take one more step to cross over on another unique journey. It was so tempting. The peace was a siren song that beckoned. In this moment he saw that his death would be ruled a heart attack. He understood that the choice of leaving his present life was his alone to make. There was an implicit lie in this revelation. If he chose to leave and if people thought that he had a heart attack, this would be untrue. There was an implicit misperception about his death that he did not want to leave behind as his final legacy.

The thought of people thinking that he died from a heart attack, when the actual cause of death was so different, was unacceptable.

Poised as he was in a near death state, he realized that he could leave this life not by dying but rather by consciously being responsible and changing all the things and beliefs that no longer worked for him and which were the cause of him reaching this crossroads in his life.

In this moment Jeffrey chose life.

He resolved to find the meaning and the answers to his life. For the following several weeks following this epiphany he was half out of his mind. His consciousness had shifted and he felt as if he was in this world but not of it. Somehow his life force moved his body but his consciousness was in another dimension. He experienced the familiar things around him as a detached observer. After several weeks the effect diminished and it felt as if his body and soul slowly integrated back into the physical world.

The time spent out of his body created an entirely new perspective of life for Jeffrey. This was the experience that led him to write this book.

Shortly prior to this time he had met his current partner, Sharda, in a union that itself was life transforming. Through a series of chance events, a maintenance man had introduced a metaphysical travel client to him, who in turn introduced Jeffrey to Sharda as a potential customer.

Sharda is a seminar leader, life coach and spiritual guide of exceptional abilities. She takes spiritual groups to sacred places. It was on one of the India tours that Jeffrey was introduced to Haidakhan, the site of venerated Indian saint, Babaji, as written about by Paramahansa Yogananda, in his book, "Autobiography of a Yogi".

At that time Sharda lived in Dallas, Texas, and it became apparent that their mutual connection transcended the physical boundaries of time. As they later found out, their connection was a wonderful occurrence of a single soul in two bodies. What did this mean? Jeffrey decided to find out.

And in doing so began one of the most magnificent journeys of Jeffrey's life.

From the world of a high-powered international business, Jeffrey's life had come full circle. He was cast back in the role of novice and student. Nothing in his prior experience was of value in understanding this new world. Nothing was certain anymore. Nothing appeared the same.

His entire life to date was simply the small steps in preparation of the greatest journey of his life.

With help, support and guidance from Sharda, Jeffery took the first tentative steps into the MIND OF GOD.

Printed in the United States
1289200006B/73-87